Educational Leadership Theory

Series Editors

Scott Eacott, School of Education, University of New South Wales, Sydney, Australia

Richard Niesche, School of Education, University of New South Wales, Sydney, Australia

The Educational Leadership Theory book series provides a forum for internationally renowned and emerging scholars whose ongoing scholarship is seriously and consequentially engaged in theoretical and methodological developments in educational leadership, management and administration. Its primary aim is to deliver an innovative and provocative dialogue whose coherence comes not from the adoption of a single paradigmatic lens but rather in an engagement with the theoretical and methodological preliminaries of scholarship. Importantly, Educational Leadership Theory is not a critique of the field—something that is already too frequent—instead, attention is devoted to sketching possible alternatives for advancing scholarship. The choice of the plural 'alternatives' is deliberate, and its use is to evoke the message that there is more than one way to advance knowledge. The books published in Educational Leadership Theory come from scholars working at the forefront of contemporary thought and analysis in educational leadership, management and administration. In doing so, the contributions stimulate dialogue and debate in the interest of advancing scholarship.

International Editorial Board
Ira Bogotch, Florida Atlantic University, USA
Fenwick W. English, University of North Carolina, USA
Gabriele Lakomski, University of Melbourne, Australia
Paul Newton, University of Saskatchewan, Canada
Izhar Oplatka, Tel Aviv University, Israel
Jae Hyung Park, Education University of Hong Kong, Hong Kong
Eugenie Samier, University of Strathclyde, Scotland
Roberto Serpieri, Università di Napoli Federico II, Italy
Dorthe Staunaes, Aarhus University, Denmark
Yusef Waghid, University of Stellenbosch, South Africa
Jane Wilkinson, Monash University, Australia

More information about this series at http://www.springer.com/series/15484

Eugenie A. Samier · Eman S. ElKaleh
Editors

Teaching Educational Leadership in Muslim Countries

Theoretical, Historical and Cultural Foundations

Springer

Editors
Eugenie A. Samier
University of Strathclyde
Glasgow, UK

Eman S. ElKaleh
Zayed University
Dubai, United Arab Emirates

ISSN 2510-1781 ISSN 2510-179X (electronic)
Educational Leadership Theory
ISBN 978-981-13-6817-2 ISBN 978-981-13-6818-9 (eBook)
https://doi.org/10.1007/978-981-13-6818-9

Library of Congress Control Number: 2019932619

© Springer Nature Singapore Pte Ltd. 2019
This work is subject to copyright. All rights are reserved by the Publisher, whether the whole or part of the material is concerned, specifically the rights of translation, reprinting, reuse of illustrations, recitation, broadcasting, reproduction on microfilms or in any other physical way, and transmission or information storage and retrieval, electronic adaptation, computer software, or by similar or dissimilar methodology now known or hereafter developed.
The use of general descriptive names, registered names, trademarks, service marks, etc. in this publication does not imply, even in the absence of a specific statement, that such names are exempt from the relevant protective laws and regulations and therefore free for general use.
The publisher, the authors and the editors are safe to assume that the advice and information in this book are believed to be true and accurate at the date of publication. Neither the publisher nor the authors or the editors give a warranty, express or implied, with respect to the material contained herein or for any errors or omissions that may have been made. The publisher remains neutral with regard to jurisdictional claims in published maps and institutional affiliations.

This Springer imprint is published by the registered company Springer Nature Singapore Pte Ltd.
The registered company address is: 152 Beach Road, #21-01/04 Gateway East, Singapore 189721, Singapore

Series Editors' Foreword

Discussions of educational leadership research are always discussions about theory. Sometimes matters of ontology, epistemological, and axiology are made explicit, other times they are not, but we cannot undertake, dialogue, and debate research without theory. What counts as theory and/or quality research in educational leadership has changed over time. From the influence of sociology and behavioural science in the establishment of university departments of educational administration (as it was known then) through to the rise of the theory movement in the mid-twentieth century and subsequent interventions such as Thomas Barr Greenfield's humanistic science, the Critical Theory of Richard Bates and William Foster, and Colin Evers and Gabriele Lakomski's naturalistic coherentism, tensions in educational leadership theory have shaped what work is conducted, legitimised, published, and ultimately advanced. This is all set in a field of inquiry where questions of relevance and/or practical significance remain dominant and enduring. The desire for immediacy and direct translation of research into practice, especially for the improvement of outcomes, means that matters of theory are often seen as peripheral at best and more often marginalised or silenced. Theory, which can unsettle assumptions, ask questions of the status quo, and recast our ways of thinking, seeing and doing, is perceived as getting in the way of instrumentalist and/or functional prescriptions of how things ought to be.

The *Educational Leadership Theory* book series is explicitly designed to address what we see happening in educational leadership scholarship. That is, an aversion to rigorous, robust, and most importantly, enduring dialogue and debate on matters of theoretical and methodological advancement. To that end, this series provides a forum for internationally renowned and emerging scholars whose ongoing scholarship is seriously and consequentially engaged in theoretical and methodological developments in educational leadership, management, and administration. Its primary aim is to deliver an innovative and provocative dialogue whose coherence comes not from the adoption of a single paradigmatic lens but rather in an engagement with the theoretical and methodological preliminaries of scholarship. Importantly, *Educational Leadership Theory* is not simply a critique of the field—something that is already too frequent—instead, attention is devoted to sketching possible alternatives for advancing scholarship. The choice of the plural "alternatives" is deliberate, and its use is to evoke the message that there is more than one way to advance knowledge. The books published in *Educational Leadership Theory* come from scholars working at the forefront of contemporary thought and analysis in educational leadership, management, and administration. In doing so, the contributions stimulate dialogue and debate in the interest of advancing scholarship. Specifically, we aim to:

- Foreground the theoretical/methodological preliminaries of educational leadership research;
- Sketch areas of relevance and possible theoretical/methodological developments that serve to extend current debates on leadership in education.

We interpret these aims widely, consistent with our goal of promoting dialogue and debate in the field. Importantly, we ask our contributors to respond to the following guiding questions:

1. What are the theoretical/methodological problems from which educational leadership is based and/or have implications for educational leadership?
2. How can we engage them?

These questions, we believe, are vital as the field of educational leadership faces increasing questions of its relevance and status within education research, and as education research itself faces increasing challenges from beyond in the audit culture of the contemporary academy. Our goal is not to bring a series of like-minded contributors together to outline the virtues of a particular research tradition. Such an undertaking would do little more than provide legitimation of existing theorisations and negate theoretical pluralism. Instead, we seek to bring a diverse group of scholars together to engage in rigorous dialogue and debate around important matters for educational leadership research and practice. This is a significant move, as instead of surrendering our thoughts to a singular, stable, and standardised knowledge base we explicitly seek to interrogate the dynamism of contradictions, multiplicities, and antinomies of a vibrant field of theories and practices.

Most importantly, we want the *Educational Leadership Theory* book series to stimulate dialogue and debate. We are broad in our meaning of the label "theory". The analytical dualism of explanation and description is a poor and weak distinction between what is and is not theory. We too are not against the absence of practical application. However, what we seek are contributions that take matters of theory and methodology (as in theory as method) serious. In short, we are more inclusive than exclusive. This also goes for what is meant by "educational leadership". We do not limit our interpretation to schools or higher education but are instead open to work discussing education in its broadest possible sense. A focus on theory travels well across geographic and disciplinary boundaries. In taking matters of theory serious, we see the *Educational Leadership Theory* book series as a key outlet for stimulating dialogue and debate by recognising the problems and possibilities of existing knowledge in the field and pushing that further. This is an undertaking that we hope you will join us on—be that as a contributor, reader, or critique—all in the interests of advancing knowledge.

Scott Eacott
Richard Niesche
Series Editors

Preface

This book is an exploration of what it means to teach educational administration and leadership in a Muslim context, based on the experiences of the editors, one of whom is a Westerner experienced in international and comparative studies who became immersed in the Islamic and local culture of her doctoral students, and the other born and raised in a Muslim country and living and working in another who studied for a number of years mostly Western management and leadership studies. We met in a doctoral programme, while the former was beginning to gain an understanding and experience in a new environment (and rapidly modifying the curriculum to achieve a more appropriate and relevant course of studies) and the latter finding ways to bring Islamic values and practices to a field dominated under globalisation by mostly Anglo-American literature. Given the convergence of our views, we co-authored an article on ethics in Islamic leadership for public administration, finding the experience mutually beneficial and much easier to do than one might think given cultural and religious differences (ElKaleh and Samier 2013).

What united our visions was the field as properly a human and humane pursuit, in a religious framework with a long humanistic tradition, highly successful historically, and one of the sources of the Renaissance and Enlightenment in Europe, therefore sharing many fundamental values with some of the Western schools of thought. In other words, approached in this manner, the bridge to cross from both directions was not insurmountable. In fact, focussed on foundational values and philosophy, it turned out to be only a few short steps, although significant ones. The common ground, we found, was much greater than what separated us. A lesson I continued to learn as the first editor increased her immersion into authentic Arab and Islamic culture, and leaving behind the (mis-)constructed polarised views that have infected much of the international discourse.

Despite the developing field of international and comparative educational leadership and administration in the last two decades, little attention has been paid to the teaching of educational administration and leadership in Muslim countries and communities that take into account the jurisdictional characteristics, culture, social system and traditions of administration, leadership, and education. What many scholars, like Ahmad (2009), have observed is that many of those in leadership positions in Islamic countries perpetuate the use of foreign and often incompatible models of leadership. In addition, education sets conceptual boundaries privileging Anglo-American knowledge (Hourani et al. 2011), a literature that is predominantly ethnocentric, although slowly evolving into a more diverse and global representation. A globalised education, according to Asfour (2006), asserts a hegemony that tends towards a conformity, which in the Middle East means to extra-Arab and non-Islamic values, negatively affecting identity and culture, often causing social institution disruption and leading to practices that fail due to their lack of societal integration. These globalisation critiques in the Middle East are also influenced by Said's (2006) critical concept of "Orientalism" which includes transplanted education curricular models, tests, teaching staff, and those from the region educated in the West who transmit that education, often unmodified, when they return to the Middle East.

This volume is designed to explore the Islamic tradition and Muslim contexts for educational administration and leadership focussing on postgraduate curriculum and pedagogy drawing on a range of theoretical foundations and approaches that are more culturally and jurisdictionally appropriate in a number of Muslim countries. The inspiration, in part, comes from authors in general management studies like Ali (1992) and Alatas (2006) who have argued for more nationally and culturally relevant teaching and research in Arab and Muslim countries that respect the values and traditions of these countries and also take into consideration their developing and nation-building challenges (Henry and Springborg 2001). This requires a modification and adjustment of Western curricula and pedagogy in all fields (Numan 2015) including postgraduate educational administration and leadership programmes that meet the values and aims of Islamic education that are intellectual, moral, and physical that serve families, communities, and humankind in a balance between the individual and society (Ahmed 1990; Shah and Baporikar 2011).

The aims of this volume contribute to an emerging specialisation in international and comparative educational administration and leadership oriented towards a broader and more diverse set of perspectives where few books exist on teaching at the postgraduate level in non-Western contexts. It also raises issues of globalised educational administration and leadership teaching, as it applies in Muslim contexts, proposes alternative approaches, and demonstrates that Islamic traditions have a strong foundation upon which to build in the field and are compatible with many aspects of Western theory and practices provided that sufficient modifications and adaptations are made. Additionally, the volume is intended to contribute to the international and comparative literature, to a greater internationalisation of university curriculum discussion, and an understanding of educational administration and leadership in Muslim countries and communities that too often have been presented through negative stereotypes, or which have required homogenisation that compromise culture, social structures, and social institutions in the developing world (Maringe and Foskett 2012).

This collection is dedicated to the many friends and colleagues in the field in the United Arab Emirates with whom we debated and discussed and from whom we learned, as well as colleagues in many Muslim countries and communities who are on the same voyage.

Glasgow, UK
Dubai, United Arab Emirates

Eugenie A. Samier
Eman S. ElKaleh

References

Ahmad, K. (2009). Leadership and work motivation from the cross cultural perspective. *International Journal of Commerce and Management, 19*(1), 72–84.

Ahmed, M. (1990). *Islamic education: Redefinition of aims and methodology.* New Delhi: Qazi.

Alatas, S. F. (2006). Alternative discourses in Asian social science: Responses to eurocentrism. New Delhi: Sage.

Ali, A. (1992). Management research themes and teaching in the Arab world. *International Journal of Educational Management, 6*(4), 7–11.

Asfour, G. (2006). An argument for enhancing Arab identity within globalisation. In J. Fox, N. Mourtada-Sabbah & M. al-Mutawa (Eds.), *Globalisation in the Gulf* (pp. 141–147). London: Routledge.

ElKaleh, E. & Samier, E. A. (2013). The ethics of Islamic leadership: A cross-cultural approach for public administration. *Administrative Culture, 14*(2), 188–211.

Henry, C. & Springborg, R. (2001). Globalization and the politics of development in the Middle East. Cambridge: Cambridge University Press.

Hourani, R., Diallo, I. & Said, A. (2011). Teaching in the Arabian Gulf: Arguments for the deconstruction of the current educational model. In C. Gitsaki (Ed.), *Teaching and learning in the Arab world* (pp. 335–355). Bern: Peter Lang.

Maringe, F. & Foskett, N. (2012). Introduction: Globalization and universities. In F. Maringe & N. Foskett (Eds.), *Globalization and internationalization in higher education: Theoretical, strategic and management perspectives* (pp. 1–13). London: Continuum.

Numan, R. (2015). Assuring quality outcomes: Best practices for higher education in Islamic countries. *HUM Journal of Educational Studies, 3*(1), 92–111.

Said, E. (2006). Orientalism now. In H. Lauder, P. Brown, J. Dillabough & A. Halsey (Eds.), *Education, globalisation, and social change* (pp. 138–142). Oxford: Oxford University Press.

Shah, I. A. & Baporikar, N. (2011). The suitability of imported curricula for learning in the Gulf states: An Oman perspective. In C. Gitsaki (Ed.), *Teaching and learning in the Arab world* (pp. 275–292). Bern: Peter Lang.

Contents

1 **Editors' Introduction: An Overview of the Educational Administration and Leadership Curriculum: Traditions of Islamic Educational Administration and Leadership in Higher Education** 1
Eugenie A. Samier and Eman S. ElKaleh

Part I   Foundational Theories and Models

2 **The Humanist Roots of Islamic Administration and Leadership for Education: Philosophical Foundations for Intercultural and Transcultural Teaching** 23
Eugenie A. Samier

3 **A Critical Approach to Developing Culturally Relevant Leadership Curricula for Muslim Students** 39
Eman S. ElKaleh

4 **Leadership Development in the UAE: Critical Perspectives on Intercultural Pedagogies in a Graduate Education Programme** 55
Barbara Harold and Lauren Stephenson

Part II   Current Controversies and Challenges

5 **The Knowledge Base on Educational Leadership and Management in Arab Countries: Its Current State and Its Implications for Leadership Development** 77
Rima Karami-Akkary and Waheed Hammad

xiv

6 Educational Administration and Leadership Curricula for Modern Nation-Building in Muslim Countries: Modernisation, National Identity and the Preservation of Values and Culture 93
Eugenie A. Samier and Eman S. ElKaleh

7 Locality, Leadership and Pedagogies for Entrepreneurship Education 113
M. Evren Tok and Cristina D'Alessandro

Part III Country Cases

8 The 'Westernised' Map of the Field of Educational Administration in Turkey and Dominant Perspectives in School Leadership Education 135
Kadir Beycioglu, Ali Çağatay Kılınç and Mahmut Polatcan

9 A Reflection on Teaching Educational Administration in Iran: A Critical Approach 153
Arash Rastehmoghadam

10 K-12 Education Reforms in Saudi Arabia: Implications for Change Management and Leadership Education 171
Bader A. Alsaleh

Editors and Contributors

About the Editors

Eugenie A. Samier is Reader in Educational Management and Leadership at the University of Strathclyde, Glasgow. Her research concentrates on administrative philosophy and theory, interdisciplinary foundations of administration, theories and models of educational leadership, and comparative educational administration. She has frequently been Guest Researcher at the Humboldt University of Berlin, was Visiting Professor in the Department of Administrative Studies at the University of Tartu, Estonia (2003), a Visiting Fellow at Oxford Brookes University, and has been a guest lecturer at universities and institutes in the USA, Germany, Estonia, Russia, Norway, Lithuania, Finland, Qatar, Bahrain, and the UAE. Her publications include chapters and articles on organisational culture and values, the new public management, the role of history and biography in educational administration, the role of humanities, aesthetics, and literary analysis in administration, and Weberian foundations of administrative theory and ethics in a number of international book collections and many leading journals in the USA, Australia, the UK, Germany, the Baltic region, and Canada. She is Founding Board Member of *Administrative Culture* journal and is editor of several book collections with Routledge on ethics, aesthetics, politics, emotions, trust and betrayal, ideologies and maladministration in educational administration. She is also Associate Editor of the four-volume master works *Educational Leadership and Administration* (Sage 2009), a contributor on authority, bureaucracy, critical theory to *Encyclopaedia of Education Law* (Sage 2008), on aesthetics and human agency to the *Handbook of Educational Leadership* (Sage, 2011), aesthetics of leadership and bureaucratic theory to the *Handbook of Educational Theory* (Information Age Publishing, 2013). She has also written a number of articles on topics like toxic leadership, passive evil, kitchification of educational leadership, the avant-garde, postcolonial educational administration, and Islamic ethics, social justice, global governance, administrative tradition, and educational change in the Middle East for several journals and book collections. She also worked as a management consultant in Canada to the public sector for a number of years on a broad variety of projects including legislation development, organisational reviews, board development, and government department restructuring and redesign.

Eman S. ElKaleh studied her MBA at the University of Wollongong followed by a Ph.D. in management, leadership, and policy at the British University in Dubai in association with Birmingham University, UK. She received an Academic Excellence Award by Dubai International Academic City for her dissertation entitled "Teaching Leadership in UAE Business and Education Programs: A Habermasean Analysis within an Islamic Context". While Eman hails from Egypt, she has worked in the UAE at two major universities for nearly twenty years. Currently, she teaches business leadership at Zayed University's College of Business in addition to overseeing the Admission and Recruitment Unit. Understanding the need to develop leadership capacity in Gulf Region countries, she is actively developing programmes and workshops to help Muslim students as well as the faculty and staff with whom they interact gain a better understanding of leadership from an Islamic perspective. She has given guest lectures on Islamic leadership at a number of universities abroad such as Oxford Brookes University, UK; the Humboldt University of Berlin, Germany; Qatar University; and at the British University and Zayed University in the UAE. She was selected to serve as the Chair of Professional Development in the MENASA NASPA Advisory Board. She is also participating in a number of international research projects in leadership studies. She also has a solid experience in reviewing research studies and serves as a reviewer for a number of international and national peer-reviewed conferences and research awards. Tasked with developing a comprehensive programme for student success, she was recognised for her innovation in 2012 by receiving Zayed University's highest honour at a university-wide ceremony.

Contributors

Bader A. Alsaleh King Saud University, Riyadh, Saudi Arabia

Kadir Beycioglu Faculty of Education, Dokuz Eylul University, Buca, Izmir, Turkey

Cristina D'Alessandro University of Ottawa, Ottawa, Canada

Eman S. ElKaleh College of Business, Zayed University, Dubai, United Arab Emirates

Waheed Hammad Educational Administration, College of Education, Sultan Qaboos University, Muscat, Oman;
Damietta University, Damietta, Egypt

Barbara Harold Center for Educational Innovation, Zayed University, Dubai, United Arab Emirates

Editors and Contributors xvii

Rima Karami-Akkary Educational Administration, Policy and Leadership, American University of Beirut, Beirut, Lebanon

Ali Çağatay Kılınç Department of Educational Sciences, Faculty of Letters, Karabuk University, Karabuk, Turkey

Mahmut Polatcan Department of Educational Sciences, Faculty of Letters, Karabuk University, Karabuk, Turkey

Arash Rastehmoghadam Allameh Tabataba'i University, Tehran, Iran

Eugenie A. Samier University of Strathclyde, Glasgow, UK

Lauren Stephenson School of Education, University of Notre Dame, Sydney, Australia

M. Evren Tok College of Islamic Studies, HBKU, Doha, Qatar

Chapter 1
Editors' Introduction: An Overview of the Educational Administration and Leadership Curriculum: Traditions of Islamic Educational Administration and Leadership in Higher Education

Eugenie A. Samier and Eman S. ElKaleh

Abstract This chapter provides an overview of several topics relevant to constructing an approach to teaching educational administration and leadership in Muslim countries. First, it places the topic in the context of the changing nature and critiques of the field that argue for a greater internationalisation to both resist some of the negative aspects of globalisation and to represent countries' traditions in the professional curriculum. Then, it identifies literature that presents the underlying principles and values of Islamic education that guide curriculum and pedagogy and shape its administration and leadership including the *Qur'an* and *Sunnah* and the classical educational literature which focuses on aims, values and goals of education as well as character development upon which a 'good' society is built. This is followed by a section on the Islamic administration and leadership traditions that are relevant to education, including the values of educational organisations and how they should be administered, identifying literature on the distinctive Islamic traditions of leadership and administrator education and training as it applies to education from the establishment of Islam and early classical scholars and senior administrators in the medieval period who laid a strong foundation for a highly sophisticated preparation and practice of administration in philosophical writings and the Mirrors of Princes writings, and subsequent authors who have built upon it up to the contemporary period. The final section provides an overview of the chapters in this collection.

E. A. Samier (✉)
University of Strathclyde, Glasgow, UK
e-mail: eugenie.samier@gmail.com

E. S. ElKaleh
Zayed University, Dubai, United Arab Emirates
e-mail: eman.salah2@gmail.com

© Springer Nature Singapore Pte Ltd. 2019
E. A. Samier and E. S. ElKaleh (eds.), *Teaching Educational Leadership in Muslim Countries*, Educational Leadership Theory,
https://doi.org/10.1007/978-981-13-6818-9_1

Introduction

Despite the developing field of international and comparative educational leadership and administration in the last two decades (e.g. Dimmock and Walker 2005), a significant body of literature from the developing and indigenous worlds, outside the Anglo-American dominant literature, has only emerged in the last decade, one region of which is the Arab world (Hammad and Hallinger 2017). Among the articles surveyed by Hammad and Hallinger, few specifically focused on teaching at the graduate level and many of those in school administration and leadership tend to use Anglo-American sources in their writings. What many scholars like Sulaiman (1985) have observed for some time is that many of those in leadership positions in Islamic countries perpetuate the use of foreign and often incompatible models of leadership that produce students who are 'deluded hybrids' (p. 32), and set conceptual boundaries privileging Anglo-American knowledge (Hourani et al. 2011), a literature that is predominantly ethnocentric (Shah 2006), although slowly evolving into a more diverse and global representation, an argument made by Dimmock and Walker (1998) since one of their earliest articles on comparative studies focussed on cross-cultural factors.

Two notable collections that do closely explore educational administration and leadership in their jurisdictional, cultural, political and social conditions are Wiseman's (2009) *Educational Leadership: Global Contexts and International Comparisons* and Miller's (2017) *Cultures of Educational Leadership: Global and Intercultural Perspectives*, as well as a small number of articles like Brooks and Mutohar's (2018) examination of Islamic values that can inform a school leadership model, Saleemad's (2015) study of Islamic school leadership competencies, and du Plessis' (2017) examination of diverse student voices in curriculum design and delivery in the field. What is needed for accuracy in the field, as well as preparing professionals to function appropriately in their own countries, is an educational administration and leadership that is much more internationalised, taking into consideration not only contextual, but also personal and interactional, factors that shape ideas and values of education, the roles constructed, and the structure and dynamics of the social institutions of society, including the interdependent relationships of educational organisations with those in other sectors which vary considerably internationally, for example, the economy and the security sectors.

This argument has been made in related fields, for example, in general management studies (Ali 1992; Alatas 2006; Jabnoun 2008), in public administration (Beekun and Badawi 1999; Farazmand and Pinkowski 2006; Gulrajani and Moloney 2012), and organisation studies (Branine 2011) that have begun to develop a modern Islamic administration and leadership tradition as well as postcolonial authors who have argued for more nationally and culturally relevant teaching and research in Arab and Muslim countries that respect the values and traditions of these countries and also take into consideration their developing and nation-building challenges (Henry and Springborg 2001). In education, generally, a body of literature has expanded on Islamic education (Zia 2006) that does provide important contextual information and underlying values, but very few sources have addressed the postgraduate teaching of educational administration and leadership in Islamic contexts. This requires a modification and adjustment of Western curricula and pedagogy in all fields (Numan 2015) while drawing on very long, complex and developed Islamic traditions, including postgraduate educational administration and leadership programmes that meet the values and aims of Islamic education that are intellectual, moral and physical that serve families, communities and humankind in a balance between the individual and society (Ahmed 1990; Shah and Baporikar 2011), while appreciating that there are many differences among Muslim states and communities through political and cultural practices and the conditions in which they operate.

The aims of this volume are to raise issues of globalised educational administration and leadership teaching as they apply in Muslim contexts, propose alternative approaches and demonstrate that Islamic educational traditions have a strong foundation upon which to build and are compatible with many principles of Western theory and practices while often taking different forms through cultural expression. It is also intended to contribute to the internationalisation literature providing a more accurate representation of educational administration and leadership in non-Western traditions such as the Islamic that have often been presented through negative stereotypes. In the Islamic, in particular, a 'clash' of civilisations' view has been promoted by some governments and scholars (e.g. Huntington 1996), but has also been criticised through a 'clash of barbarisms' by Achcar (2006) and a clash of 'ignorance' by Eid and Karim (2014) and Karim and Eid (2014) who argue that a long history of collaboration and constructive influences in many sectors including education have been overshadowed by conflict and hostility. As one of the first volumes to explore the teaching of the Islamic tradition and Muslim contexts for educational administration and leadership, the focus here is on postgraduate curriculum and pedagogy drawing on a range of theoretical foundations and approaches culturally and jurisdictionally appropriate in a number of Muslim countries, drawing on the aspects of the Islamic tradition that have provided the collaborative and constructive influences.

This chapter provides an overview of several topics relevant to constructing an approach to teaching educational administration and leadership in Muslim countries. The first section places the topic of the book in the context of the changing nature and critiques of the field that argue for a greater internationalisation to both resist some of the negative aspects of globalisation like homogenisation that compromises culture, social structures and social institutions in the developing world (Maringe and Foskett 2012), and to represent countries' traditions in the professional curriculum. The second section identifies the literature that presents the underlying principles and values of Islamic education that guide curriculum and pedagogy and also shape its administration and leadership including the *Qur'an* and *Sunnah* and the classical educational literature which focuses on aims, values and goals of education as well as character development upon which a 'good' society is built. This is followed by a section on the Islamic administration and leadership traditions that are relevant to education, including the values of educational organisations and how they should be administered, identifying literature on the distinctive Islamic traditions of leadership and administrator education and training as it applies to education from the establishment of Islam and early classical scholars and senior administrators in the medieval period who laid a strong foundation for a highly sophisticated preparation and practice of administration in philosophical writings and the Mirrors of Princes writings, and subsequent authors who have built upon it up to the contemporary period. The rationale for examining this tradition is threefold: first, to present traditions that are more consistent with and have embedded in them important societal values in Muslim contexts; to address the lack of theoretical foundation for the field in non-Western countries (Hallinger and Hammad 2017); and finally, to address concerns raised by a number of scholars about how educational administration and leadership are taught with an overreliance on Anglo-American ideas and practices are misapplied in very different contexts (e.g. Dimmock and Walker 2005; Guenther 2006). The final section provides an overview of the chapters in this collection.

The Changing Nature and Critiques of the Field

Higher education in Muslim countries, as in many parts of the world, has expanded considerably in recent years, and often, as in the United Arab Emirates and throughout the Arabian Gulf, is seen to be part of nation-building and modernisation (Fox 2008). At the same time, students from many Muslim countries travel to countries like Germany, Canada, the UK, Australia and the USA (although this has lessened significantly in the last couple of years) to acquire degrees that are either not available in home countries, or which are not considered to be of high enough quality. Many enter the programmes of Western university branches, the highest proportion in the Middle East (Ahmad and Hussain 2017), that may be low in quality in terms of learning resources, lack of continuity due to high turnover, poor rates of research and a questionable quality of faculty (Wilkins 2010), and which can also cause problems of cultural identity (Haj-Yehia and Erez 2018). This is taking place during a number of sociopolitical and economic forces that have either encouraged or pressured the adoption of Western curriculum (Romanowski 2017) and teaching even if the governance and administration is culturally different, for example, the top-down management styles typical of Arab and other countries evident in a number of cross-cultural studies (Chhokar et al. 2007; Trompenaars and Hampden-Turner 2012).

Globalisation, as Farazmand (2006) has explained, means different things in different disciplines, although coalescing around a central ideology of a global system that reflects Western corporate capitalist values: in economics, it generally means 'a fully integrated world market; to political science, the decline of state sovereignty and the rise of 'supranational and global governing bodies under a new world order'; in business, it means a 'borderless world' for corporate opportunity; and for others a world driven by 'private-sector corporations, not governments' (p. 13). The results of globalisation Farazmand (2006) argue to be the following:

> No matter what perspective is adopted, the end results have been increasing fiscal crisis of the state, accompanied by a serious crisis of governability, insecurity in the midst of increased militarization of the world, and further crises of human insecurity worldwide, a vicious cycle that only feeds into more crises in the age of globalization and increasing inequality. (p. 11)

Sadly, too, Islamophobia, negative stereotyping of all things Islamic, affects educational provision in many countries in the West where an increasing rejection of Islamic values and practices and the segregation of Muslim students is taking place (Barakat 2018), a view in part influenced by Huntington's (1996) 'clash of civilizations' theory promoting Western hegemony globally, which Farazmand (2006) argues 'will produce nothing but a catastrophe for the world' (p. 7).

The problem of globalisation is essentially an exported form of Western education (Burbules and Torres 2000; Donn and Al Manthri 2010; Spring 2014), usually of neoliberal character promoting corporate capitalist economic values and accountability regimes imported from the private sector, subjecting national systems, regardless of character or age to a tyranny of international rankings and Western accreditation (Altbach 2003). A globalised education, according to Asfour (2006), asserts a hegemony that tends towards a conformity, which in the Middle East means to extra-Arab and non-Islamic values, negatively affecting identity and culture. As part of the transformations taking place is the need for a large proportion of the younger generations to acquire a higher education. An additional factor is the common practice of people from these countries taking postgraduate degrees in Western countries where usually only Western theories and experiences are studied, and then return to Muslim countries and teach what they were taught, in many cases without integrating local knowledge and content into their curriculum (Mullen et al. 2013). The impact of this on students, in the UAE for example, of a curriculum that promotes Western values and identity and the English language causes them to increasing behave in a Western manner and become detached from Arabic and their culture (Khelifa 2010).

This ideology can be seen in those Westerners, for example, who teach a completely foreign curriculum in countries with distinctively different societal traditions and arrangements, eschewing any opportunities to learn from the new countries they are in, essentially violating the human rights of their students to their own culture, and using a curriculum which carries a hidden curriculum (Giroux 1983) of Westernising colonisation, a not-so-well masked 'orientalism' in Said's sense (1978) of attributing to only one tradition the values of civilisation and knowledge. Even the attempts to internationalise curriculum often do not authentically represent diverse traditions, by making 'add-ons' to a predominantly Western, or Anglo-American, curricular theoretical structure and foundation. If educational administration and leadership also have to prepare professionals to administer and lead in their own countries, they need a grounding in knowledge, skills and role construction that has cultural, organisational and legal integrity, is comprehensive and demonstrates how their knowledge traditions can 'stand independent' in the sense of not having to be propped up by foreign knowledge systems, except in cases where they are engaged in multicultural and international affairs (Samier 2014a, b).

Globalisation critiques in many parts of the world reflect a growing and more diversified postcolonial literature, most initially influenced by Said's (1978) critical concept of 'Orientalism' which includes transplanted education curricular models, tests, teaching staff and those from the region educated in the West who transmit that education, often unmodified, when they return to the Middle East. These include a broad range of psychological, social, cultural and political approaches: cultural imperialism by Satterthwaite and Atkinson (2005), Mignolo (2011) and Naidoo (2007); neocolonisation by Memmi (2003), Quist (2001) and Nkrumah (2009); colonisation of mind by Thiong'o (1986); epistemicide by Hall and Tandon (2017), Gandhi (1998) and de Sousa Santos (2007) who views it as a cognitive injustice; subaltern identities by Gramsci (1971), Guha (1982) and Spivak (1992); symbolic violence by Bourdieu and Wacquant (1992); necrocapitalism by Banerjee (2008); and a cultural security problem by Samier (2015). Applied to educational administration and leadership, these critiques emphasise the neglect of both the conditions, values and culture of societies and communities (e.g. aboriginal) and their valuable intellectual traditions which themselves carry knowledge of leadership, administration and education, due in part to the heritage of colonisation, and more recently, a neoliberal style globalisation.

The remedies have been in development for a number of years now including a number of approaches that examine educational and deeper societal efforts such as decolonisation by Mignolo (2007, 2011) and Saffari et al. (2017) including in education (Barongo-Muweke 2016), and actionable postcolonial theory in education by Andreotti (2011) and Stein and Andreotti (2016). A broader inclusive approach has also been pursued through internationalising the field (Dimmock and Walker 2005; Vavrus and Bartlett 2009) and conducting comparative and cross-cultural studies (Miller 2017; Wiseman 2009; Zajda et al. 2009) that extend well beyond Western borders and that examine education in its societal context and through its contributions to national development. Relevant to this discussion is a body of literature on internationalising higher education curriculum that has been evolving since the 1990s, broadening its scope and advocates an incorporation of content reflecting many more countries' knowledge and practice traditions (Larsen 2016), particularly important for branch campuses of Western universities.

Being more inclusive and representative internationally has also affected the research methods literature. While some forms of research already took into account context and the participant's perspective such as hermeneutics and phenomenology (e.g. Glesne 2011; Van Manen 1990), since the early 1990s a movement within research methods to contextualise research practices that are more appropriate to social, political and cultural conditions has been taking shape, as well as examining risk levels in some countries where the laws are restrictive. This includes a large body of aboriginal research methods, mostly originating in Canada, Australia, New Zealand and the USA (e.g. Graveline 2000; Haig-Brown and Archibald 1996; Rigney 1999; Smith 1999), and culturally sensitive research methods literature that has global representation now (e.g. Johnstone 2019; Silverman 2017; Wilson 2003), including historiography important in examining the development of educational systems in transcultural context (Herren et al. 2012). Many of these issues and principles also apply to minorities where culture and identity are different and where colonisation has occurred (e.g. Tillman 2002).

There are a few other bodies of literature that are not used as extensively as they could be for curricular and pedagogical use, for example, international public administration (Farazmand 2002), policy transfer literature in public administration (Dolowitz and Marsh 2000; Hadjiisky et al. 2017; Ventriss 1989), now being researched in education (Scott et al. 2016), and sometimes referred to as policy borrowing (Portnoi 2016; Steiner-Khamsi 2004) where major modifications and adjustments should be made when using policy precedents from other countries; multiple modernities (Sachsenmaier et al. 2002) and that demonstrate how a local and indigenous form of educational administration and leadership would be far more effective (Minthorn and Chavez 2015), and organisation studies that examine cross-culturalism, interculturalism and transculturalism (e.g. Dimmock and Walker 2005). This does not mean an utter rejection of any Western research principles and practices, but there are better ways to conduct research that preserves the integrity, dignity and traditions of other countries.

Education in the Islamic Traditions

An examination of educational administration and leadership teaching has to be done within the context of Islamic education. This includes an understanding of the foundational philosophies and principles for relevant curriculum and pedagogy in the *Qur'an* and *Sunnah* and those developed by classical scholars, as well as an understanding of the nature of education and its role in society. The aim of education established in its primary sources is both practical and fulfils religious values and requirements of Islam which requires education that produces good people in the virtue tradition. This requires a balanced growth in personality by holistically educating and training the spirit, intellect, rationality, feelings and body to serve *Allah*, the community and humankind (Yasin and Jani 2013) with the emphasis being on character-centred leadership that Beekun (2012) argues reflects the concept of 'practical wisdom,' defined by Nonaka and Takeuchi (2011) as 'tacit knowledge acquired from experience that enables people to make prudent judgments and take actions based on the actual situation, guided by values and morals' (p. 60).

Al-Attas (1980) emphasises this wholistic nature of Islamic education that includes reasoning, meaning-making, heart, intellect and mind, and aiming at a properly ordered society. Sarwar (1996) also presents an Islamic philosophy of education that is wholistic and which should prepare for adult responsibilities in society and preparation to participate in its social institutions. The results from a number of international conferences are relatively consistent with moderate Muslim scholars who trace their theories of education and its management and leadership to the primary texts and practices of Islam including the 'articulation of Islamic values, Qur'an and Hadith as foundational texts, promotion of science for the good of mankind, promotion of Islamic theories in economics, politics, sociology and philosophy, making sharia the core, and establishing a provisional body of Muslim thinkers and educators to monitor and drive education' (Erfan and Zahid 1995, p. 62).

Islamic education is also oriented towards one's civil rights and civic responsibilities (Merry 2007). It is these fundamental values of education that also have to inform educational administration and leadership with responsibilities for evaluation and monitoring of educational organisation and practices as well as professional staff development and an oversight of curriculum.

While there has been a continuous tradition in scholarship of the Islamic educational tradition since its medieval development by authors like Ibn Sina, Ibn Rushd and Al-Farabi, there is renewed interest appearing in a number of countries that are either Muslim or have large Muslim minorities where independent or private schools have been established by these communities aimed at improving the quality of education, reasserting its traditional values, and addressing identity and citizenship issues (e.g. Abbas 2011; Abdalla et al. 2006; Al Zeera 2001; Sahin 2013) and providing a foundation for the development of educational administration and leadership for a modern world. An important dimension of Islamic education is the growing number of Muslim schools in non-Muslim countries, for example, in the UK (Scott-Baumann and Cheruvallil-Contractor 2015), France (Bourget 2019), and Europe generally and South Africa (Tayob et al. 2011). Some of this literature also tackles Islamophobic problems they are encountering in countries like the UK (Breen 2018), and more broadly (Van Driel 2004).

Administration and Leadership in the Islamic Traditions

A discussion in the Islamic tradition of administration and leadership begins with relevant passages in the *Qur'an*. There are several that present the Prophet Muhammad as a role model for leadership, to which people should strive to follow that include an emphasis on 'an exalted standard of character' using the term *khuluq* which connotes the acquisition of custom or habits rather that inborn qualities, his suitability as an excellent model and one from whom wisdom can be learned (Beekun 2012). Those qualities associated with an exemplary character suitable for leadership include truthfulness and the integrity associated with not lying, trustworthiness in not compromising values and not cheating others, being just towards all, being benevolent towards all even those who have behaved unjustly or unfairly towards one, exhibiting humility and kindness and exercising patience. Such individuals need to be able to inspire others, demonstrate relevant competences and be willing to authentically engage in consultation. What is notable in this tradition is that leadership depends upon the voluntary participation of followers and cannot issue from compelling others to act against their will issuing from an understanding of leadership as both a servant to one's people and a protector or guardian from tyranny and oppression (Beekun and Badawi 1999; ElKaleh and Samier 2013).

Part of character is in the motivation for being a leader—those who are enamoured with it and pursue it out of self-interest should not be leaders nor should those who enjoy the exercise of power and who are not willing or capable of continuous self-improvement. These kinds of requirements mean that anyone qualified for leadership must have a high level of self-awareness, self-reflection and self-critique. These are necessary for the accountabilities that have to be met and the quality and rigour of one's intentions. For Beekun (2012), many of the character traits correspond to those of a servant leadership model as well as how Burns defined transforming leadership in helping others strive to be better people and providing them the guidance and support they need to do so.

Based on these principles, and the *Sunnah*, the speech and actions of the Prophet Muhammad, the Islamic classical tradition evolved through several centuries in the medieval period through scholarship and practice that also incorporated many pre-Islamic practices that were not in conflict with Islamic values. The scholars include such figures as Ibn Khaldun (1969) who created a sociological tradition that examined roles and structures in Arab societies, Al-Farabi (1997), who recommended an integrated curriculum of foreign and Islamic content in higher education aimed at developing the active intellect as the cause of existence emphasising comprehension and conceptualisation and taught with imagination, Ibn Rushd (Davidson 1992), al-Kindi and al-Ghazali who focussed on the development of 'heart' in students aimed at higher-order values and happiness in their acquisition of theoretical and practical knowledge (Giladi 1987). These principles translate into educational leadership as a role modelling position from which one ensures that knowledge is respected and used for the public good, in teachers and students working towards a higher level of self-characterisation by moral principle and emulating the Islamic virtues of character (see ElKaleh and Samier 2013; Shah 2016).

There are many classical sources that inform teaching practices, professionalism, a culture of learning, the necessary conditions for learning including constructive relationships among teacher, student and parent, and the responsibilities of the state in providing and governing education. Guenther (2005) provides a detailed discussion of many of the most important authors in these respects such as Ibn-Sahnun who wrote the first handbook for teachers from the Maliki school of jurisprudence emphasising the just and fair treatment of students and challenging their minds. Al-Jahiz emphasised student-centred learning, teacher professionalism and dynamic interpretive learning over rote memorisation and Al-Mawardi from the Umayyad Caliphate who promoted scholarship and books as necessary to learning. Al-Qabisi wrote on the conditions that teachers and students need for effective education as well as al-Tusi, a philosopher–vizier, who focussed on education as a process-involving teacher, student and parents as a cohesive dynamic aimed at the enjoyable acquisition of knowledge leading to happiness. Finally, the role of the state in governing and managing the emerging educational systems in the first centuries of Islam was a concern for many scholars and administrators in shaping this social institution (Makdisi 1961; Rosenthal 1962; Talbani 1996).

For most countries in the Middle East, this heritage changed significantly starting in the seventeenth century with the beginnings of the colonial period which advanced a secular education to prepare colonial bureaucrats (Talbani 1996), often at odds with Islamic principles (Cook 1999), and postcolonial periods in which reconstituting the Islamic education tradition that also meets the needs of modernisation (Merry 2007) and nation- and institution-building.

One of the most significant bodies of literature in the Islamic administrative tradition is the 'Mirror of Princes' literature written by scholars and senior administrative officials which served not only rulers and their viziers but all leadership and administrative posts. These writings that identify not only personal qualities, knowledge, skills and character traits, and the values that underpin them, but also the type of education and training needed to fulfil these roles including those responsible for educational organisations. The main aim of this literature was to translate the principles in the *Qur'an* and *Sunnah* into character requirements, ways of making decisions, who to recruit as staff and how to work with them and the population in providing effective organisations for the public good. In this sense also, the Prophet Muhammad (p) through the *Hadith* and *Sunnah* provides a role model, his essential purpose in Islam to emulate the *Qur'an*, in this interpretive process and in constructing the model for leaders and administrators. Beekun (2012) argues that his example provides virtues and moral alternative to two of the dominant approaches which have in part led to problems of corruption: the transactional, which is self-centred, the transformational, value-neutral, and the responsible model that is unidimensional and incomplete, focussing on one virtue only.

This body of writings is very large, leadership and administration being critical to nation and empire building as well as principles guiding the evolution of social institutions. However, the use of this literature to inform contemporary practice is not well developed and only emerging as a main factor in internationalising leadership and administration fields with examples like Boroujerdi (2013). The main relevant texts of contemporary interest are the following: the eleventh-century *Qābūs-nāma* (*A Mirror for Princes*) by ibn Qābūs and ibn Washmgīr (1951); the eleventh-century *The Ordinances of Government* (*al-Ahkam as-Sultaniyyah*) by Abu'l-Hasan Al-Mawardi (2002); the eleventh-century *The Book of Government or Rules for Kings* (*Siyar al-Mulūk or Siyāsat-nāma*) by Nizām. A-Mulk (2002); the eleventh-century Turko-Islamic *Wisdom of Royal Glory* (*Kutadgu Bilig*) by Yusuf Khass Hajib (1983); the anonymously authored mid-twelfth-century Persian *The Sea of Precious Virtues* (*Bahr. al-Favā'id*) (1991); and ibn Zafar al-Siqilli's (2005) twelfth-century *Consolation for the Ruler During the Hostility of Subjects* (*Sulwan al-Muta' fi "Udwan al-Atba"*) in *The Just Prince*.

Many of these texts were intended to be used as training manuals and as guidelines for practice much in the same sense that modern policies, regulations and procedures are used. For example, the eight-century Abdullah Ibn al-Muqaffa, in his rules for the court, the *al-Adab al-Kabir*, stressed values of friendship, cooperation and solidarity with others, and the ability to assume responsibility reflecting both religious values and reason derived in part from his use of Aristotle's *Nicomachean Ethics*, that should govern the relations between those with power and position and those who are governed or led (Daiber 2013). Also emphasised in this text is the importance of learning, including the acquisition of foreign knowledge, that produces the moral dispositions and social responsibilities producing administrative and leadership ability from which rulers in the caliphates of the medieval period recruited their viziers and other administrative staff a theme that runs through many of the later, and more famous mirrors of princes. Some of these authors, like Al-Mawardi, established training programmes and schools for the public sector, including those responsible for the education sector. An additional importance to this literature for educational administration is that it is during the Islamic classical period that one of the earliest university systems was created (Rosenthal 1962).

A close reading of this literature contains many similarities with particularly humanistically oriented Western theories that emphasise the roles of higher-order values, community service, kinds of sources that are valuable, such as biographies (English 1995) and the importance of role modelling for principled, collaborative and visionary leadership for the common good (see Jubran 2015). This is not surprising given the close relationships intellectually between Europe and the Islamic world and the strong influence the latter's tradition had on scholarship (Huff 2003; Watt 1982) and the rise of universities (Makdisi 1981). Some authors like Beekun (2012) look to the Islamic tradition as a way of improving leadership since so many of the models that have been used are deficient in a number of ways particularly morally and in character development. His argument is that even in non-Muslim contexts, the Islamic model has aspects that are transferable.

Chapter Overviews

While the field of educational administration has grown remarkably over the last few decades, Anglo-American perspectives have still been dominating the field, although there have been increasing requests (e.g. Alatas 2006; Ali 1992; Mullen et al. 2013) to develop more nationally and culturally relevant curricula that represent and respect the traditional knowledge and values of Muslim and other countries. This volume responds to these requests by investigating the development of the educational administration and leadership field in a number of Muslim countries and proposing different approaches and theoretical foundations to integrate indigenous knowledge, culture and values into its curricula. To this end, chapters included in this volume examine various approaches to and issues in teaching educational administration and leadership in Muslim countries and in the Muslim world generally, including contextual and conceptual factors and relevant curricular and pedagogical theories and practices.

The first section, 'Foundational Theories and Models', offers theoretical foundations for developing educational administration and leadership curricula in Muslim countries. It starts with Samier's examination of the Islamic humanist tradition and its application to the teaching of educational administration and leadership in Muslim countries. She first compares the basic principles of the Islamic humanist tradition with the classical to the contemporary times and the Western humanist tradition, explaining how both traditions relate to conceptions of the good, ethics, and higher-order values that are grounded in human qualities such as autonomy, freedom and emancipation. Then, she discusses the principles of ideal leadership and administration that humanism aims at in its preparation of leaders and official administrators. Finally, she concludes with an argument of how the Islamic humanist tradition can contribute to intercultural and transcultural graduate teaching in international educational administration.

In the following chapter, ElKaleh proposes a theoretical model that offers a critical and holistic approach to leadership teaching using Habermas' theories of communicative action and knowledge and human interests. The model adopts an intercultural and interdisciplinary approach to learning that can be used for developing culturally relevant and critically reflective leadership curricula in Muslim and other countries. The chapter starts with a critical review of Habermas' account of critical theory, focussing on his theories of communicative action and knowledge and human interests in particular, and then provides a critical discussion of the theoretical model including the content and teaching practices recommended by leadership scholars and leadership literature worldwide to provide students with a balanced and pluralistic learning experience that addresses both spiritual and intellectual aspects of knowledge. ElKaleh concludes the chapter with a critical reflection of her own experience in using the model with Muslim students.

This section ends with Harold and Stephenson's discussion on the development and implementation of an educational leadership graduate programme in a Middle Eastern tertiary institution and its theoretical foundation using the social-constructivist perspective and Habermas' theory of communicative action. Using a Bourdieuian framework, they first provide a contextual overview of the nature of neoliberal policy enactments and their impact on teaching and learning in Middle Eastern higher education. Then, they discuss an educational leadership programme that they have developed and implemented for postgraduate Emirati students using content from Western and Islamic research and literature and pedagogical approaches informed by a social-constructivist perspective and Habermas' theory of communicative action. The chapter concludes with the successes and challenges of this programme and lessons learned through the development and implementation phases.

In the second section, 'Current Controversies and Challenges', Karami-Akkary and Hammad investigate the challenges and opportunities that educational leadership and management scholars face in Arab societies to establish an indigenous knowledge base that is connected to the global international scholarly discourse and their implications for leadership development in Arab countries. They argue that developing effective educational leadership programmes in the Arab countries must be based on a solid knowledge base that is well connected to international literature and research but also sensitive to traditional cultural values and responsive to the needs of indigenous practitioners. The first part of this chapter discusses the importance of research in leadership preparation programmes and highlights the major research themes found in the existing international literature. The second section investigates the current indigenous knowledge available on educational leadership and management literature in the Arab societies. In the final section, Karami-Akkary and Hammad discuss the implications of the current state of indigenous knowledge for educational leadership preparation and propose some future directions for educational leadership research and practice in the Arab region.

This is followed by Samier and Elkaleh's discussion on educational leadership for nation building in Muslim countries. They argue that there are no inherent conflicts or contradictions, as claimed by some scholars, between Islam and modernisation and those Muslim countries, using the conception of multiple modernities, can find their own path to modernisation—one that is based on Islamic values and principles with *Shura* as a political ideology. They discuss the leadership characteristics and qualities that Muslim leaders need to contribute effectively to economic development, social cohesion, cultural appropriateness and national solidarity. The conclusion suggests that nation-building efforts should involve an extensive use of historical events, traditional narratives and literature that aim to explain and convey cultural values and national ideologies to the new generations. This can be achieved through a hybrid curriculum model where international literature can be combined with material in the field reflecting the nature and character of Muslim countries, particularly if one is presenting the field in an interpretive and critical manner and taking into account the collective nature of Muslim societies.

The final chapter in this section by Tok and D'Alessandro argues that embeddedness and local cultures and contexts are key elements that should be included in entrepreneurship education, training and curricula. It contends that entrepreneurs should be able to understand and translate values and culture as well as territories knowledge into their work and practices. In this chapter, Tok and D'Alessandro investigate the entrepreneurial training and teaching in Qatar as an example of how leadership and policy may have a great role in designing and sustaining entrepreneurship education in line with national needs and aspiration. They start with an overview of entrepreneurship education and discuss embeddedness as a theoretical framework for the study. Then, they discuss entrepreneurship as an embedded process and its implications in Qatar. They conclude the chapter with lessons learned from the Qatari experience.

The third and final sections of country cases discuss educational administration and leadership in three Muslim countries, Turkey, Iran and Saudi Arabia. The first chapter by Beycioğlu, Cağatay Kılınç and Polatcan discusses the historical development of the educational administration and leadership in Turkey including the dominant leadership preparation approaches and practices. It presents the various factors that inhibit the development of educational administration as a professional field in Turkey and use Hofstede's cultural dimensions to investigate the behaviour of school administrators and the extent to which cultural values influence leadership preparation and practices in Turkey. The authors start with a historical overview of the development of educational administration in Turkey followed by a discussion on the preparation and appointment processes of school leaders. Then, they use Hofstede's cultural dimensions to investigate the behaviour of school leaders in Turkey and examine the extent to which culture and values of society affect the preparation of educational leaders.

In the next chapter, Rastehmoghadam uses the analytical-critical method to review the teaching status of educational administration in Iran and to analyse the constraints governing this process. He starts with an overview of the history of the traditional and modern education systems in Iran including the formation of educational studies and educational administration. Then, he discusses the factors that hinder the development of the field at the macro (historical and sociopolitical) and micro (research and curricula) levels.

Finally, Alsaleh investigates the waves of K-12 education reform in Saudi Arabia using Rogers' (2003) and Ely's (1990, 1999) Models of innovation and proposes curriculum outlines for leadership preparation in Saudi Arabia. The chapter discusses the various challenges that educational administrators face during the implementation processes and attributes the shortcomings to a lack of change management and leadership that failed to address the internal and external innovation factors during the implementation stages. The chapter starts with an overview of the Saudi education system and the Tatweer education reform project followed by an overview of Rogers (2003) and Ely's (1990, 1999) proposed frameworks. Next, it critically reviews Saudi education reforms and proposes curriculum outlines in change management and leadership for the preparation of future educational leaders at Saudi universities.

References

Abbas, T. (2011). *Islam and education: Major themes in education*. New York: Routledge.
Abdalla, A., Abu-Nimer, M., Nasser, I., Kadayific, A., Kunkle, L., & el-Kilani, S. (2006). *Improving the quality of Islamic education in developing countries: Innovative approaches*. Washington DC: Creative Associates International.
Achcar, G. (2006). *The clash of barbarisms: The making of the new world disorder*. London: Paradigm.
Ahmad, S., & Hussain, M. (2017). An investigation of the factors determining student destination choice for higher education in the United Arab Emirates. *Studies in Higher Education, 42*(7), 1324–1343.
Ahmed, M. (1990). *Islamic education: Redefinition of aims and methodology*. New Delhi: Qazi.
Al Zeera, Z. (2001). *Wholeness and holiness in education: An Islamic perspective*. London: The International Institute on Islamic Thought.
Al-Attas, S. (1980). *The Concept of Education in Islam: A framework for an Islamic philosophy of education*. Kuala Lumpur: ISTAC.
Al-Farabi, A. N. (1997). *On the perfect state*. Chicago: Kazi Publications.
Al-Mawardi, A. (2002). *The ordinances of government: Al-Ahkam as-Sultaniyyah w'al-Wilayat al-Diniyya*. Reading: Garnet Publishing.
Al-Mulk, N. (2002). *The book of government or rules for kings (Siyar al-Mulūk or Siyāsat-nāma)*. Abingdon: Routledge.
Alatas, S. F. (2006). *Alternative discourses in Asian social science: Responses to Eurocentrism*. New Delhi: Sage.
Ali, A. (1992). Management research themes and teaching in the Arab world. *International Journal of Educational Management, 6*(4), 7–11.
Altbach, P. (2003). American accreditation of foreign universities: Academic colonialism in action. *International Higher Education, 32,* 5–7.
Andreotti, V. (2011). *Actionable postcolonial theory in education*. New York: Palgrave Macmillan.
Anonymous. (1991). *The sea of precious virtues*. Salt Lake City: University of Utah Press.
Asfour, G. (2006). An argument for enhancing Arab identity within globalisation. In J. Fox, N. Mourtada-Sabbah & M. al-Mutawa (Eds.), *Globalisation in the Gulf* (pp. 141–147). London: Routledge.
Banerjee, S. (2008). Necrocapitalism. *Organization Studies, 29*(12), 1541–1563.

Barakat, M. (2018). Advocating for Muslim students: If not us, then who? *Journal of Educational Administration and History, 50*(2), 82–93.

Barongo-Muweke, N. (2016). *Decolonizing education: Towards reconstructing a theory of citizenship education for postcolonial Africa*. Wiesbaden: Springer.

Beekun, R. (2012). Character centered leadership: Muhammad (p) as an ethical role model for CEOs. *Journal of Management Development, 31*(10), 1003–1020.

Beekun, R., & Badawi, J. (1999). *Leadership: An Islamic perspective*. Beltsville, MD: Amana.

Boroujerdi, M. (Ed.). (2013). *Mirror for the Muslim prince: Islam and the theory of statecraft*. Syracuse, NY: Syracuse University Press.

Bourdieu, P., & Wacquant, L. (1992). *An invitation to reflexive sociology*. Chicago: University of Chicago Press.

Bourget, C. (2019). *Islamic schools in France: Minority integration and separatism in Western society*. Cham: Springer.

Branine, M. (2011). *Managing across cultures*. Los Angeles: Sage.

Breen, D. (2018). *Muslim schools, communities and critical race theory: Faith schooling in an islamophobic Britain?*. London: Macmillan.

Brooks, M., & Mutohar, A. (2018). Islamic school leadership: A conceptual framework. *Journal of Educational Administration and History, 50*(2), 54–68.

Burbules, N., & Torres, C. (Eds.). (2000). *Globalization and education: Critical perspectives*. Abingdon: Routledge.

Chhokar, J., Brodbeck, J., & House, R. (Eds.). (2007). *Culture and leadership across the world*. New York: Lawrence Erlbaum.

Cook, B. (1999). Islamic versus Western conceptions of education: Reflections on Egypt. *International Review of Education, 45*(3/4), 339–357.

Daiber, H. (2013). Humanism: A tradition common to both Islam and Europe. *Filozofija I Društvo, 24*(1), 293–310.

Davidson, H. (1992). *Alfarabi, Avicenna, and Averroes on intellect: Their cosmologies, theories of the active intellect, and theories of human intellect*. New York: Oxford University Press.

Dimmock, C., & Walker, A. (1998). Towards comparative educational administration: Building the case for a cross-cultural school-based approach. *Journal of Educational Administration, 36*(4), 379–401.

Dimmock, C., & Walker, A. (2005). *Educational leadership: Culture and diversity*. London: Sage.

Dolowitz, D., & Marsh, D. (2000). Learning from abroad: The role of policy transfer in contemporary policy-making. *Governance, 13*(1), 5–24.

Donn, G., & Al Manthri, Y. (2010). *Globalisation and higher education in the Arab Gulf States*. Oxford: Symposium Books.

Eid, M., & Karim, K. (Eds.). (2014). *Re-imagining the other: Culture, media, and Western-Muslim intersections*. Basingstoke: Palgrave Macmillan.

ElKaleh, E., & Samier, E. A. (2013). The ethics of Islamic leadership: A cross-cultural approach for public administration. *Administrative Culture, 14*(2), 188–211.

Ely, D. P. (1990). Conditions that facilitate the implementation of educational technology innovations. *Journal of Research on Computing in Education, 23*(2), 298–305.

Ely, D. P. (1999). *New perspectives on the implementation of educational technology innovations*. https://files.eric.ed.gov/fulltext/ED427775.pdf (accessed 15 May 2018).

English, F. (1995). Toward a reconsideration of biography and other forms of life writing as a focus for teaching educational administration. *Educational Administration Quarterly, 31*(2), 203–223.

Erfan, N., & Valie, Z. (Eds.). (1995). *Education and the Muslim world, challenge and response: Recommendation of the Four World conferences on Islamic education*. Islamabad: Institute of Policy Studies.

Farazmand, A. (Ed.). (2002). *Administrative reform in developing nations*. Westport, CT: Praeger.

Farazmand, A. (2006). Globalization: A theoretical analysis with implications for governance and public administration. In A. Farazmand & J. Pinkowski (Eds.), *Handbook of globalization, governance, and public administration* (pp. 3–25). Boca Raton, FL: CRC Press.

Farazmand, A. & Pinkowski, J. (2006). Preface. In A. Farazmand & Pinkowski, J. (Eds.), *Handbook of globalization, governance, and public administration*. Boca Raton: CRC Press.

Fox, W. (2008). The United Arab Emirates and policy priorities for higher education. In C. Davidson & P. Smith (Eds.), *Higher education in the Gulf States: Shaping economies, politics and culture* (pp. 110–125). London: Saqi.

Gandhi, L. (1998). *Postcolonial theory: A critical introduction*. New York: Columbia University Press.

Giladi, A. (1987). Islamic educational theories in the Middle Ages: Some methodological notes with special reference to al-Ghazali. *Bulletin (British Society for Middle Eastern Studies), 14*(1), 3–10.

Giroux, H. (1983). *Hidden curriculum and moral education*. Richmond, CA: McCutchan.

Glesne, C. (2011). *Becoming qualitative researchers: An introduction*. Boston: Allyn & Bacon.

Gramsci, A. (1971). *Selections from the prison notebooks*. New York: International Publishers.

Graveline, F. J. (2000). Circle as methodology: Enacting an Aboriginal paradigm. *Qualitative Studies in Education, 13*(4), 361–370.

Guenther, S. (2006). Be masters in that you teach and continue to learn: Medieval Muslim thinkers on educational theory. *Comparative Education Review, 50*(3), 367–388.

Guenther, S. (2005). Advice for teachers: The 9th century Muslim scholars Ibn Sahnun and Al-Jahiz on pedagogy and didactics. In S. Guenther (Ed.), *Ideas, images and methods of portrayal: Insights into classical Arabic literature and Islam* (pp. 79–116). Leiden: Brill.

Guha, R. (1982). *Subaltern studies I*. Delhi: Oxford University Press.

Gulrajani, N., & Moloney, K. (2012). Globalizing public administration: today's research and tomorrow's agenda. *Public Administration Review, 72*(1), 78–86.

Hadjiisky, M., Pal, L., & Walker, C. (Eds.). (2017). *Public policy transfer: Micro-dynamics and macro-effects*. Cheltenham: Edward Elgar.

Haig-Brown, C., & Archibald, J. (1996). Transforming First Nations research with respect and power. *Qualitative Studies in Education, 9*(3), 245–267.

Haj-Yehia, K., & Erez, M. (2018). The impact of the ERASMUS program on cultural identity: A case study of an Arab Muslim female student from Israel. *Women's Studies International Forum, 70*, 32–38.

Hajib, Y. K. (1983). *Wisdom of royal glory: A Turko-Islamic mirror for princes*. Chicago: University of Chicago Press.

Hall, B., & Tandon, R. (2017). Decolonization of knowledge, epistemicide, participatory research and higher education. *Research for All, 1*(1), 6–19.

Hallinger, P. & Hammad, W. (2017). Knowledge production on educational leadership and management in Arab societies: A systematic review of research. *Educational Management, Administration & Leadership*. https://doi.org/10.1177/1741143217717280.

Hammad, W., & Hallinger, P. (2017). A systematic review of conceptual models and methods used in research on educational leadership and management in Arab societies. *School Leadership & Management, 37*(5), 434–456.

Henry, C., & Springborg, R. (2001). *Globalization and the Politics of Development in the Middle East*. Cambridge: Cambridge University Press.

Herren, M., Rüesch, M., & Sibille, C. (Eds.). (2012). *Transcultural history: Theories, methods, sources*. Berlin: Springer.

Hourani, R., Diallo, I., & Said, A. (2011). Teaching in the Arabian Gulf: Arguments for the deconstruction of the current educational model. In C. Gitsaki (Ed.), *Teaching and learning in the Arab world* (pp. 335–355). Bern: Peter Lang.

Huff, T. (2003). *The rise of early modern science: Islam, China, and the West*. Cambridge: Cambridge University Press.

Huntington, S. P. (1996). *The clash of civilizations and the remaking of world order*. New York: Simon and Schuster.

Ibn Khaldun, A. (1969). *The Muqaddimah: An introduction to history*. Princeton: Princeton University Press.

1 Editors' Introduction: An Overview of the Educational …

Jabnoun, N. (2008). *Islam and Management*. Riyadh: International Islamic Publishing House.

Johnstone, L. (2019). *The politics of conducting research in Africa: Ethical and emotional challenges in the field*. Cham: Springer.

Jubran, A. (2015). Educational leadership: A new trend that society needs. *Procedia, 210,* 28–34.

Karim, K., & Eid, M. (Eds.). (2014). *Engaging the other: public policy and Western-Muslim intersections*. Basingstoke: Palgrave Macmillan.

Khelifa, M. (2010). Trading culture: Have Western-educated Emirati females gone Western? *OIDA International Journal of Sustainable Development, 1,* 19–29.

Larsen, M. (2016). *Internationalization of higher education: An analysis through spatial, network, and mobilities theories*. New York: Palgrave Macmillan.

Makdisi, G. (1961). Muslim institutions of learning in eleventh century Baghdad. *Bulletin of Oiental and African Studies, 24*(2), 1–56.

Makdisi, G. (1981). *The rise of colleges: Institutions of learning in Islam and the West*. Edinburgh: Edinburgh University Press.

Van Manen, M. (1990). *Researching lived experience: Human science for an action sensitive pedagogy*. Albany: SUNY Press.

Maringe, F., & Foskett, N. (2012). Introduction: Globalization and universities. In F. Maringe & N. Foskett (Eds.), *Globalization and internationalization in higher education: Theoretical, strategic and management perspectives* (pp. 1–13). London: Continuum.

Memmi, A. (2003). *The colonizer and the colonized*. London: Earthscan.

Merry, S. (2007). *Culture, identity, and Islamic schooling: A philosophical approach*. Houndmills: Palgrave Macmillan.

Mignolo, W. (2007). Delinking: The rhetoric of modernity, the logic of coloniality and the grammar of decoloniality. *Cultural Studies, 21*(2), 449–514.

Mignolo, W. (2011). *The darker side of Western modernity: Global future, decolonial options*. Durham: Duke University Press.

Miller, P. (Ed.). (2017). *Cultures of educational leadership: Global and intercultural perspectives*. London: Palgrave Macmillan.

Minthorn, R., & Chavez, A. F. (Eds.). (2015). *Indigenous leadership in higher education*. New York: Routledge.

Mullen, C. A., English, F. W., Brindley, S., Ehrich, L., & Samier, E. A. (2013). Neoliberal issues in public education. *Interchange, 43,* 181–186.

Naidoo, R. (2007). *Higher education as a global commodity: The perils and promises for developing countries*. London: Report for the Observatory on Borderless Higher Education.

Nkrumah, N. (2009). *Neo-colonialism: The last stage of imperialism*. New York: International Publishers.

Nonaka, I., & Takeuchi, H. (2011). The wise leader. *Harvard Business Review, 89*(5), 58–67.

Numan, R. (2015). Assuring quality outcomes: Best practices for higher education in Islamic countries. *IIUM Journal of Educational Studies, 3*(1), 92–111.

du Plessis, A. E. (2017). Design and intervention of an educational-leadership program: Student voice and agency, expectations and internationalization. *International Journal of Higher Education, 6*(1), 251–268.

Portnoi, L. (2016). *Policy borrowing and reform in education: Globalized processes and local contexts*. New York: Palgrave Macmillan.

Quist, H. (2001). Cultural issues in secondary education development in West Africa: Away from colonial survivals, toward neocolonial influences? *Comparative Education, 37*(3), 297–314.

Qābūs, Ibn, & Ibn Washmgīr, K. (1951). *A Mirror for Princes: The Qābūs-nāma*. New York: E. P. Dutton & Co.

Rigney, L. (1999). Internationalization of an indigenous anticolonial cultural critique of research methodologies: A guide to indigenist research methodology and its principles. *Wicazo Sa Review, 14*(2), 109–121.

Rogers, E. M. (2003). *Diffusion of innovations*. New York: Free Press.

Romanowski, M. (2017). Neoliberalism and Western accreditation in the Middle East: A critical discourse analysis of educational leadership constituent council standards. *Journal of Educational Administration, 55*(1), 70–84.

Rosenthal, E. (1962). *Political thought in medieval Islam.* Cambridge: Cambridge University Press.

Sachsenmaier, D., Riedel, J., & Eisenstadt, S. (Eds.). (2002). *Reflections on multiple modernities: European, Chinese and other interpretations.* Leiden: Brill.

Saffari, S., Abdolmaleki, K., & Akhbari, R. (2017). Unsettling colonial modernity: Islamicate contexts in focus. In S. Saffari, R. Akhbari, K. Abdolmaleki, & E. Hamdon (Eds.), *Unsettling colonial modernity in Islamicate contexts* (pp. 1–26). Newcastle upon Tyne: Cambridge Scholars Publishing.

Sahin, A. (2013). *New Directions in Islamic Education: Pedagogy and Identity Formation.* Turkey: KUBE.

Said, E. (1978). *Orientalism.* New York: Vintage Books.

Saleemad, K. (2015). Leadership competency model for Islamic school leaders. *International Journal of Humanities and Management Sciences, 3*(2), 86–88.

Samier, E. A. (2014a). Designing public administration curriculum for the United Arab Emirates: Principles for graduate PA programmes for a modernising Arab Islamic state. *Administrative Culture, 15*(2), 222–246.

Samier, E. A. (2015). Is the globalization of higher education a societal and cultural security problem? *Policy Futures in Education, 13*(5), 683–702.

Samier, E. A. (2014b). Western doctoral programmes as public service, cultural diplomacy or, intellectual imperialism? Teaching educational management & leadership in the United Arab Emirates. In A. Taysum & S. Rayner (Eds.), *Investing in our education? Leading, learning, researching and the doctorate* (pp. 93–123). Scarborough: Emerald.

Sarwar, G. (1996). *Issues in Islamic education.* London: Muslim Education Trust.

Satterthwaite, J., & Atkinson, E. (2005). *Discourses of education in the age of imperialism.* Stoke-on-Trent: Trentham Books.

Scott, D., Terano, M., Slee, R., Husbands, C., & Wilkins, R. (2016). *Policy transfer and educational change.* London: Sage.

Scott-Baumann, A., & Cheruvallil-Contractor, S. (2015). *Islamic education in Britain: New pluralist paradigms.* London: Bloomsbury.

Shah, S. (2006). Educational leadership: An Islamic perspective. *British Educational Research Journal, 32*(3), 363–385.

Shah, S. (2016). *Education, leadership and Islam: Theories, discourses and practices from an Islamic perspective.* Abingdon: Routledge.

Shah, I. A., & Baporikar, N. (2011). The suitability of imported curricula for learning in the Gulf states: An Oman perspective. In C. Gitsaki (Ed.), *Teaching and Learning in the Arab World* (pp. 275–292). Bern: Peter Lang.

Silverman, H. (Ed.). (2017). *Research ethics in the Arab region.* Cham: Springer.

Smith, L. T. (1999). *Decolonizing methodologies: Research and indigenous peoples.* London: Zed Books.

de Sousa Santos, B. (2007). Beyond abyssal thinking: From global lines to ecologies of knowledges. *Review of the Fernand Braudel Center, 30*(1), 45–89.

Spivak, G. (1992). Can the subaltern speak? In P. Williams & L. Chrisman (Eds.), *Colonial discourse and post-colonial theory* (pp. 66–111). New York: Columbia University Press.

Spring, J. (2014). *Globalization of education.* New York: Routledge.

Stein, S., & Andreotti, V. (2016). Postcolonial insights for engaging different in educational approaches to social justice and citizenship. In A. Peterson, R. Hattam, M. Zembylas, & J. Arthur (Eds.), *The Palgrave international handbook of education for citizenship and social justice* (pp. 229–245). London: Palgrave Macmillan.

Steiner-Khamsi, G. (Ed.). (2004). *The global politics of educational borrowing and lending.* New York: Teachers College Press.

Sulaiman, I. (1985). Education as imperialism. *Afkar Inquiry, 2*(7).

Talbani, A. (1996). Pedagogy, power and discourse: Transformation of Islamic education. *Comparative Education Review, 40*(1), 66–82.

Tayob, A., Niehaus, I., & Weisse, W. (Eds.). (2011). *Muslim schools and education in Europe and South Africa*. Münster: Waxmann.

Thiong'o, N. (1986). *Decolonizing the mind: The politics of language in African literature*. Oxford: James Currey.

Tillman, L. C. (2002). Culturally sensitive research approaches: An African-American perspective. *Educational Researcher, 31*(9), 3–12.

Trompenaars, F., & Hampden-Turner, C. (2012). *Riding the waves of culture*. London: Nicholas Brealey.

Van Driel, B. (Ed.). (2004). *Confronting islamophobia in educational practice*. London: Trentham Books.

Vavrus, F., & Bartlett, L. (Eds.). (2009). *Critical approaches to comparative education: Vertical case studies from Africa, Europe, the Middle East, and the Americas*. New York: Palgrave Macmillan.

Ventriss, C. (1989). The internationalization of public administration and public policy: Implications for teaching. *Policy Studies Review, 8*(4), 898–903.

Watt, M. (1982). *The influence of Islam on medieval Europe*. Edinburgh: Edinburgh University Press.

Wilkins, S. (2010). Higher education in the United Arab Emirates: An analysis of the outcomes of significant increases in supply and competition. *Journal of Higher Education Policy and Management, 32*(4), 389–400.

Wilson, S. (2003). Progressing toward an indigenous research paradigm in Canada and Australia. *Canadian Journal of Native Education, 27*(2), 161–178.

Wiseman, A. (2009). *Educational leadership: Global contexts and international comparisons*. Emerald: Bingley.

Yasin, R., & Jani, M. (2013). Islamic education: The philosophy, aim, and main features. *International Journal of Education and Research, 1*(10), 1–18.

Zafar, Ibn, & Al-Siqill, M. (2005). *The just prince: A manual of leadership*. Singapore: Horizon Books.

Zajda, J., Daun, H., & Saha, L. (Eds.). (2009). *Nation-building, identity and citizenship education: Cross-cultural perspectives*. Dordrecht: Springer.

Zia, R. (Ed.). (2006). *Globalization, modernization and education in Muslim countries*. New York: Nova Science.

Eugenie A. Samier is Reader in Educational Management and Leadership at the University of Strathclyde, Glasgow. Her research concentrates on administrative philosophy and theory, interdisciplinary foundations of administration, theories and models of educational leadership and comparative educational administration. She has frequently been Guest Researcher at the Humboldt University of Berlin, was Visiting Professor in the Department of Administrative Studies at the University of Tartu, Estonia (2003), Visiting Fellow at Oxford Brookes University and has been Guest Lecturer at universities and institutes in the USA, Germany, Estonia, Russia, Norway, Lithuania, Finland, Qatar, Bahrain and the UAE. Her publications include chapters and articles on organisational culture and values, the New Public Management, the role of history and biography in educational administration, the role of humanities, aesthetics and literary analysis in administration and Weberian foundations of administrative theory and ethics in a number of international book collections and many leading journals in the USA, Australia, the UK, Germany, the Baltic region and Canada. She is Founding Board Member of *Administrative Culture* journal and is Editor of several book collections with Routledge on ethics, aesthetics, politics, emotions, trust and betrayal, ideologies and maladministration in educational administration. She is also Associate Editor of the four-volume Master Works *Educational Leadership and Administration* (Sage 2009), a contributor on authority, bureaucracy, critical theory to *Encyclopaedia of Education Law* (Sage

2008), on aesthetics and human agency to the *Handbook of Educational Leadership* (Sage, 2011), aesthetics of leadership and bureaucratic theory to the *Handbook of Educational Theory* (Information Age Publishing, 2013). She has also written a number of articles on topics like toxic leadership, passive evil, kitschification of educational leadership, the avant-garde, postcolonial educational administration, and Islamic ethics, social justice, global governance, administrative tradition and educational change in the Middle East for several journals and book collections. She also worked as a management consultant in Canada to the public sector for a number of years on a broad variety of projects including legislation development, organisational reviews, board development and government department restructuring and redesign.

Eman S. ElKaleh studied her MBA at the University of Wollongong followed by a Ph.D. in Management, Leadership and Policy at the British University in Dubai in association with Birmingham University, UK. She received an Academic Excellence Award by Dubai International Academic City for her dissertation entitled 'Teaching Leadership in UAE Business and Education Programs: A Habermasean Analysis within an Islamic Context'. While Eman hails from Egypt, she has worked in the UAE at two major universities for nearly twenty years. Currently, she teaches business leadership at Zayed University's College of Business in addition to overseeing the Admission and Recruitment Unit. Understanding the need to develop leadership capacity in Gulf-Region countries, she is actively developing programmes and workshops to help Muslim students as well as the faculty and staff with whom they interact gain a better understanding of leadership from an Islamic perspective. She has given guest lectures on Islamic leadership at a number of universities abroad such as University of Oxford Brookes, UK, the Humboldt University of Berlin, Germany, Qatar University and at the British University and Zayed University in the UAE. Eman was selected to serve as the Chair of Professional Development in the MENASA NASPA Advisory Board. She is also participating in a number of international research projects in leadership studies. Eman also has a solid experience in reviewing research studies and serves as a reviewer for a number of international and national peer-reviewed conferences and research awards. Tasked with developing a comprehensive programme for student success, Eman was recognised for her innovation in 2012 by receiving Zayed University's highest honour at a university-wide ceremony.

Part I
Foundational Theories and Models

Chapter 2
The Humanist Roots of Islamic Administration and Leadership for Education: Philosophical Foundations for Intercultural and Transcultural Teaching

Eugenie A. Samier

Abstract This chapter examines the Islamic humanist tradition as it relates to the teaching of educational administration and leadership in a Muslim context, with implications for intercultural and transcultural use and to show correspondences with Western humanism. The initial section is a comparison of the central principles of the Islamic humanist tradition from the classical through to contemporary times with the Western humanist tradition as they relate to conceptions of the good, ethics, the construction of meaning and a set of higher order values predicated upon human dignity, integrity, empathy, well-being and the public good. In both, professions are viewed as meaningful work that allow for large measures of decision-making, and are grounded in human qualities and needs including autonomy, freedom and emancipation balanced with responsibilities, obligations and duties to society. These are compared with principles of knowledge in Western humanism. Secondly, the chapter examines the principles of good or ideal leadership and administration that humanism aims at in its preparation of officials, including those in the educational sector in the classical Islamic tradition. The chapter concludes with a discussion of how the Islamic humanist tradition can contribute to intercultural and transcultural graduate teaching in international educational administration.

Introduction

For a number of decades, humanism has been a minor but persistent approach in the Western field of administrative and leadership studies, and only recently has broadened to include other international humanist traditions (Dierksmeier et al. 2011). However, the development in education, particularly in non-Western contexts (e.g. Arar and Haj-Yehia 2018), is not as developed as humanism in business manage-

---

E. A. Samier (✉)
University of Strathclyde, Glasgow, UK
e-mail: eugenie.samier@gmail.com

© Springer Nature Singapore Pte Ltd. 2019
E. A. Samier and E. S. ElKaleh (eds.), *Teaching Educational Leadership in Muslim Countries*, Educational Leadership Theory,
https://doi.org/10.1007/978-981-13-6818-9_2

ment, which has produced a number of books that provide a comprehensive approach (e.g. Spitzeck et al. 2009; Von Kimakowitz et al. 2011) including management and leadership education (Amann et al. 2011). There are humanist texts in educational studies relevant to administration and leadership such as early theoretical foundations (Greenfield and Ribbins 1993; Samier 2005), humanisation as a necessary precondition for peace education often associated with critical perspectives like that of Freire (Gill and Niens 2014), in McLaren and Jamillo's (2007) promotion of a critical humanistic approach to the effects of global capitalism on education, and recently in the critique of neoliberal managerial administration of education that undermines humanistic foundations (Plum 2012). There are also international and comparative educational leadership arguments like those of Wong (1998) that moral humanism is a central feature of other cultures like Chinese which do not receive enough attention in the field in the West. A fuller exploration of humanism's effect on pedagogy and curriculum needs both a broader development in the contemporary world and a more comprehensive appreciation of several historical traditions—here its Islamic roots are explored.

Arguments for a return to humanism include the lack of intellectual depth and domination by a market-based business model (Niesche 2018). Another comes from the critique of neoliberalism and its internationalisation through globalised education where all but economic values are held as a priority and even serve as the underlying foundation for management and leadership models (Mullen et al. 2013), which also account for damaging effects on indigenous systems of belief critiqued in the post-colonial literatures, for example, the marginalisation of humanist Ubuntuism in a number of African communities (Barongo-Muweke 2016). Beekun (2012, p. 1003) sees, for example, the Islamic emphasis on character, morality and related values as a more valuable foundation for management than the current business(-derived) models that are predicated upon 'self-serving, individualistic and narcissistic tendencies'. Humanism has been a foundational philosophy from which other theories of education and its management have derived in many parts of the world, some of which still have influence in their communities like Confucianism and Islam which have given rise to intellectual traditions, research, the formation of educational systems and from which we can learn in an increasingly diversified world (Samier forthcoming).

The focus in this chapter is on the Islamic humanist tradition as it relates to the teaching of educational administration and leadership in a Muslim context, with implications for intercultural and transcultural use. As a number of scholars are beginning to point out, educational administration and leadership is not solely an Anglo-American topic as it has tended to be framed for the last few decades, but has many historical and international antecedents (Arar and Haj-Yehia 2018). The second purpose of the chapter is to show the correspondences that exist between the Islamic and Western humanist traditions in terms of human values, knowledge and educational ideal, which in this chapter are argued to be close in many ways to the Western Idealist tradition and the German Bildung conception of education, despite significant differences that may provide avenues of understanding in multicultural environments.

Humanistic Principles in Islam and the West

The purpose of this section is to identify the core values and principles of humanism in the West and Islam, including their historical relationship, and to discuss in more detail the forms it takes in Islamic leadership and administration. Although the traditions in the West and Islam are related, through similar ideas of the good, ethics, the construction of meaning and a set of higher order values predicated upon human dignity, integrity, empathy, well-being and the public good (Goodman 2003), they do differ in a few significant ways. But in both, professions are viewed as meaningful work that allow for large measures of decision-making, and are grounded in human qualities and needs including autonomy, freedom and emancipation balanced with responsibilities, obligations and duties to society.

Humanism in the West

The concept of humanism in the West refers primarily to the Renaissance movement of valuing human beings and the culture and values that place humanity in the centre of considerations, coming to mean a non-religious or secular perspective by the modern period, although by the mid-twentieth century, took on a broader view that reflected interest internationally in systems of thought as a recognition that the values associated with Western humanism were shared by other traditions (Copson 2015). What is shared is a moral and political concern for the welfare of human beings, their ability to use reason, express their views and concerns, and work to construct a world in which individuals can reach their full human potential. The degree to which this rests on a 'scientific' approach to reality has been disputed by interpretive and critical approaches that distinguish between science as a value and method for knowing the natural world and understanding that is used to learn about human life and whether humanism is necessarily secular and non-religious (see Nasr 2006; Oldmeadow 2004) is a contentious point, with which some have taken issue, particularly in humanism's development historically within religious systems of thought (Zimmerman 2012). However, the view taken here is that early humanism and continuing as a tradition within the field is that humanistic knowledge can be grounded in direct spiritual experience. The historical relationship of Western and Islamic scholarship (e.g. Al-Rodhan 2012; Essa 2010) is a close shared tradition through humanist and liberal arts traditions where the influence is strongest with respect to conceptions of peace and cosmopolitanism (Küng 2008; March 2009; Said 2004; Tampio 2012) with respect to conceptions of peace and cosmopolitanism, and in principles of public policy (Karim and Eid 2014).

Depending on the form of humanism, a variety of character and personality traits as well as styles of social interaction are considered in the human interest. The main values of humanism focus on the human condition as they relate to peace, justice, equality and human rights along with tolerance and personal responsibility in a world that is humanly created at least on a sociopolitical and cultural level. This necessitates the cultivation of human reason, awareness, decision-making and choice in order for people to achieve their ideals and aspirations, create meaning and cultivate virtues of character. What is also closely associated with this approach are capacities of sympathy and empathy as well as a critical and interpretive understanding of society and its social institutions (Grayling 2015).

Humanism, as it is interpreted for application to leadership and management studies, focuses on a few key principles: respect for the dignity of each person to prevent exploitation and abuse (Pirson and Kostera 2017); ethical decision-making as the foundation of business practices that derives from a Kantian-type view that people are ends in themselves rather than means to goals, an approach that characterises many management models; and normative legitimacy in business for contributing positively to society and meeting corporate responsibilities rather than the self-interest that often dominates corporate culture (Von Kimakowitz et al. 2011). The shift in perspective is one from the market, efficiency and exchange values to human and societal well-being as intrinsic values focused on human rights, the elevation of ethics to a position of primacy and the use of the humanities in education and research in constructing knowledge and achieving cultural sensitivity. Amann and Stachowicz-Stanusch (2013) emphasise integrity as a core humanistic value that should govern organisations in achieving dignity, through three means that affect social interaction particularly affecting leadership roles: overcoming organisational inconsistencies in 'actions, values, methods, measure, principles, expectations, and outcomes' in humanism; closing gaps that exist between behaviour and appropriate societal norms; and overcoming the incompatibilities between the organisation's structures and practices that compromise moral principles (p. 3).

A humanistic approach initially developed in many Western countries as an investigation of their administrative systems focused on the (quasi-humanistic) human relations movement followed by organisational humanism (Kaplan and Tausky 1977) and subsequently by more participatory forms of leadership, debureaucratising to humanise public agencies (Gagliardi and Czarniawska 2006), and managing with integrity (Amann and Stachowicz-Stanusch 2013) while emphasising interpretivism, hermeneutic and phenomenological approaches as well as emancipatory critical theory (Box 2005) and using the humanities in teaching management fields (e.g. Brown 1994; Czarniawska-Joerges and Guillet de Monthoux 1994). Similar concepts have been explored in educational administration (Greenfield and Ribbins 1993; Samier 2005). While it is common in the literature to find humanism associated with the 'Western' tradition (Antweiler 2012), there are other humanisms in addition to the Islamic which also have relevance for administrative studies, such as African, Indian and Chinese societies (e.g. Copson and Grayling 2015; Dierksmeier et al. 2011; Leoussi 2000; Schiele 1990).

Humanism in educational administration and leadership in the West rest partly on the foundation of the literature on humanism in education generally, such as Veugelers (Veugelers 2011; see also Aloni 2007; Steiner 2004) for whom autonomy combined with humanity in education allows one to have agency and assume personal responsibility guided by moral principle, developing one's capacity and contributing to the welfare of others. In more politically radical form, it is aimed at emancipation in Freire (Roberts 2000). In educational administration, the first major scholar to open the door theoretically and practically to humanism was Thom Greenfield (Greenfield and Ribbins 1993) who began his transformation from the dominant structural functionalism towards a humanistic perspective in the 1970s developing towards an existential view grounded in classical thought and mostly the idealist intellectual tradition, followed by a few authors like Maxcy and Liberty (1983) and Ribbins (2003). While the field has not engaged in detail in humanism, it has produced a body of the literature that strives for a 'humane' model (e.g. Aloni and Weintrob 2017; Giancola and Hutchison 2005), is associated with neo-Marxist (Smyth 1989) and critical theory (Foster 1986) humanism through feminist critiques (Blackmore 1999), social justice (Lumby and Coleman 2007), and a broad range of critical perspectives like Bourdieu (Thomson 2017), Foucault (Gillies 2013) and Arendt (Gunter 2014), and is reflected in many postcolonial approaches (e.g. Rhea 2015) encompassing the main values of humanism regarding dignity, freedom, peace, tolerance, equality and a sensitivity to human qualities, both positive and negative.

Humanism in Islam

Humanism's relevance to leadership and management is not new to the Islamic tradition. Many passages in the Qur'an and Hadith were intended to apply to the economic sector by seeking to ground business practices in morality as an application of fundamental principles of rights, justice and equity, tolerance and harmoniousness for society. The texts are specific in their application itemising guidelines for contracts, transactions, jurisprudential guidelines and procedures, and identifying forms of business that were morally desirable as well as character traits that met these standards (Mohammed 2013). One can also infer from the Prophet Muhammad's actions and speech that his purpose of inviting others to the good and right, provides a model of appropriate leadership in others, which in an organisational context can be understood as creating a culture and work that allows others to develop into their full potential within a moral framework. A broad range of behaviour was itemised as undesirable and therefore immoral (haram) such as greed, the misuse of wealth in damaging others and the community, using violence and maligning others, all of which are inconsistent with the Qur'anic conception of good character consisting of goodness, righteousness, equity, harmony and justice, the truth and the right, and piety (Mohammed 2013). Those in leadership positions should be governed by integrity and honesty with a duty to compassion and protecting others (ElKaleh and Samier 2013).

Social justice is at the heart of this tradition, observed by Mir (2010) to consist of a vision for leadership of shaping a society that is just, egalitarian, and welfare-oriented and free from oppression and discrimination. Mir compares the Islamic leadership model consisting of the attributes of piety, humility, social responsibility, self-development and mutual consultation, as most closely related to Burns' (1978) conception of transforming leadership since its primary responsibility is that of raising others to higher moral and motivational levels.

These central humanistic Islamic concepts were expressed by a large number of scholars beginning in the earliest years of the Islamic medieval intellectual tradition, among the best known being Al-Farabi, Al-Ghazali, Ibn Khaldun, Al-Kindi, Ibn Miskawayh, Ibn Sina and Ibn Rushd (Goodman 2003; Pormann 2010) reflecting a constructivist view of reality (Makdisi 1990; Morgan 1980), and heavily grounded in classical philosophy, particularly Plato and Aristotle. The religious philosophy of Al-Farabi and Ibn Sina, for example, was influenced heavily by the work of Aquinas, Augustine, Spinoza and Leibniz and the scientific writing in turn of Ibn Sina influenced Bacon among many others (Al-Khalili 2010; Lyons 2009; Masood 2009; Morgan 2007) particularly from the ninth through to the thirteenth centuries in what is referred to as the European Renaissance. During this period, many Christian, Jewish and Muslim scholars and monks visited centres of learning like Baghdad, Basra, Isfahan and in Al Andalus for whom knowledge was regarded as belonging to all of humanity (Leaman 1996; Ljamai 2015). It was a scholarly tradition that formed mostly in the Abbasid caliphate where rulers and senior officials heavily patronised education, the establishment of research centres and universities, and a community of scholars during which the major disciplines and scholarly schools formed and whose work translated classical philosophy and built upon its foundation. In the midst of this explosion of research and thought, the humanistic character of Islam was expanded on and formed the basis of the humanities and social sciences as well as some of the legal and religious commentary traditions.

What unites them, to varying degrees in their emphases, is the role of reason in producing knowledge and morality (Kraemer 1984) (although there was and still is controversy within Islamic scholarship on the relationship been rationality and religious doctrine of revelation), a concentration on the nature of humanity and its capacities, and the possibilities of education in producing the cultured, enlightened and knowledgeable human being, as well as a tradition of 'perennial wisdom' (Leaman 1996). What also distinguished them was their understanding of education and its essential role in producing a good and moral society through shaping individuals in education morally and intellectually as well as acquiring the knowledge and skills to participate fruitfully in society (Kraemer 1984).

The Humanistic Ideal of Islamic Educational Administration and Leadership

The central concept of '*adib*'—what education and experience is necessary in producing refined and cultured individuals—is roughly equivalent to the Greek notion of 'paideia' and the later German concept of 'Bildung', regarded as a necessary preparation in the Abbasid caliphate for the civil servants who served the empire (Leaman 1996). The main difference between the two Leaman argues is not significant, with the Greek oriented towards the state, and the Muslim towards service to Allah in community and societal forms. What unites the two is the belief that reason is a path to morality and the social good, requiring an educational process that provides the capabilities and knowledge to perfect oneself in a union of theory and practice, and is a lifelong pursuit that in Islam is a religious obligation in both the Qur'an and the Hadith (Günther 2006). It is in this tradition, producing a number of mirrors of princes that defined good rulership and public servant that Islamic humanistic models of leadership and administration are formed. It is during this period as well that Aristotle's work among other classical writers on the nature and relationship of various bodies of knowledge were built upon in forming the disciplines and curriculum.

The close humanistic correspondence between Islamic and Western humanism is also evident in education through key concepts, approaches to fundamental human values, the construction of knowledge and educational ideal as well as the kind of teaching practices that distinguish these traditions (Daiber 2013; Dossett 2014; Makdisi 1990) as they apply to humanistically oriented educational administration and leadership. This tradition is still evident in contemporary scholars who advocate a humanistic educational ideal (Afsaruddin 2016; Al-Attas 1980; Halstead 2004; Yasin and Jani 2013).

These principles were synthesised into a large body of curricular and pedagogical literature as scholarship expanded and an Islamic philosophy of education formed which discussed not only the aims and goals of education, but also teaching methods, how learning takes place, and the requisite actions and behaviour of students and teachers, particularly moral principles, which was understood to apply to all of those involved with education (Günther 2006) including those we would now identify as educational administrators and leaders. For example, Ibn Sahnun, whose influential 'Rules of Conduct for Teachers' (*Adab al-mu'allimin*) in the ninth century, specifies practices that overlap heavily into the educational administration role:

> Ibn Sahnun provides to (medieval) elementary-school teachers a number of specific instructions and rules that range from aspects of the curriculum and examinations to practical legal advice in such matters as the appointment and payment of the teacher, the organization of teaching and the teacher's work with the pupils at school, the supervision of pupils at school and the teacher's responsibilities when the pupils are on their way home, the just treatment of pupils (including, e.g., how to handle trouble between pupils), classroom and teaching equipment, and the pupils' graduation. (Günther 2006, p. 370)

The principles of good or ideal leadership and administration that humanism aims at in its preparation of officials discussed above apply equally to those in the educational sector. The classical Islamic tradition has been explored for its role in schools connected to the leadership of the governing powers and their administrators including the role of humanist texts and the style of education used such as the 'work–study course' practice (Hassi 2012; Kashif et al. 2015; Makdisi 1990).

Arar and Haj-Yehia (2018) have investigated conceptions of Islamic medieval educational leadership and its potential value to contemporary multiculturalism. While the goals in Islamic education are not only for this life, but for the Day of Judgment, there are other values and concerns that are consistent with values one finds in a humanism that can be more broadly shared: ethical education, the influence on personality, supporting tolerance and diversity aimed at the social good, and moral behaviour. In general, leaders in the tradition of Muslim communities should be oriented towards improving society and bringing cohesion to communities, including educational organisations, as well as practicing a form of praxis—in part derived from Aristotle in the classical Islamic tradition. Arar and Haj-Yehia (2018) have identified how in education, as in other spheres of life, how Muslim leaders should be governed by a set of values and characteristics: practice collaboration, and encourage cooperation and collective responsibility; operate in accordance with Islamic values and Shari'ah law, including equality and justice; serve responsibly (derived from faith) and as a role model for the educational community; exhibit compassion, honesty, integrity and modesty, avoid deceit and discrimination, and other harmful practices; use hope and support to motivate teachers; and carry out administrative duties such as setting goals and putting into motion implementation through appropriate means, while using the principle of appointing the suitable person to the appropriate position. The character and disposition embedded in the conception of leader in the Islamic tradition have very high and multiple standards consisting of courage, durability, reliability, determination, stability, a scholarly orientation and have patience and inner peace with a well-developed ability in rhetoric.

Of most importance to this chapter are the principles of tolerance and pluralism embedded in Islam, and codified in the *Shurūṭ 'Umar* or the pact of Umar, which established the security and rights of minorities in an Islamic state, considered to be part of good governance (Krämer 2013). Even though its observance varied under individual regimes, many of the caliphs not only protected the rights of non-Muslims but appointed non-Muslims to very high positions in the bureaucracy (Sirry 2011) and later the Ottoman Empire maintained comparatively high levels of tolerance (Barkey 2005). Maintaining these principles in government and society are central responsibilities of those in political or institutional leadership positions.

Conclusion

There are a number of ways in which knowledge of the Islamic humanist tradition's view of educational administration and leadership can contribute to both the scholarship and knowledge in the field as well as valuable practice-based understanding. On a more theoretical level, the Islamic tradition, along with many other traditions internationally and historically, can not only demonstrate that the field is contextually shaped, but also that some core conceptions and values, like humanistic ones, can transcend cultural and historical boundaries. Secondly, it contributes to our understanding of other cultures and systems of thought and values, and intercultural and transnational knowledge from which we can learn. This can provide an important prophylaxis against ethnocentrism, bias and even bigotry in both knowledge and value construction and in how this applies to shaping others' conceptions and practices in teaching the field, hopefully informing governance and policy-making actors. It is a way in which a society can achieve the most fundamental rights of social justice; recognising other knowledge traditions is, I would argue, essential to respecting the dignity and integrity of others.

One way in which this can be done is to remember that the 'Western' tradition did not arise in isolation but rests upon foundations built by other parts of the world in intellectual history and is continually influenced by other traditions and scholars. This included a heavy debt to the classical period of Islamic scholarship, which not only conveyed large bodies of knowledge from classical Greek and Roman literature, their own advances in knowledge built upon this base and others, for example, India and China (Nasr 2001), but also the structure and organisation of the university as a social institution (Makdisi 1981) to Europe beginning in the late medieval period and continued through into the modern period. Given this foundational character of Western knowledge, it is argued here that some Islamic and Western traditions should be seen as related, or, as Apostolov (2004) argues, zones of contact. It is this that allows for Islamic humanistic values to also serve as lessons in pursuing intercultural and transcultural practices and provide human commonality and bridges of understanding and cooperation.

This understanding can also help inform how the many critiques from other parts of the world than the West, and, mostly, Anglo-American scholarship in educational administration and leadership, in recognising them as valid, relevant and legitimate concerns under historical and contemporary imperialism and globalisation: Orientalism, postcolonialism, subalternity, epistemicide, neo-imperialism, colonisation of mind, cultural imperialism, necrocapitalism, decolonisation, cultural security and symbolic violence (Samier and Milley unpublished paper). It is to these ruptures of neo-imperialism, aided by the reduction of all things to economic values in neoliberalism and seemingly the current world order, that inter- and transculturalism can speak. Even more of concern is the rising populist nationalism in many countries that builds walls, shuts down academic programmes and shuts out many groups of people, erecting exclusions that compromise social justice and contribute to violence (López-Alves and Johnson 2018).

One can see that the humanistic dimension of the Islamic tradition provides the necessary values, knowledge and abilities for interculturalism and transculturalism to form in social relationships, and within professional roles and responsibilities. Interculturalism and transculturalism are two related but different phenomena. While definitions vary across the literature in the field, in general terms, 'interculturalism' means having the values, knowledge and attitudes enabling people to engage in dialogue, exchange and interaction while maintaining their own cultural heritages, argued by many to reduce conflict and prejudice while increasing positive attitudes and evolve into solidarity (Loobuyck et al. 2016)—in other words producing what Portera (2011) calls a 'new synthesis' that allows one to interact morally across differences and can enter relationships on equal terms without having to sacrifice parts of their cultural identity. In effect, it is the ability for those of different cultures to engage in Habermasean (1984–1989) communicative action by equally exchanging ideas. However, as Cantle (2012) points out, intercultural dialogue by itself does not necessarily produce interculturality of community relations. The implications for educational administration and leadership are that knowledge and ability, as well as large measures of understanding and empathy, associated with humanism are required to engage interculturally with diverse colleagues, staff, students and parents. The measure of one's interculturality is not just an ability to be civil and tolerate other's views, but to engage in a formational relationship, even mentorship, with those from other cultural backgrounds, requiring a sense of common humanity and the cultural literacy and competencies (Cantle 2012) to do so. The record of the Islamic administrative tradition in its more humanistic phases, such as that of many periods in the Abbasid Caliphate, is evidence of a very high degree of intercultural cooperation and collaboration, as populations with the caliphate had the rights and protections for their national cultures and living alongside neighbours from other backgrounds, as well as the highly diverse senior bureaucracy drawn from many cultures and religious backgrounds who worked effectively together at high levels of administrative and leadership ability (Afsaruddin 2007; Samier 2017; Sirry 2011).

'Transculturalism', instead, refers to those elements of culture that travel across cultural boundaries, such as values like respect, honesty, peace and justice—in other words, values like those associated with humanism. But transculturalism also takes other forms of more materialist and anti-humanistic values that connect some cultures, and more recently populist nationalism. However, as Éigeartaigh and Berg (2010) argue, transculturalists who are able to adapt to new cultures and transcend their own by being able to function well within other cultures may be requirements for educational administration and leadership in increasingly diverse societies and in a more globalised world. And they need more than the popular 'intercultural communication' skills; engaging in meaningful social relationships interculturally requires a much deeper understanding and facility with values, attitudes, behaviour, mores and standards.

Because culture plays a large part in the construction of our personal and professional identities affecting our dispositions and behaviour (Grant and Brueck 2011), being confronted with other ways of being can be disruptive, and needing to respond in other cultural forms can be regarded as threatening to identity. At this point, the notion of 'cosmopolitan' comes into play. On a global level, there are degrees of 'cosmopolitanisation' taking place on individual and societal levels, and often including materialistic, individualistically self-centred, and pleasure fulfilment orientations (Portera 2011), not always welcome, consciously aware of, nor warranted due to globalisation effects and neo-colonisation, but there is also the 'cosmopolitanism' phenomenon of the conscious individual or group who intentionally interacts and participates in more than one culture and which may be a position adopted that carries a moral position of our obligations to others and valuing these differences, while not needing to achieve a consensus on principles and practices (Grant and Brueck 2011). It also, of course, can refer to someone who is able to easily participate in more than one culture—with significant differences in family structures and roles, notions of friendship, authority and obedience, and boundaries of behaviour—and has senses of attachment and belongingness to them—certainly abilities and states of being that historically the senior administrators within the Islamic empires had to be able to do.

In practical or applied terms, understanding of the Muslim communities that make up a large proportion of the world's population both in Muslim states and as minority groups in diverse societies can contribute to multiculturalism and the complex practices and dynamics in intercultural social interactions and relations (Arrar and Haj-Yehia 2018). Its values and practices can contribute to better achieving inclusivity and diversity, which can help resolve educational problems of dropout, marginalisation (such as helping refugee groups integrate, not assimilate) into their new countries and shaping citizens for a multicultural world in which people feel engaged and socially responsible for others regardless of their differences. Integrating the Islamic humanist tradition can also, as Tibi (2009) argues, contribute to intercultural and transcultural graduate teaching in international educational administration. One possible pedagogical means is in aiming to achieve the fusion of horizons possible as Gadamer (1989) and Ricoeur (2004) have explained (themselves the result of a long tradition that predates its European forms).

On a larger, political scale, there is potential benefit in internationalising educational administration and leadership so that it is more inclusive and tolerant, and sees value in practices from other parts of the world that may contribute to the field's development in ways in which historically, knowledge and skills have previously travelled enriching their host societies. In the contemporary period, plagued with problems of 'post-truth' politics (e.g. Kavanagh and Rich 2018; Levitin 2017) and in the current context of Islamophobia in the 'West' (Allan 2010; Esposito and Kalin 2011; Lean 2012; Sayyid and Vakil 2011; Zempi and Chakraborti 2014), there are many books that benefit from and have contributed to the development of misconceptions, misrepresentations and negative stereotyping of Islam, its principles, contributions to the intellectual history of the 'West' and its current practices for the vast majority of Muslims (Badran 2001; Shaheed 1999). In contrast, it is a long tradition of peaceful relations that issued from the Islamic humanistic period in the writings of Al-Ghazali, Ibn Khaldun and Ibn Rushd as well as the cosmopolitan and multicultural fabric of early periods of Islamic history during which a broad global view and appreciation of cultural differences were a valued source of knowledge and understanding (Euben 2006; Samier 2018), still evident in the work of contemporary Muslim scholars who emphasise this dimension of Islam in the Qur'an and Sunna (e.g. Abu-Nimer 2003; Esposito and Yilmaz 2010; Hashmi 2002; Sashedina 2007).

References

Abu-Nimer, M. (2003). *Nonviolence and peace building in Islam: Theory and practice*. Gainsville, FL: University Press of Florida.

Afsaruddin, A. (2007). *The first Muslims: History and memory*. Oxford: Oneworld.

Afsaruddin, A. (2016). Muslim views on education: parameters, purview, and possibilities. *Journal of Catholic Legal Studies, 44*(1), 143–178.

Al-Attas, S. (1980). *The concept of education in Islam: a framework for an Islamic philosophy of education*. Kuala Lumpur: ISTAC.

Al-Khalili, J. (2010). *Pathfinders: The golden age of Arabic science*. London: Penguin.

Al-Rodhan, N. (Ed.). (2012). *The role of the Arab-Islamic world in the rise of the west: Implications for contemporary trans-cultural relations*. Basingstoke: Palgrave Macmillan.

Allan, C. (2010). *Islamophobia*. Farnham: Ashgate.

Aloni, N. (2007). *Enhancing humanity: The philosophical foundations of humanistic education*. Dordrecht: Springer.

Aloni, N., & Weintrob, L. (Eds.). (2017). *Beyond bystanders: Educational leadership for a humane culture in a globalizing reality*. Rotterdam: Sense.

Amann, W., Pirson, M., & Dierksmeier, C. (Eds.). (2011). *Business schools under fire: Humanistic management education as the way forward*. Houndmills: Palgrave Macmillan.

Amann, W., & Stachowicz-Stanusch, A. (2013). Introduction: Why the business world needs more integrity. In W. Amann & A. Stachowicz-Stanusch (Eds.), *Integrity in organizations: Building the foundations for humanistic management* (pp. 1–16). Houndmills: Palgrave Macmillan.

Antweiler, C. (2012). *Inclusive humanism: Anthropological basics for a realistic cosmopolitanism*. Göttingen: V & R.

Apostolov, M. (2004). *The Christian-Muslim frontier: A zone of contact, conflict or cooperation*. London: Routledge.

Arar, K., & Haj-Yehia, K. (2018). Perceptions of educational leadership in medieval Islamic thought. *Journal of Educational Administration and History, 50*(2), 69–81.

Badran, M. (2001). Understanding Islam, Islamism and Islamic feminism. *Journal of Women's History, 13*(1), 47–52.

Barkey, K. (2005). Islam and toleration: Studying the Ottoman imperial model. *International Journal of Politics, Culture, and Society, 19*, 5–19.

Barongo-Muweke, N. (2016). *Decolonizing education: Towards reconstructing a theory of citizenship education for postcolonial Africa*. Wiesbaden: Springer.

Beekun, R. (2012). Character centered leadership: Muhammad (p) as an ethical role model for CEOs. *Journal of Management Development, 31*(10), 1003–1020.

Blackmore, J. (1999). *Troubling women: Feminism, leadership, and educational change*. Ballmore: Open University Press.

Box, R. (2005). *Critical social theory in public administration*. Armonk, NY: M. E. Sharpe.

Brown, J. (1994). Leadership education through humanistic texts and traditions: The Hartwick classic leadership cases. *Journal of Leadership & Organizational Studies, 1*(3), 104–116.

Burns, J. M. (1978). *Leadership*. New York: Harper & Row.

Cantle, T. (2012). *Interculturalism: The new era of cohesion and diversity*. New York: Palgrave Macmillan.

Copson, A. (2015). What is humanism? In A. Copson & A. Grayling (Eds.), *The Wiley Blackwell handbook of humanism* (pp. 1–33). Chichester: Wiley.

Copson, A., & Grayling, A. (Eds.). (2015). *The Wiley Blackwell handbook of humanism*. Chichester: Wiley.

Czarniawska-Joerges, B., & Guillet de Monthoux, P. (Eds.). (1994). *Good novels, better management: reading organizational realities*. Chur: Harwood Academic.

Daiber, H. (2013). Humanism: A tradition common to both Islam and Europe. *Filozofija I Društvo, 24*(1), 293–310.

Dierksmeier, C., Amann, W., von Kimakowitz, E., Spitzeck, H., & Pirson, M. (Eds.). (2011). *Humanistic ethics in the age of globality*. Houndmills: Palgrave Macmillan.

Dossett, R. (2014). The historical influence of classical Islam on western humanistic education. *International Journal of Social Science and Humanity, 4*, 88 91.

ElKaleh, E., & Samier, E. A. (2013). The ethics of Islamic leadership: a cross-cultural approach for public administration. *Administrative Culture, 14*(2), 188–211.

Esposito, J., & Kalin, I. (2011). *Islamophobia: The challenge of pluralism in the 21st century*. Oxford: Oxford University Press.

Esposito, J., & Yilmaz, I. (Eds.). (2010). *Islam and peacebuilding*. New York: Blue Dome Press.

Essa, A. (2010). *Studies in Islamic civilization: The Muslim contribution to the renaissance*. Herndon, VA: International Institute of Islamic Thought.

2 The Humanist Roots of Islamic Administration and Leadership …

Euben, R. (2006). *Journeys to other shore: Muslim and western travellers in search of knowledge*. Princeton: Princeton University Press.

Foster, W. (1986). *Paradigms and promises: New approaches to educational administration*. Buffalo, NY: Prometheus.

Gadamer, H. (1989). *Truth and method*. New York: Continuum.

Gagliardi, P., & Czarniawska, B. (Eds.). (2006). *Management education and humanities*. Cheltenham: Edward Elgar.

Giancola, J., & Hutchison, J. (2005). *Transforming the culture of school leadership: Humanizing our practice*. Thousand Oaks: Corwin.

Gill, S., & Niens, U. (2014). Education as humanization. *Compare, 44*(1), 10–31.

Gillies, D. (2013). *Educational leadership and Michel Foucault*. Abingdon: Routledge.

Goodman, L. (2003). *Islamic humanism*. Oxford: Oxford University Press.

Grant, C., & Brueck, S. (2011). A global invitation: Toward the expansion of dialogue, reflection and creative engagement for intercultural and multicultural education. In C. Grant & A. Protera (Eds.), *intercultural and multicultural education* (pp. 3–11). New York: Routledge.

Grayling, A. (2015). The good and worthwhile life. In A. Copson & A. Grayling (Eds.), *The Wiley Blackwell handbook of humanism* (pp. 87–93). Chichester: Wiley.

Greenfield, T., & Ribbins, P. (1993). *Greenfield on educational administration: Towards a humane science*. London: Routledge.

Gunter, H. (2014). *Educational leadership and Hannah Arendt*. Abingdon: Routledge.

Günther, S. (2006). Be masters in that you teach and continue to learn: Medieval Muslim thinkers on educational theory. *Comparative Education Review, 50*(3), 367–388.

Habermas, J. (1984–1989). *The theory of communicative action*. Boston: Beacon Press.

Halstead, M. (2004). An Islamic concept of education. *Comparative Education, 40*(4), 517–529.

Hashmi, S. (Ed.). (2002). *Islamic political ethics: Civil society, pluralism, and conflict*. Princeton: Princeton University Press.

Hassi, A. (2012). Islamic perspectives on training and professional development. *Journal of Management Development, 31*(10), 1035–1045.

Kaplan, H., & Tausky, C. (1977). Humanism in organizations: A critical appraisal. *Public Administration Review, 37*(2), 171–180.

Karim, K., & Eid, M. (2014). *Engaging the other: Public policy and western-Muslim intersections*. Basingstoke: Palgrave Macmillan.

Kashif, M., De Run, E., Rehman, M., & Ting, H. (2015). Bringing Islamic tradition back to management development: A new Islamic Dawah based framework to foster workplace ethics. *Journal of Islamic Marketing, 6*(3), 429–446.

Kavanagh, J., & Rich, M. (2018). *Truth decay*. Santa Monica, CA: RAND.

Von Kimakowitz, E., Pirson, M., Dierksmeier, C., Spitzeck, H., & Amann, W. (2011). Introducing this Book and Humanistic Management. In E. Von Kimakowitz, M. Pirson, H. Spitzeck, C. Dierksmeier, & W. Amann (Eds.), *Humanistic management in practice* (pp. 1–12). Houndmills: Palgrave Macmillan.

Kraemer, J. (1984). Humanism in the renaissance of Islam. *Journal of the American Oriental Society, 104*(1), 135–164.

Krämer, G. (2013). Pluralism and tolerance. In G. Bowering, P. Crone, W. Kadi, D. Stewart, & M. Zaman (Eds.), *The Princeton encyclopaedia of Islamic political thought* (pp. 419–427). Princeton: Princeton University Press.

Küng, H. (2008). *Islam: Past, present and future*. Oxford: Oneworld Publications.

Leaman, O. (1996). Islamic humanism in the fourth/tenth century. In S. Nasr & O. Leaman (Eds.), *History of Islamic philosophy* (pp. 295–306). London: Routledge.

Lean, N. (2012). *The islamophobia industry: How the right manufactures rear of Muslims*. London: Pluto Press.

Leoussi, A. (2000). *Classical humanism and modern societies*. Society, 37(5), 70–77.

Levitin, D. (2017). *Weaponized lies: How to think critically in the post-truth era*. New York: Dutton.

Ljamai, A. (2015). Humanistic thought in the Islamic world of the middle ages. In A. Copson & A. Grayling (Eds.), *The Wiley Blackwell handbook of humanism* (pp. 153–169). Hoboken, NJ: Wiley-Blackwell.

Loobuyck, P., Meer, N., Modood, T., & Zapata-Barrero, R. (2016). Towards an intercultural sense of belonging together. In N. Meer, T. Modood, & R. Zapata-Barrero (Eds.), *Multiculturalism and interculturalism: Debating the dividing lines*. Edinburgh: University of Edinburgh Press.

Lumby, J., & Coleman, M. (2007). *Leadership and diversity: Challenging theory and practice in education*. London: Sage.

Lyons, J. (2009). *The house of wisdom: How the Arabs transformed western civilization*. London: Bloomsbury.

López-Alves, F., & Johnson, D. (Eds.). (2018). *Populist nationalism in Europe and the Americas*. New York: Routledge.

Makdisi, G. (1981). *The rise of colleges: Institutions of learning in Islam and the West*. Edinburgh: Edinburgh University Press.

Makdisi, G. (1990). *The rise of humanism in classical Islam and the Christian west*. Edinburgh: University Press.

March, A. (2009). *Islam and liberal citizenship: The search for an overlapping consensus*. Oxford: Oxford University Press.

Masood, E. (2009). *Science & Islam: A history*. London: Icon Books.

Maxcy, S., & Liberty, L. (1983). Should education leaders be humanistic? *Journal of Thought, 18*(4), 101–106.

McLaren, P., & Jamillo, N. (2007). *Pedagogy and praxis in the age of empire: Towards a new humanism*. Rotterdam: Sense.

Mir, A. M. (2010). Leadership in Islam. *Journal of Leadership Studies, 4*(3), 69–72.

Mohammed, J. A. (2013). The Islamic paradigm of morality: Toward a humanism approach. In S. Khan & W. Amann (Eds.), *World Humanism* (pp. 151–164). Houndmills: Palgrave Macmillan.

Morgan, C. H. (1980). Paradigms, metaphors, and puzzle solving in organization theory. *Administrative Science Quarterly, 25*(4), 605–622.

Morgan, M. H. (2007). *Lost history: The enduring legacy of Muslim scientists, thinkers, and artists*. Washington DC: National Geographic Society.

Mullen, C., English, F., Brindley, S., Ehrich, L., & Samier, E. A. (2013). Neoliberal issues in public education. *Interchange, 43*(3), 181–186.

Nasr, S. (2001). *Science and civilisation in Islam*. Chicago: ABC International Group.

Nasr, S. (2006). *Islamic philosophy from its origin to the present: Philosophy in the land of prophecy*. Albany, NY: SUNY Press.

Niesche, R. (2018). Critical perspectives on educational leadership: a new 'theory turn'? *Journal of Educational Administration and History, 50*(3), 145–158.

Oldmeadow, H. (2004). *Journeys east: 20th century western encounters with eastern religious traditions*. Bloomington, IN: World Wisdom.

Pirson, M., & Kostera, M. (2017). Introduction to dignity and organization. In M. Kostera & M. Pirson (Eds.), *Dignity and the organization* (pp. 1–9). Houndmills: Palgrave Macmillan.

Plum, M. (2012). Humanism, administration and education: the demand for documentation and the production of a new pedagogical desire. *Journal of Education Policy, 27*(4), 491–507.

Pormann, P. (2010). The continuing tradition of Arab humanism. *International Journal of the Classical Tradition, 17*(1), 95–106.

Portera, A. (2011). intercultural and multicultural education. In C. Grant & A. Protera (Eds.), *intercultural and multicultural education* (pp. 12–30). New York: Routledge.

Rhea, A. (2015). *Leading and managing indigenous education in the postcolonial world*. Abingdon: Routledge.

Ribbins, P. (2003). Biography and the study of school leaders: towards a humanistic approach. In M. Brundrett, N. Burton, & R. Smith (Eds.), *Leadership in education* (pp. 55–73). Thousand Oaks: Sage.

Ricoeur, P. (2004). *Memory, history, forgetting*. Chicago: University of Chicago Press.

Roberts, P. (2000). *Education, literacy, and humanization: Exploring the work of Paulo Freire*. Westport: Bergin & Garvey.

Said, E. (2004). *Humanism and democratic criticism*. New York: Columbia University Press.

Samier, E. A. (2005). Toward public administration as a humanities discipline: a humanistic manifesto. *Administrative Culture, 6*, 6–59.

Samier, E. A. (2017). The Islamic public administration tradition: Historical, theoretical and practical dimensions. *Administrative Culture, 18*(1), 53–71.

Samier, E. A. (2018). Philosophical and historical origins and genesis of Islamic global governance. In L. Pal & M. E. Tok (Eds.), *Global governance and Muslim organizations* (pp. 83–104). Cham: Palgrave Macmillan.

Samier, E. A. & Milley, P. (unpublished paper). What (Theoretically) is an international education administration curriculum: Postcolonial critiques for sustaining national and cultural identities.

Samier, E. A. (forthcoming). Missing non-western voices on social justice for education: A postcolonial perspective on traditions of humanistic marginalized communities. In R. Papa (Ed.), *Handbook on promoting social justice in education*. New York: Springer.

Sashedina, A. (2007). *The Islamic roots of democratic pluralism*. Oxford: Oxford University Press.

Sayyid, S., & Vakil, A. (Eds.). (2011). *Thinking through islamophobia: Global perspectives*. New York: Columbia University Press.

Schiele, J. (1990). Organization theory from an Afrocentric perspective. *Journal of Black Studies, 21*(2), 145–161.

Shaheed, F. (1999). Constructing identities: culture, women's agency and the Muslim world. *International Social Science Journal, 51*(159), 61–73.

Sirry, M. (2011). The public role of Dhimmīs during 'Abbāsid times. *Bulletin of the SOAS, 74*(2), 187–204.

Smyth, J. (Ed.). (1989). *Critical perspectives on educational leadership*. New York: Routledge-Falmer.

Spitzeck, H., Pirson, M., Amann, W., Kahn, S., & Kimakowitz, E. (Eds.). (2009). *Humanism in business*. Cambridge: Cambridge University Press.

Steiner, R. (2004). *Human values in education*. Great Barrington, MA: Anthroposophic Press.

Tampio, N. (2012). *Kantian courage: Advancing the Enlightenment in contemporary political theory*. Bronx, NY: Fordham University Press.

Thomson, P. (2017). *Educational leadership and Pierre Bourdieu*. Abingdon: Routledge.

Tibi, B. (2009). Bridging the heterogeneity of civilisations: reviving the grammar of Islamic humanism. *Theoria, 56*(120), 65–80.

Veugelers, W. (Ed.). (2011). *Education and humanism: Linking autonomy and humanity*. Rotterdam: Sense Publishers.

Wong, K.-C. (1998). Culture and moral leadership in education. *Peabody Journal of Education, 73*(2), 106–125.

Yasin, R., & Jani, M. (2013). Islamic education: the philosophy, aim, and main features. *International Journal of Education and Research, 1*(10), 1–18.

Zempi, I., & Chakraborti, N. (2014). *Islamophobia, victimization and the veil*. Basingstoke: Palgrave Macmillan.

Zimmerman, J. (2012). *Humanism and religion*. Oxford: Oxford University Press.

Éigeartaigh, A., & Berg, W. (2010). Editors' Introduction: Exploring transculturalism. In W. Berg & A. Éigeartaigh (Eds.), *Exploring transculturalism* (pp. 7–16). Wiesbaden: Springer.

Eugenie A. Samier is Reader in Educational Management and Leadership at the University of Strathclyde, Glasgow. Her research concentrates on administrative philosophy and theory, interdisciplinary foundations of administration, theories and models of educational leadership and comparative educational administration. She has frequently been Guest Researcher at the Humboldt University of Berlin, was Visiting Professor in the Department of Administrative Studies at the University of Tartu, Estonia (2003), was Visiting Fellow at Oxford Brookes University and has been Guest Lecturer at universities and institutes in the USA, Germany, Estonia, Russia, Norway, Lithuania, Finland, Qatar, Bahrain and the UAE. Her publications include chapters and articles on organisational culture and values, the New Public Management, the role of history and biography in educational administration, the role of humanities, aesthetics and literary analysis in administration, and Weberian foundations of administrative theory and ethics in a number of international book collections and many leading journals in the USA, Australia, the UK, Germany, the Baltic region and Canada. She is Founding Board Member of *Administrative Culture* journal and is Editor of several book collections with Routledge on ethics, aesthetics, politics, emotions, trust and betrayal, ideologies and maladministration in educational administration. She is also Associate Editor of the four-volume Master Works *Educational Leadership and Administration* (Sage 2009), a contributor on authority, bureaucracy, critical theory to *Encyclopaedia of Education Law* (Sage 2008), on aesthetics and human agency to the *Handbook of Educational Leadership* (Sage, 2011), aesthetics of leadership and bureaucratic theory to the *Handbook of Educational Theory* (Information Age Publishing, 2013). She has also written a number of articles on topics like toxic leadership, passive evil, kitschification of educational leadership, the avant-garde, postcolonial educational administration, and Islamic ethics, social justice, global governance, administrative tradition, and educational change in the Middle East for several journals and book collections. She also worked as Management Consultant in Canada to the public sector for a number of years on a broad variety of projects including legislation development, organisational reviews, board development and government department restructuring and redesign.

Chapter 3
A Critical Approach to Developing Culturally Relevant Leadership Curricula for Muslim Students

Eman S. ElKaleh

Abstract The secular and materialistic values imported to Muslim countries through globalisation and the uncritical application of Western models and theories are changing societies from being Muslim towards a materialistic and secular one where economic value is the most critical factor that drives people's behaviour and decisions. The real challenge for Muslim countries, then, is to develop and implement higher education curricula that reflect Islamic and cultural values while incorporating global knowledge developed by Western and other scholars. This chapter aims to achieve this balance by proposing a theoretical model that can be used for developing culturally relevant and critically reflective leadership curricula. The model is derived from Habermas' account of critical theory and offers a critical and holistic approach to leadership teaching. It adopts an intercultural and interdisciplinary approach to learning and aims to start a dialogue between Western and indigenous sources of knowledge. The model also proposes the content and teaching practices recommended by leadership scholars and leadership development literature internationally to provide students with a balanced and pluralistic learning experience that addresses both the spiritual and the intellectual aspects of knowledge.

Introduction

The main role of higher education worldwide traditionally was to maintain cultural values while providing students with valuable knowledge that enables them to reach their full potential and make remarkable contributions to their society. However, the increasing influence of neoliberalism and globalisation on higher education, with their greater emphasis on commercial values, private interests, and competition over moral and sacred values, has resulted in a shift of educational goals from being humanistic, where the focus is on students' intellectual, cultural, and moral development, to becoming socio-economic where the focus is on economic benefits, career

---

E. S. ElKaleh (✉)
Zayed University, Dubai, United Arab Emirates
e-mail: eman.salah2@gmail.com

© Springer Nature Singapore Pte Ltd. 2019
E. A. Samier and E. S. ElKaleh (eds.), *Teaching Educational Leadership in Muslim Countries*, Educational Leadership Theory,
https://doi.org/10.1007/978-981-13-6818-9_3

advancement, and private interests (Cesari 2004; Donn and Al-Manthri 2010; Giroux 2002; Lipman 2011). This raises cultural security issues for Muslim nations and acts as a threat to Islamic and national identity mainly because the secular, commercial and materialistic values imported to Muslim countries through globalisation are contradictory to Islamic values that promote collectivism, dedication, self-denial and working for the well-being of society as a form of worship. Cultural security, as defined by Tehranian (2004, p. 7), is 'the freedom to negotiate one's identity'. However, this is not possible to achieve when one's cultural and religious values are excluded from higher education through the intensive use of Western knowledge and staff who are mostly secular oriented and use predominantly secular curricular material. Such a domination by Western knowledge and practices is changing societies from being Muslim, where Islam is a wholistic way of life, towards a materialistic and secular one where economic value is God.

A good example of how Western education can change one's soul and identity can be seen in Blanks' (1998) reflection on his teaching experience at the American University in Cairo. He noticed that the more his students were involved in liberal arts and Western education, the more they move away from their original identity as Egyptians. Eventually, he admits that globalisation, although driven by good intentions, is a form of cultural imperialism because 'there is something in the project that affirms Western values and undermines local cultural autonomy' (p. 5). Similarly, Adams (1958) concludes, from his teaching experience at the American University of Beirut, that the main problems that professors may face when teaching American curricula in foreign contexts are: a lack of knowledge and use of local traditions and practices; a lack of a common language and cultural heritage that hinder effective communication with students; and a natural antagonism of students to foreign curricula due to the textbooks that frequently refer to the American experiences which are of little help to foreign students who are not familiar with American life. This, according to Adams, runs the risk of imported curricula to be either misinterpreted or meaningless. He believes that for such knowledge to be meaningful to students, it must be linked to their own experiences. Stenberg (2004) also argues that Islam has an epistemology derived from the belief that God created the world and humans as his followers have the duty of studying it, and this is what makes seeking knowledge and science discovery a form of worship; therefore, Islamic principles and values cannot be left out of any curricula.

The real challenge for Muslim countries and higher education institutions, then, is to develop and implement a hybrid curriculum that reflects Islamic and cultural values while incorporating global knowledge established by Western and other scholars. This chapter attempts to achieve this balance by proposing a theoretical model that can be used for developing culturally relevant and critically reflective leadership curricula. This model may help higher education institutions in Muslim countries achieve their strategic goal of equipping students with the latest international knowledge that enables them to compete effectively in the global market without sacrificing or being alienated from their cultural and Islamic identity. The model adopts a holistic and interdisciplinary approach to knowledge and uses Habermas' (1971, 1984) account of critical theory as a theoretical foundation, focusing on his theories of knowledge and human interests and communicative action in particular, due to its wide applications in higher and adult education (Brookfield 2005a; Murphy and Fleming 2010). The first section of the chapter discusses Habermas's work and how his account of critical theory offers a holistic and pluralistic approach to knowledge in which all sources and forms of information are regarded as complementary with equal importance and respect. The second section discusses how the planning and designing of the curriculum should be informed by a deep understanding of how people create knowledge through three cognitive interests: technical, practical, and emancipatory. The third section of the chapter discusses Habermas' theory of communicative action and how it contributes to developing people's communicative competencies. Finally, the chapter concludes with a discussion of the proposed theoretical model that can be used as a foundation for developing value oriented and culturally relevant leadership curricula and the author's own experience in using the model.

Habermas' Critical Theory

Critical theory is an intellectual tradition developed with an emancipatory and social justice goal by a group of scholars from the Institute of Social Research at University of Frankfurt. It was developed in response to the economic challenges, instability and the rise of Fascism that Germany was facing. Critical theory investigates social problems by combining a range of disciplines such as philosophy, social psychology, sociology, political economy and science (Murphy 2010). A critical theory for adult learning, according to Brookfield (2005b), will increase student awareness of social and political phenomena and help them challenge dominant ideology, power, and hegemony and reclaim reason by emphasising critical approaches to learning and deemphasising instrumental and technical learning. One distinction of the German philosopher and sociologist Jürgen Habermas' work is that it combines philosophy with science to bridge the gap between theory and practice (values and facts). He is a strong advocate of the Enlightenment tradition and the modernity project to the extent that he has been called the theorist or philosopher of democracy (Brookfield 2005a; Fleming 2010). Habermas' account of critical theory offers a holistic and pluralistic approach to knowledge in which all sources and forms of information (Western vs. indigenous, objective vs. subjective) are regarded as complementary with equal importance and respect. He explains that scientific and practical knowledge are 'connected by the common form of critical enquiry' (1970, p. 10). His approach appreciates different perspectives and perceives diversity as an opportunity for developing a deep and comprehensive understanding of a certain phenomenon. Habermas' work has significantly contributed to our understanding of social change and social conflict. His work encourages us to challenge our own assumptions and make genuine efforts to understand other perspectives with tolerance and respect.

Habermas' (1970, 1987b) theories of knowledge and human interests and communicative action can provide a powerful framework for developing critically reflective curricula that leads to holistic learning experiences and positive social changes.

Englund (2010) argues that the implications of Habermas' work for education provide a solid framework for analysing the relationship between education and society. Adult education, according to Habermas (1970, 1987b), should help people realise their emancipatory cognitive interest in their professional and personal lives (see also Brookfield 2005a), and this, while achieved through the involvement of communicative action, may lead to significant positive changes in society. Habermas' (1970, 1979, 1987b) ideas have been of great influence in developing critical adult education discourses and in encouraging educators to critically reflect on their educational practices (Gouthro 2006). For example, Brookfield (2005b) points out that teaching from a critical theory perspective involves a social transformation intent. He believes that critical teaching is concerned with helping students realise their emancipatory cognitive interest, embrace self-criticism, and establish a more just, liberal, and ethical society. Critical teaching should also help in reclaiming reason by involving people in ideology and hegemony critique. Many authors like Brookfield (2005a), Endres (2006), Ewert (1991), Gouthro (2006), Heslep (2001), and Welton (1991) discuss the use of Habermas' theories in adult learning and adult education. Mezirow (1981) also developed his transformational learning theory based on Habermas' ideas. This chapter adds to this body of literature by using his theories of knowledge and human interests (1971, 2005) and communicative action (1984, 1987a, 2001) as a theoretical foundation for developing culturally relevant leadership curricula within a Muslim context. Following is a discussion of both theories.

Knowledge and Human Interests

Habermas' theory of knowledge and human interests (1971) has been frequently cited in adult and higher education literature. In this theory, Habermas suggests a model of three cognitive interests (technical, practical and emancipatory) that constitute how human knowledge is generated. According to Habermas (1971), the technical interest addresses the scientific aspect of knowledge and is concerned with the knowledge we need to predict, control and manipulate our environment. Such knowledge finds its roots in the empirical-analytic sciences where there is great emphasis on experimentation, hypothesis, and deduction and can be gained through empirical research, instrumental reasoning (finding the best techniques to achieve objectives), cognition (developing intellectual capacity) and skills. As discussed by Romanowski (2014), this interest assumes that science is neutral and objective. Therefore, human actions are informed by universal laws with less concern for the moral and ethical aspects of knowledge since decisions are based on empirical data rather than moral values.

The practical interest addresses the moral aspect of knowledge and is concerned with the knowledge we need to communicate with others in just and reasonable ways. This knowledge is rooted in the historical-hermeneutic 'sciences' and can be gained through interpretive research, moral reasoning, and ethical judgment. This approach does not aim to manipulate the environment but rather to understand and interpret social phenomena and to attain possible consensus among social actors. According to this interest, ethical judgment and decisions are made through dialogue and discussion rather than proved rules or laws (Habermas 1971; Milley 2004; Romanowski 2014).

Finally, the emancipatory interest is concerned with the knowledge we need to free ourselves from domination and taken-for-granted assumptions. This knowledge is rooted in critical social sciences and can be gained through critical self-reflection that examines how past experiences may inform current ones (Butler 1997; Milley 2004; Romanowski 2014). According to Habermas (1971), 'In self-reflection knowledge for the sake of knowledge attains congruence with the interest in autonomy and responsibility. The emancipatory cognitive interest aims at the pursuit of reflection as such' (p. 314). Therefore, the emancipatory interest is considered to be the highest form of knowledge that higher education institutions and adult education programmes should aim for (Butler 1997; Habermas 1971).

As suggested by Brookfield (2001), a critical theory for adult education should start with understanding how people learn to free themselves from ideological manipulation. Understanding how people learn helps us make informed decisions when planning and designing curricula. A balanced educational programme is expected to address those three cognitive interests proposed by Habermas in order to create a balanced human experience that leads to social evolution. Habermas (1971) points out that modern societies put a great emphasis on developing the scientific and technical aspect of knowledge to accelerate their economic development, at the expense of moral and reflection aspects. This creates imbalanced learning experiences that eventually result in losing one's capacity for making moral choices and expressing oneself in an authentic manner (Milley 2004). Consequently, a good and balanced leadership curriculum would contain sophisticated scientific knowledge, moral and cultural values, and opportunities for self-reflection and self-discovery. Such a curriculum would provide a balanced learning experience leading to social evolution, as indicated by Habermas (1979). For Habermas (1984), social evolution means that people live in harmony despite their cultural and ideological differences (cultural rationalisation) where they work towards establishing productive economic and administrative systems (social modernisation).

Communicative Action

The theory of communicative action (Habermas 1984, 1987a, 2001) is another important theory that has been extensively cited and used in adult education (e.g. Brookfield 2005a; Gouthro 2006; Milley 2004; Murphy and Fleming 2010) as it provides a comprehensive framework for developing critical and participatory approaches to learning (Gouthro 2006). For Habermas (1984), communicative action is the action or activity taken by two or more individuals to reach mutual understanding or agreement that leads to consensual decisions. He believes that mutual understanding lies at the heart of human speech. According to him, 'reaching mutual understanding is the inherent telos of human speech' (p. 287) and this understanding allows people to enjoy 'the intersubjective mutuality of reciprocal understanding, shared knowledge, mutual trust, and accordance with one another' (1979, p. 3). He further explains that for communicative action to happen, three validity claims have to be satisfied: 'communicative action can continue undisturbed only as long as participants suppose that the validity claims they reciprocally raise are justified' (1979, p. 3). Validity claims are the assumptions people make about the truth and sincerity of speech. The three validity claims identified by Habermas are: truth as the 'obligation to provide certain grounds'; rightness as the 'obligation to provide justification'; and truthfulness as the 'obligation to provide trustworthy' (1979, p. 65). Habermas argues that when people engage in conversation, they learn to assess those validity claims. Therefore, dialogic teaching and collective creation of knowledge should be central pedagogical practices in adult learning.

Habermas (1970) asserts that universities have a moral responsibility to bring back to 'consciousness, through reflection, the relation of living generations to active cultural traditions' (p. 9). For him, the main mission of higher education is to help learners develop the critical reasoning and communicative competency required for democracy (Fleming 2010). Habermas (1984) also argues that capitalism distorted learning to reason because it gives priority to instrumental rationality at the expense of communicative rationality by emphasising market values over socialisation and cultural reproduction. He also argues that capitalism invaded the lifeworld and contributed to the collapse of the public sphere. The public sphere is the common area where people gather to discuss their issues, problems or concerns (e.g. *Majlis* in Arab Muslim countries) while lifeworld is the basic assumptions and beliefs that frame our understanding and interpretation of the world (e.g. moral and cultural values). In Habermas' (1987a) view, lifeworld 'forms a horizon and at the same time offers a store of things taken for granted' (p. 298). As capitalism encourages self-interest and pursuing private goals with little consideration of how this would affect others, a colonisation of lifeworld by system took place through the great emphasis on money, power, and technical rationality (which what globalisation is doing in Muslim countries). As people become involved in communicative action, lifeworld is recreated and renewed. Thus, he argues that colonisation processes of lifeworld can be resisted through the re-cultivation of ethical, democratic and caring values in system (Habermas 1987a; Murphy and Fleming 2010), which can be achieved through the practice of communicative action. According to Gouthro (2006), communicative action offers a mechanism for developing critical and participatory approaches to learning, which can take place in higher education.

Habermas (1984) also points out that when people communicate, new meanings and concepts emerge leading to change in perspectives and the creation of new ideas. Thus, communicative action serves as a medium for reproducing lifeworld (p. 337). He argues that we should think of societies as a combination of systems and lifeworlds. Colonisation of lifeworld by administrative and economic systems takes place when instrumental and strategic communication (technical rationality) take priority over communicative action (communicative rationality). Therefore, when people develop their rational communicative competences through communicative action, they will be able to disrupt the repressive structures of system (Gouthro 2006; Habermas 1987a). He also argues that colonisation processes of lifeworld can be resisted through the re-cultivation of ethical, democratic and caring values in the system (Murphy and Fleming 2010). This colonisation of lifeworld is currently taking place through the neoliberalisation and commodification of higher education where knowledge is being treated as a commodity or service for those who can afford it rather than a developmental process that enriches one's life (Gibbs 2010). Neoliberalism was identified by Giroux (2002) as the most dangerous ideology of our time because it promotes market and commercial values over sacred and social justice values leading to 'self-interested individuals' (p. 425). Consequently, Habermas (1987b) argues that universities should foster discourse and communicative action as higher education is an important context for developing people's communicative competences and ethical values that help them achieve progressive social evolution (Milley 2004). Habermas' theory is more concerned with undistorted communication through which equality, willing to accept better arguments, and free dialogue are needed more than transparent communication.

Morrow (2010) argues that Habermas' theory of communicative action provides a reasonable and practical framework that distinguishes between strategic and rational communication and allows for dialogical negotiation between indigenous knowledge and technical rationality embedded in Western science. Also, Habermas' theory offers an ethical and just form of discourse that recognises diverse and different forms of life allowing it to transcend gender differences and cultural differences. Similarly, Gouthro (2006) claims that Habermas' account provides a comprehensive and proactive analytical approach that should inform critical discourses in adult education. Furthermore, Habermas' account of critical theory is congruent with Islamic principles and practices, which make it very applicable at Muslim countries. For example, *Shura* (consultation) is a form of communicative action as both aim to achieve mutual understanding and consensual decisions. New ideas and knowledge are produced through the practice of both *Shura* and communicative action as both processes lead to higher levels of critical thinking. Khalifa Omar Ibn Abdul Aziz has argued that 'Both the ability to consult and debate leads to enlightenment and are the keys to intellectual clarity' (in Ali 2005, p. 118). Therefore, Habermas' work provides an excellent framework for developing culturally relevant curricula that offer balanced learning experiences between Western and indigenous knowledge and materialistic and moral values, and this balance is realised through critical thinking and self-reflection of what works best in certain societies or cultures. These values and practices are inherent to the Islamic intellectual tradition, found in the work of great scholars like Ibn Khaldun, Ibn Sina, and Ibn Rushd.

A Critical Theory Model for Developing Culturally Relevant Curricula

The model proposed below in Fig. (3.1) offers a critical approach to leadership education and aims to serve as a foundation for developing culturally relevant and critically reflective leadership curricula. It is based on Habermas' theories of communicative action and knowledge and human interest and aims to look for content and teaching practices that broaden 'the meaning of learning beyond the acquisition of knowledge and skills' (Petriglieri et al. 2011, p. 446). The model adopts an intercultural and interdisciplinary perspective and attempts to start a dialogue between Western and indigenous sources of knowledge to show how different perspectives may interact to deepen our understanding of social phenomena including educational administration and leadership. As Brookfield (2005a) points out, teaching from a critical theory perspective is not only about how we teach but also about what we teach. Therefore, the model was designed to propose the content and teaching practices that are recommended by leadership scholars and leadership development literature worldwide. For example, Hotho and Dowling (2010) argue that leadership development programmes should move away from emphasising the technical aspect of knowledge and provide more opportunities for interaction and critical discourses. The model, through its four dimensions, addresses this point and aims to provide students with a balanced and pluralistic learning experience that includes the universal and the particular, the feeling and the intellect, the spiritual and material needs of human being (Nash and Scott 2009). As shown in Fig. (3.1), the first three sections of the model address the technical, practical and emancipatory aspects of knowledge as identified by Habermas' (1971) while the fourth refers to the practice of communicative action (Habermas 1984, 1987a) through which students develop their communicative competency and fully realise the emancipatory interest. The technical dimension of the model includes the scientific knowledge of leadership such as the most dominant theories and models from global, indigenous, and Islamic/religious perspectives, current research on leadership, emotional intelligence, motivation, effective communication and conflict resolution. This aspect should allow students develop a solid and universal understanding of leadership literature.

The practical part deals with the moral and practical or applied aspects of knowledge by discussing the ethics of leadership, selecting topics from history and philosophy and discussing how they would benefit students as leaders, conducting interpretive research to understand effective leadership practices in their country, inviting business and educational leaders as guest lectures to speak about their experiences, inviting Muslim scholars to speak about leadership from an Islamic perspective, and conducting community service projects through which students can develop their leadership skills and experience the value of living for higher goals. This section follows scholars' recommendations to complement head learning with 'heart' learning. According to Nash and Scott (2009) and Samier (2009), leadership is an interdisciplinary field that is strongly connected to psychology, philosophy, history, literature, art, and religion studies. Those subjects foster heart learning more than head learning

3 A Critical Approach to Developing Culturally Relevant ...

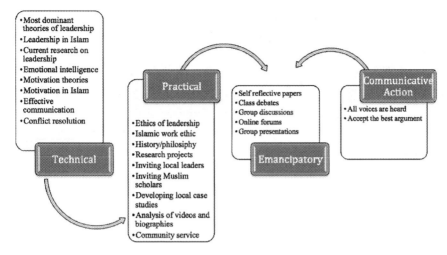

Fig. 3.1 A critical theory model for developing culturally relevant curricula

(Nash and Scott 2009), which is essential for developing a holistic learning experience and more complete leadership. Small (2004) also argues that teaching philosophy in leadership programmes develops students' critical thinking capacity which allows them to deal with uncertain situations, rapid changes, and the increasing challenges in the workplace. It also helps them find innovative and creative solutions to work problems. Similarly, Olivares (2011) argues that the use of autobiographies in leadership programmes informs student behaviour for a long time because they include personal memories and momentous events that are specific, detailed, and emotionally charged. He also believes that reflecting on those historical events, which has been addressed in the third and fourth dimensions of the model, will allow students to make sense of themselves and others because the inferences we make from real-life experiences are influenced by the assumptions, images, and stories we have in mind about ourselves and others (Petriglieri et al. 2011). Reflection and critical teaching techniques help students draw meaning from past and current experiences and become more conscious of those assumptions and images.

The third dimension of the model represents the emancipatory interest, which can be realised through reflective and critical thinking of the knowledge and information obtained by the technical and practical aspects as well as the practice of communicative action. Activities such as class debates, role-play, simulations, group discussions, online forums, group presentation, and reflective writing that includes students' life stories will help students question assumptions and think of their own leadership strategies. According to Reynolds (1999), critical reflection techniques help students question the taken-for-granted assumptions and raise moral questions about the ends as well as the means. This can be realised through the use of literature, role-play, simulations, and experiential learning. Finally, the practice of communicative action, which is the fourth dimension of the model, will develop student communicative competences, help them to be open to new ideas and practices, and help them realise the emancipatory interest 'by steering the discussion toward the meaning making that underpins leaders' decisions and actions' (Petriglieri et al. 2011, p. 446).

Since the model aims to start a dialogue between different sources of knowledge and to select the practices that work best in a certain society given its unique cultural and religious values, it can also be used as a theoretical framework in Muslim and other countries worldwide to develop culturally relevant and critically reflective curricula that incorporate indigenous and Western perspectives of leadership.

Author's Own Experience in Using the Model

In Spring 2015, I was asked to teach two business leadership classes for 4th-year undergraduate male students at one of the United Arab Emirate's (UAE) higher education institutions. It was a great opportunity to test the model since I had the freedom to design the course content and to select materials that would support this design as long as they achieve the course outcomes required in the course common syllabus. The design of the model allowed me to combine Western models and theories of leadership with indigenous and Islamic perspectives. Under the technical aspect, I used Northouse (2013) and Zehndorfer (2014) as the core textbooks in addition to articles that address leadership from an Islamic perspective such as Ali (2009), Beekun (2012) and ElKaleh and Samier (2013). Also, during class discussions and presentations, I summarised the work of Ibn Khaldun (1967) and Ibn Taymiyyah (2005) on the Islamic perspective of leadership. Those teaching materials included the dominant theories of leadership from Western and Islamic perspectives and discussed other topics that are related to leadership development such as emotional intelligence, motivation, giving feedback, effective communication, and conflict resolution. Under the practical aspect, I used articles that discuss the ethical and moral values of leadership such as Abeng (1997), Ali and Al-Owaihan (2008), and Beekun and Badawi (2005). Also, to incorporate the current and indigenous practices of leadership, I invited an Emirati leader to speak about her leadership experience and the leadership challenges Emirati leaders may go through. Students enjoyed this activity a lot because they had the opportunity to interview a local leader and to analyse her leadership style based on the theories we discussed in class.

Course assignments were also designed to facilitate more learning about leadership in the UAE and Islam. I asked students to select one of these options: create a short video (8–10 min) on a work or leadership issue/problem (e.g. lack of motivation, coming late to work, ineffective use of resources) and how leadership can contribute to solving this problem; select a Muslim leader and analyse his/her leadership behaviours based on the theories and concepts discussed in class; or interview two or three leaders and analyse what effective leadership means to them and compare this with class theories and concepts. This assignment was group work where each group had to prepare a presentation and to write a research paper on their project. Most students selected Muslim leaders such as the Prophet Muhammad, Abu Bakr, and Sheikh Zayed to write about. This assignment actually helped them to realise the practical and emancipatory aspects of knowledge by interpreting leaders' behaviours, linking them to class concepts and reflecting on what lessons they have learned from them. Also, a few of the students (7 out of 42) were working and that helped in bringing real cases to class discussions and to compare between current and past practices of leadership.

Since the students and I agreed from the beginning to practice leadership, rather than learning about leadership, students were expected to behave as leaders who act as responsible professionals, contributing effectively to class discussions, respecting other opinions and being open to learning from others. We also agreed to practice *Shura* (consultation) since it is central to leadership in Islam. Following the principles of *Shura*, I discussed with them the course outline, listened to their ideas and tried to accommodate their requests. Throughout the course, students were actively contributing to course content by suggesting new ideas and/or topics. The significance of listening to students' ideas and trying to accommodate their requests is that they had ownership in the course, and they were happy that their voices were being heard as long as they had good arguments to support their points and adhered to the basic requirements of the course and sound principles for quality and type of readings and work at the expected senior university level. Throughout the course, I also realised that students became more motivated and participative when we either worked on one of their ideas or discussed a local video or work issue in class. Being bilingual has been a privilege because I can watch and analyse videos of local leaders with them (however, other instructors may find these videos with English subtitles or ask for budget to get them translated). At the end of the course, students were grateful for being treated as professional leaders and for their ideas and opinions being listened to, which was a good opportunity to discuss that this is what leaders do, they involve followers, listen to their ideas, and act on them.

Community service was another important practice to use in helping students build their leadership skills and experience the value of serving and living for higher goals. We organised an open day for high school students in order to introduce them to university life. Most of leadership class students participated in this day where they talked to high school students about their own experiences and took them on tours around the campus. In reflecting on this activity, one of the students said, 'it was a great experience, I felt that I can make a difference and add value to their future. When I was a high school student nobody did that with me so I did many mistakes'. Other students were happy with this leadership experience and recognised how good leadership, even on a simple level, can really make a difference.

The third and fourth aspects of the model allowed me to use interactive and critical teaching techniques that help students think critically of the leadership concepts and what they mean to them as leaders. Using interactive methods such as class debates, role-play, and simulations keep students motivated and help them think critically about the different approaches to leadership and select the ones that work best in their local environment. While students sometimes resist any ideas that contradict their own views, I found that using critical and reflective practices broadens their minds and helps them be more open to new ideas and become more tolerant to contradictory perspectives. For example, at the beginning of the course we conducted a debate on whether leaders are born or made. Before the class, I asked them to read broadly about the topic and come prepared to defend both perspectives. In the beginning, they were very resistant to this proposal. They believed that they should stick to only one perspective, which they believe is the right one. I asked them to try it just for fun and promised that they would enjoy the experience. On the debate day, they came motivated and excited. They were less concerned about which perspective was right and more concerned to win the debate. We divided the class into two groups, and each selected a leader to represent them. Then, we conducted a draw based upon which the winning group selected the perspective they wanted to defend. I gave them a few minutes to work together as a group to organise their ideas before starting the debate. In the beginning, they were not sure how to do it and they were not listening to each other with many students speaking at the same time. However, by the end of the first session they learned gradually how to defend their ideas and how to listen to others and respond to them.

In the second half of the class, we switched group roles—the group that was defending the leaders are born argument had to defend the position that they are made. This is the part of the activity that some students found very challenging. However, one group did a very impressive job in bringing evidence from research that supports ideas from both perspectives. Since they provided good justifications for each view, students learned a lot from their arguments and became more open to new ideas. After the debate, we spent some time reflecting on this experience. Some students pointed out that they had learned how to defend their ideas and bring evidence to support their views. Others believed that this activity helped them to realise that their views are not always right and that they should listen to others because they may have a more valid point. While this activity helped in increasing student motivation, curiosity, and interest in the topic, it also helped them to be more open and flexible in learning from each other. Furthermore, it resulted in more trust and harmony within the group. In each following class, students used to ask me whether leaders are born or made and my response was that 'this is what we are going to discover throughout the semester'. The debate actually sets the ground for an ongoing research journey and created a context and purpose to course readings and critique. Also, the class sizes (17 and 25) were suitable for effective application of the model because it allowed for communicative action and reflection to take place.

Finally, reflective writing that includes student stories and life experiences allowed them to analyse their own style of leadership and to think of themselves as leaders and how this learning experience may inform their current and future behaviour. Throughout the course, students were involved in different reflective writing assignments, in addition to the final exam where they were asked to develop their own approach to leadership using all the knowledge they gained from this class. That is, an approach that they believe would work well in UAE business organisations. That exam helped them think critically about the leadership concepts we discussed throughout the semester and how to combine the most useful ideas into one theory. Students' answers really impressed me. Most of them discussed very important and critical leadership issues in their theories. They were able to process and combine different sources of information to create their own approaches to leadership. In their final comments on the course, many mentioned that this was one of the best courses they had in the university since it was about them and allowed them to think and act as leaders.

References

Abeng, T. (1997). Business ethics in Islamic context: Perspectives of a Muslim business leader. *Business Ethics Quarterly, 7*(3), 47–54.

Adams, J. (1958). On the teaching of public administration abroad. *Public Administration Review*, pp. 124–128.

Ali, A. (2005). *Islamic perspectives on management and organization.* Cheltenham: Edward Elgar.

Ali, A. (2009). Islamic perspectives on leadership: A model. *International Journal of Islamic and Middle Eastern Finance and Management, 2*(2), 160–180.

Ali, A., & Al-Owaihan, A. (2008). Islamic work ethic: a critical review. *Cross cultural management: An international Journal, 15*(1), 5–19.

Beekun, R. (2012). Character centered leadership: Muhammad (p) as an ethical role model for CEOs. *Journal of Management Development, 31*(10), 1003–1020.

Beekun, R., & Badawi, J. (2005). Balancing ethical responsibility among multiple organizational stakeholders: The Islamic perspective. *Journal of Business Ethics, 60,* 131–145.

Blanks, D. (1998). Cultural diversity or cultural imperialism: Liberal education in Egypt. *Liberal Education, 84*(3), 30–35.

Brookfield, S. (2001). Repositioning ideology critique in a critical theory for adult learning. *Adult Education Quarterly, 52*(1), 7–22.

Brookfield, S. (2005a). Learning democratic reason: The adult education project of Jürgen Habermas. *Teachers College Record, 107*(6), 1127–1168.

Brookfield, S. (2005b). *The power of critical theory: Liberating about learning and teaching.* San Francisco, CA: Jossey-Bass.

Butler, S. (1997). Habermas' cognitive interests: Teacher and student interests and their relationship in an adult education setting. D.Ed. Thesis. Auburn University.

Cesari, J. (2004). Islam in the West: Modernity and globalization revisited. In B. Schaebler & L. Stenberg (Eds.), *Globalization and the Muslim world: Culture, religion and modernity* (pp. 80–92). Syracuse, NY: Syracuse University Press.

Donn, G., & Manthri, Y. (2010). *Globalisation and higher education in the Arab Gulf states.* Oxford: Symposium Books.

ElKaleh, E., & Samier, E. (2013). The ethics of Islamic leadership: A cross-cultural approach for public administration. *Administrative Culture, 14*(2), 188–211.

Endres, B. (2006). Education for economic life: The role of communicative action. *Teachers College Record, 108*(10), 2001–2020.

Englund, T. (2010). Educational implications of the idea of deliberative democracy. In M. Murphy & T. Fleming (Eds.), *Habermas, critical theory and education* (pp. 19–32). New York: Routledge.

Ewert, G. (1991). Habermas and education: A comparative overview of the influence of Habermas in educational literature. *Review of Educational Research, 61*(3), 345–378.

Fleming, T. (2010). Condemned to learn: Habermas, university and the learning society. In M. Murphy & T. Fleming (Eds.), *Habermas, critical theory and education* (pp. 111–124). New York: Routledge.

Gibbs, P. (2010). The commodification and standardization of higher education. In N. Foskett & F. Maringe (Eds.), *Globalisation and internationalisation in higher education: Theoretical, strategic and management perspectives* (pp. 241–253). London: Bloomsbury Academic.

Giroux, H. (2002). Neoliberalism, corporate culture and the promise of higher education: The university as a democratic public sphere. *Harvard Educational Review, 72*(4), 1–31.

Gouthro, P. (2006). Reason, communicative learning, and civil society: The use of Habermasian theory in adult education. *Journal of Educational Thought, 40*(1), 5–22.

Habermas, J. (1970). *Toward a rational society: Student protest, science, and politics.* Boston, MA: Beacon Press.

Habermas, J. (1971). *Knowledge and human interests.* Boston, MA: Beacon Press.

Habermas, J. (1979). *Communication and the evolution of society.* Boston, MA: Beacon Press.

Habermas, J. (1984). *The theory of communicative action: Reason and the rationalisation of society* (Vol. 1). Boston, MA: Beacon Press.

Habermas, J. (1987a). *The theory of communicative action: Lifeworld and system—A critique of functionalist reason* (Vol. 2). Boston, MA: Beacon Press.

Habermas, J. (1987b). The idea of the university: Learning Processes. *New German Critique, 41,* 3–22.

Habermas, J. (2001). *On the pragmatics of social interaction: Preliminary studies in the theory of communicative action.* Oxford: Blackwell.

Habermas, J. (2005). Knowledge and human interests: A general perspective. *Continental Philosophy of Science,* 310–320.

Heslep, R. (2001). Habermas on communication in teaching. *Educational Theory, 51*(2), 191–207.

Hotho, S., & Dowling, M. (2010). Revisiting leadership development: The participant perspective. *Leadership and Organization Development Journal, 31*(7), 609–629.

Ibn Khaldun, A. (1967). *The Muqaddimah: An introduction to history.* Princeton: Princeton University Press.

Ibn Taymiyyah, T. (2005). *The political Shariyah on reforming the ruler and the ruled.* Dar ul Fiqh.

Lipman, P. (2011). Neoliberal education restructuring: Dangers and opportunities of the present crisis. *Monthly Review, 63*(3), 114–127.

Mezirow, J. (1981). A critical theory of adult learning and education. *Adult Education Quarterly, 32*(1), 3–24.

Milley, P. (2004). The social and educational implications of university cooperative education: A Habermasian perspective. Ph.D. Thesis. University of Victoria.

Morrow, R. (2010). Habermas, eurocentrism and education: The indigenous knowledge debate. In M. Murphy & T. Fleming (Eds.), *Habermas, critical theory and education* (pp. 63–77). New York: Routledge.

Murphy, M. (2010). Forms of rationality and public sector reform: Habermas, education and social policy. In M. Murphy & T. Fleming (Eds.), *Habermas, critical theory and education* (pp. 79–93). New York: Routledge.

Murphy, M., & Fleming, T. (2010). *Habermas, critical theory and education.* New York: Routledge.

Nash, R., & Scott, L. (2009). Spirituality, religious pluralism, and higher education leadership development. In A. Kezar (Ed.), *Rethinking leadership in a complex multicultural and global environment* (pp. 131–150). Sterling, VA: Stylus Publishing.

Northouse, P. (2013). *Leadership theory and practice* (6th ed.). Thousand Oaks, CA: Sage.

Olivares, O. (2011). The formative capacity of momentous events and leadership development. *Leadership and Organization, 32*(8), 837–853.

Petriglieri, G., Wood, J., & Petriglieri, J. (2011). Up close and personal: Building foundations for leaders' development through the personalization of management learning. *Academy of Management Learning and Education, 10*(3), 430–450.

Reynolds, M. (1999). Critical reflection and management education: Rehabilitating less hierarchical approaches. *Journal of Management Education, 23*(5), 537–553.

Romanowski, M. (2014). The Qatar national professional standards for school leaders: A critical discourse analysis using Habermas' theory of knowledge constitutive interests. *International Journal of Leadership in Education, 17*(2), 174–199.

Samier, E. (2009). Toward public administration as a humanities discipline: A humanistic manifesto. *Administrative Culture, 6*(2005), 6–59.

Small, M. (2004). Philosophy in management: A new trend in management development. *Journal of Management Development, 23*(2), 183–196.

Stenberg, L. (2004). Islam, knowledge and the West: The making of a global Islam. In B. Schaebler & L. Stenberg (Eds.), *Globalization and the Muslim world: Culture, religion and modernity* (pp. 93–112). Syracuse, NY: Syracuse University Press.

Tehranian, M. (2004). Cultural security and global governance: International migration and negotiations of identity. In J. Friedman & S. Randeria (Eds.), *Worlds on the move: Globalization, migration and cultural security* (pp. 3–22). London: IB Tauris.

Welton, M. (1991). *Toward development work: The workplace as a learning environment.* Melbourne: Deakin University Press.

Zehndorfer, E. (2014). *Leadership: A critical introduction.* London: Routledge.

Eman S. ElKaleh studied her MBA at the University of Wollongong followed by a Ph.D. in Management, Leadership and Policy at the British University in Dubai in association with Birmingham University, UK. She received an Academic Excellence Award by Dubai International Academic City for her dissertation entitled 'Teaching Leadership in UAE Business and Education Programs: A Habermasean Analysis within an Islamic Context'. While she hails from Egypt, she has worked in the UAE at two major universities for nearly twenty years. Currently, she teaches business leadership at Zayed University's College of Business in addition to overseeing the Admission and Recruitment Unit. Understanding the need to develop leadership capacity in Gulf-Region countries, she is actively developing programmes and workshops to help Muslim students as well as the faculty and staff with whom they interact gain a better understanding of leadership from an Islamic perspective. She has given guest lectures on Islamic leadership at a number of universities abroad such as University of Oxford Brookes, UK, the Humboldt University of Berlin, Germany, Qatar University and at the British University and Zayed University in the UAE. She was selected to serve as the Chair of Professional Development in the MENASA NASPA Advisory Board. She is also participating in a number of international research projects in leadership studies. She also has a solid experience in reviewing research studies and serves as a reviewer for a number of international and national peer-reviewed conferences and research awards. Tasked with developing a comprehensive programme for student success, she was recognised for her innovation in 2012 by receiving Zayed University's highest honour at a university-wide ceremony.

Chapter 4
Leadership Development in the UAE: Critical Perspectives on Intercultural Pedagogies in a Graduate Education Programme

Barbara Harold and Lauren Stephenson

Abstract Perspectives on the interaction between people of different cultures has changed considerably over recent decades alongside significant changes in higher education worldwide as the policies of globalisation and internationalisation have become widespread and neoliberalism has become prevalent in higher education, characterised by economic imperatives and a trend towards standardised curricula and pedagogy. Responding to the call of Mullen et al. (Interchange 43:181–186, 2013) for a 're-centering of [the] field towards orienting leadership practice … around issues of pedagogy as opposed to those of management' (p. 183), this chapter critically analyses the application of theoretical perspectives to the development and implementation of elements of an actual graduate leadership programme in a Middle Eastern tertiary institution. Using a Bourdieuian framework, it first provides a contextual overview of the nature of neoliberal policy enactments and their impact on teaching and learning in that higher education setting. It then discusses how the authors developed and implemented courses within the leadership programme with Emirati students, drawing on content from Western and Arabic and Islamic research and based on a social-constructivist perspective and a Habermasian 'communicative action' standpoint where it was important for the students to engage in critical conversations and discussions to compare and contrast ideas and to adapt them to their own leadership context. Finally, the chapter reviews the successes and challenges of the graduate coursework drawing on theoretical views of cultural difference, intercultural education and communicative action, to examine the 'fit' between theory and pedagogical practice in leadership development.

B. Harold (✉)
Center for Educational Innovation, Zayed University, Dubai, United Arab Emirates
e-mail: Barbara.Harold@zu.ac.ae

L. Stephenson
School of Education, University of Notre Dame, Sydney, Australia
e-mail: lauren.stephenson@nd.edu.au

© Springer Nature Singapore Pte Ltd. 2019
E. A. Samier and E. S. ElKaleh (eds.), *Teaching Educational Leadership in Muslim Countries*, Educational Leadership Theory,
https://doi.org/10.1007/978-981-13-6818-9_4

Introduction

Perspectives on the interaction between people of different cultures have changed considerably over recent decades from that of multi-culturalism (referring to exchanges amongst two or more cultures within a nation state) to what is now termed 'interculturalism' referring to exchange and dialogue between cultures outside the nation state (Besley and Peters 2015). Other terminology has been used, sometimes interchangeably, including cross-cultural and transcultural to reflect shifts in cultural patterns arising from increased globalisation and population movements. One outcome of these cultural 'shifts' particularly in the last two to three decades has been significant changes in education worldwide as the policies and practices of neoliberalism have been 'unleashed' on education systems (Mullen et al. 2013, p. 182). There has been a corresponding process of internationalisation particularly in higher education (HE) (Altbach and Knight 2007). On the one hand, this has resulted in greater student diversity in classrooms following the outflow of students moving freely from their own countries of origin to the 'market' of universities elsewhere in the world. On the other, rapidly developing nation states such as the United Arab Emirates and other Gulf nations have also seen inflows of international expatriate faculty (Kirk 2010). These faculties are seen as helping to make their universities more competitive in relation to their international counterparts and/or to develop a market for branch campuses of well-known universities from elsewhere. In both these contexts, however, student and faculty cultural diversity can run counter to the prevalent neoliberal project in HE characterised by a push for increasingly standardised and convergent curricula and pedagogy.

Recent studies attest to a 'cultural divide' that occurs when pedagogies reflect the dominant culture and policy environment and students' own cultural perspectives are ignored, misunderstood or undervalued (see Hatherley-Green 2012). Jiang (2011), for example, writing about the experiences of Chinese students at New Zealand universities, discusses the 'intercultural incompatibility' that occurs in attitudes to knowledge, learning strategies and student/faculty expectations. Her views are echoed in Hamdan's (2014) study of expatriate teachers in Saudi Arabian higher education. The very concept of 'intercultural education' is rife with semantic complexities, practical pitfalls and thorny theoretical problems (Coulby 2006) within which the advancement of understandings of theory and practice can take a range of analytical pathways.

Mullen et al. (2013) have recently called for a 're-centering of [the] field towards orienting leadership practice and teacher preparation around issues of pedagogy as opposed to those of management' (p. 183). This chapter is a response to their call but rather than offering suggestions about how this might be done it will critically analyse the application of theoretical perspectives to the development and implementation of elements of an actual graduate leadership programme in a Middle Eastern tertiary institution. Using a Bourdieuian framework, it first provides a contextual overview of the nature of neoliberal policy enactments and their impact on teaching and learning in a Middle Eastern higher education setting. The second section of the chapter discusses how the authors (two Australasian expatriate faculty) developed and implemented courses within a graduate leadership programme with Emirati students, drawing on content from western (e.g. Crippen 2005; Fullan 2004) and Arabic and Islamic (e.g. Al Hinai and Rutherford 2002; Sarayrah 2004; Shah 2006, 2010) research and literature.

McLoughlin's (2001) view that 'culture pervades learning and in designing instructional environments there needs to be serious debate about issues concerning the social and cultural dimensions of task design, communication channels and structuring of information if the needs of culturally diverse learners are to be met' (p. 9) informed the planning of the programme. The pedagogical approaches evolved from a social-constructivist perspective exemplified in Lave and Wenger's (1991) view of learning as a social phenomenon and characterised as 'active, constructive, collaborative, intentional, conversational, contextual and reflective' (Jonasson and Peck 1999, cited in McLoughlin 2001, p. 14). The authors brought a significant level of intercultural competence (Deardoff 2009) to their work with graduates, having taught in an Arab/Emirati context for several years prior. The graduate programme was based on a Habermasian perspective where it was important for the students to engage in critical conversations and discussions to compare and contrast ideas and to adapt them to their own leadership context. What was important was the nature of the dialogue or what Habermas (1984) termed 'communicative action' between the western teachers and Emirati students that served to 'transmit and renew cultural knowledge in a process of achieving mutual understandings' (Besley and Peters 2011, p. 8). Dialogue alone is not sufficient for intercultural education; it needs to occur in an affective context where attitudes such as empathy, curiosity and respect are evident (Perry and Southwell 2011). A further element in the pedagogical approach was the integration of technology in a blended face-to-face and online design drawing on Seimens' (2004) notion of 'connectivism'.

The third section of the chapter reviews the successes and challenges of the graduate programme and draws on theoretical views of cultural difference (Trompenaars and Hampden-Turner 1998), intercultural education (Coulby 2006) and Habermas's concept of communicative action, to examine the 'fit' between theory and pedagogical practice in leadership development in a Middle Eastern context.

Neoliberal Impact on Higher Education in the Middle East

In this section of the chapter, we provide a contextual overview of the nature of neoliberal policy enactments and their impact on teaching and learning in Middle Eastern higher education, specifically in the UAE context and then use a Bourdieuian framework to analyse some apparent contradictions.

Although the land now known as the United Arab Emirates has been inhabited for centuries by Bedouin tribes and itinerant traders and merchants its birth and development as a federation of seven emirate entities has been recent and rapid. Population growth reflects this; in just over 40 years, the population has grown from approximately a half million (mostly Emirati nationals) to the current nine and a half million, of which 1.4 million are Emirati nationals (Dubai Online n.d.). This growth has been fuelled by the wealth generated by the export of oil beginning in 1962 which led a change from a largely subsistence economy based on agriculture, pearl diving and fishing to its current basis of commerce and trade, oil and gas, financial and business services, real estate, construction and manufacturing, and tourism. During the latter half of the twentieth century, sons (mainly) of the ruling elites typically completed higher education at prestigious Western institutions, bringing those ideas and perspectives with them on their return to the UAE and their movement into positions of influence within commerce and government. The rapidity of growth has impacted all sectors of Emirati society and in particular the education system. Here, we will examine policy activity in this field, specifically in relation to higher education.

It was during this latter part of the twentieth century that the emergence of an economic orthodoxy and political ideology known as neoliberalism occurred. Although its roots can be traced to the nineteenth century concept of classical liberalism, this revised idea ran rampant throughout governments around the world, particularly from the 1970s, in response to social and economic 'crises' (both real and manufactured). At its core, the ideology of the free market was paramount characterised by minimal intervention from government, including the privatisation of state-owned enterprises (e.g. transport and utilities). Checks and balances such as unionised labour and social welfare were minimised. By the 1990s, many negative results of the neoliberal project became evident including increased disparity between high and low socioeconomic sectors, increased unemployment and poverty, reductions in wages, and fraud and inefficiencies across institutions (Harvey 2007).

The academic literature dealing with the concept of neoliberalism is replete with examples and critique, much of which highlights the negative impact of neoliberal policy and practice. Bourdieu himself was particularly critical of neoliberalism calling it a 'new type of conservative revolution that claims connection with progress, reason and science… [that] ratifies and glorifies the rule of what we call the financial markets, a return to a sort of radical capitalism answering to no law except that of maximum profit; an undisguised, unrestrained capitalism' (Bourdieu 1998, p. 125). Its impact on education policy has also been referred to as 'social Darwinism' (Tienken 2013) where certain policy implementations that appear to be objective (e.g. standardised testing) may actually discriminate against certain groups of students. On the other hand, Rowlands and Rawolle (2013) warn that while the term is mentioned frequently in academic literature, its 'complex and multifaceted nature makes it difficult to define and describe' (p. 1) and that other more nuanced explanations are needed for economic and political influences on education policy.

During the last two decades of growth and expansion, significant changes have occurred in the higher education sector in the UAE and it was impacted by several factors where the influence of neoliberal ideology became apparent in specific ways. First, within the government sector, was the rapid growth of international consultancies involving 'policy borrowing' from predominantly Western perspectives and curricula. The higher education national sector was modelled largely on North

American structure and curriculum content and during the late 1990s and the initial decade of the new century the consultation 'industry' was very active. Consultants were also brought in from the United Kingdom and Australia. A key driver behind the adoption of international structures and curricula was the desire of the government to join the international movement for educational reform and to raise the status of local universities in world ranking systems. Despite the volume of consultancies, the process was not uncontested and concerns about its impact emerged from early on. For example, a prominent tertiary educator warned that:

> All higher education colleges and universities are following curriculum of foreign universities. Instead of following foreign universities, UAE institutions should adopt a local curriculum, ideally suited for the country's environment. (Nazzal 2001)

This view aligns with Bourdieu's concern about how 'globalisation' and uncritical policy borrowing can lead to policy and practice disassociated from its original cultural and socio-historical milieu:

> … these commonplaces of the great new global vulgate that endless media repetition progressively transforms into universal common sense manage in the end to make one forget that they have their roots in the complex and controversial realities of a particular historical society, now tacitly constituted as a model for every other and a yardstick for all things. (Bourdieu and Wacquant 1999, p. 42)

Their view is echoed in more recent commentary by Samier (2013, in Mullen et al. 2013) who notes that external neoliberal and modernisation forces impacting on the UAE society have led to a shift from traditional social values such as hospitality, loyalty and tolerance (alongside moral and religious ones) to those such as materialism and secularism associated with neoliberal-related practices of industrialisation, urbanisation and technologisation (p. 216). Samier's view has been reaffirmed more recently by Warner and Burton (2017) who note the inherent challenges to, and potential undermining of local/indigenous forms of knowledge by what they term 'Western-oriented modernization' (p. 10) undertaken throughout the wider region.

Currently, there are three government-funded federal HE institutions; UAE University, Zayed University and the Higher Colleges of Technology, but a second major neoliberal impact on higher education was the rapid entry of branch campuses of private international universities and other tertiary institutions. Ahmed and Abdalla Alfaki (2013), for example, note that in a ten-year period from 1997 to 2008, the number of licensed higher education institutions increased from 5 to 58, including some branch campuses of foreign universities, attracted by the high economic growth and private sector investments in higher education. This figure had increased to 71 by 2013 (Ashour and Fatima 2016). Accompanying the rapid growth in HE institutions was the influx of Western-educated faculty in both national and international institutions. The impetus to employ well-qualified international faculty arose from four original policy pillars in the 1970s (Fox 2007) and was reinforced by the Ministry of Higher Education and Scientific Research and underpinned by the economic imperative to prepare graduates to contribute to economic growth and development in the expanding globalised position of the UAE.

In the flux and flow of the UAE economy, what was termed the 'education gold rush' (Ashour and Fatima 2016) resulted, for some institutions, in some unanticipated problems of low enrolment, poorly qualified faculty and inferior curricula (Wilkins 2010). The immediate outcome of this was a government requirement for both external international accreditation of public tertiary entities and the development of internal accreditation processes to regulate the private institutions (Goodwin 2006). This aligns with Connell's (2013) view that the neoliberal project underpins the recent growth of 'managerialism' in universities, where the processes for quality assurance together with an increased focus on compliance with government regulatory requirements have led to a reduction in academic democracy, more centralised decision making, and a view of students as customers (p. 103).

A perusal of key policy and strategic planning documents over the last decade and a half provides clear evidence of the impact of neoliberal thinking in the UAE. The Office of Higher Education and Planning in the Ministry of Higher Education and Scientific Research (MOHESR; now subsumed within a broader Ministry of Education), for example, published two key reports focusing on the importance of access to higher education by Emirati students (MOHESR 2004a), and on the role of higher education in the future of the UAE (MOHESR 2004b). Two other key reports from the Office of Higher Education and Planning followed in 2007, one of which discussed the status of science and engineering education in the UAE (MOHESR 2007a). Neoliberal perspectives were evident here including a comparative ranking with other countries, and a focus on the need for a competitive workforce, programme quality consistency with international standards and participation in the global economy. The second report (MOHESR 2007b) set an ambitious direction for the country, underpinned again with clear neoliberal perspectives. It sets three goals—to provide educational opportunity for all Emiratis, to ensure high quality education and to contribute to the UAE economic development. The report also included two action items calling for regular programme review at the institutional level and institutional accountability and reporting of student outcomes to the Ministry of Higher Education. These particular items foreshadowed the more recent quality assurance, managerialist regime now embedded in federal institutions. During this period, the UAE government also issued major policy documents outlining key strategic goals and directions for the country, within which higher education featured strongly.

The most recent government initiative for higher education, entitled the National Strategy for Higher Education 2030, was launched by the Ministry of Education in September 2017 (Ministry of Education n.d.). The recurrence of specific terminology clearly identifies its neoliberal underpinnings where the focus is clearly on development of the kinds of technical and practical skills that will support economic growth, the labour market, the knowledge economy and entrepreneurship. The initiative's four main pillars—quality, efficiency, innovation and harmonisation—also reflect a neoliberalist agenda which is evidenced further by the inclusion of managerialist practices such as assessment-based standards, quality control, classification of outputs and reports to establish transparency to support achievement of the initiative.

It is clear that the neoliberal perspective still underpins higher education policy development in the UAE. At a recent Leaders Forum in Abu Dhabi, for example, speakers commented on the need for specialised education courses that aligned with the needs of the job market, and for partnerships to be formed between education institutions, private sector industries, and government bodies (Zaatari 2017). However, the degree to which neoliberal policy and practice has been actually implemented within higher education and wider social and economic sectors remain somewhat ambivalent.

For example, in a recent analysis of the level of success of neoliberal policies in transforming the UAE federal bureaucracy into a 'new public management' (NPM) system, Mansour (2017) argues that the government has achieved success in some economic areas (e.g. privatisation of water and electricity utilities, telecommunications and public transport). However, social services to UAE citizens (free education, health care, and social welfare) have resisted privatisation due to the nature of government–citizen relationships in the tribal-based society. In Bourdieuian terms, the *habitus* of individual citizens within the *field* of social services is resistant to a free market approach to the structure and delivery of those services. What is unique to the UAE is the co-existence of culturally defined 'patron–client' relationships alongside the NPM tools such as e-government, competition, privatisation and quality assurance (Mansour 2017). The influence of local cultural elements on the neoliberalism process has been discussed elsewhere. Elyas and Picard (2013), in their discussion of the Saudi Arabian educational context, suggest that greater scrutiny is needed of the impact of neoliberal reforms on wider social relations (p. 38). While the concept of 'globalisation' implies and standardisation of policy they observe that a concept of 'glocalisation', where local cultural needs impacts the selection, processing and consumption of neoliberal policy, provides a better explanation of what is happening in higher education (p. 38).

The foregoing commentary provides an overview of how a neoliberalist agenda derived from a globalised policy field has influenced policy and practice in a localised field of higher education in the UAE. In analysing its origin and progress, a Bourdieuian perspective can provide some insights. Lingard et al. (2005), while noting that Bourdieu did not actually write about education policy, claim that his key concepts of *field*, *habitus* and *capitals* can provide a useful theoretical framework for understanding policy development and implementation. Lingard (2006) further argues that:

> Bourdieu's theoretical stance and methodological disposition allow a way beyond such spatial and national constraints, a necessary position for analyzing and understanding global effects in contemporary educational policy and the emergence of a global policy field in education. (p. 291)

In Bourdieu's conception, individual social 'agents' operate within a particular *habitus* of values, beliefs, and dispositions and possess varying levels of economic, social, cultural and symbolic *capital* that allows them to interact within the structured social spaces or *fields* comprising their own logics, laws of practice, hierarchies and power relations (Lingard et al. 2005).

Lingard et al. (2005) posit the global field of educational policy as not only an economic-related field but also a political project within a process of 'flows' of people and ideas across national borders. They go on to argue that while different nation states possess greater or lesser levels of power 'the amount of 'national capital' possessed by a given nation within these global fields is a determining factor in the spaces of resistance and degree of autonomy for policy development within the nation' (p. 8). Burden-Leahy (2009) develops this idea further in discussing the conundrum of higher education in the UAE, a wealthy developing nation which possesses the economic, social and cultural capital to use its education system to 'reinforce messages about the region, country and religion' (p. 540) but has not yet achieved the higher education success expected from extensive consultancies with Western ideas. She suggests that other global fields are in play that operate to limit the UAE and other developing nations from entering the globalised policy discourse. Lingard et al. (2005) suggest a widening of Bourdieu's concepts to include a category of 'cross-field effects' that would thus allow investigation of the ways that fields and sub-fields interconnect and impact each other (e.g. the national education policy field and the bureaucratic field and the social field and the globalised education policy field) to explain the apparent contradictions that can occur.

Pedagogical Approaches to the Teaching of Educational Leadership in the UAE

In this section, we discuss how we co-constructed and implemented courses within a graduate leadership programme with Emirati students as we worked together over an eight-year period. We had observed students who arrived with a willingness to learn, and yet the educational opportunities presented to them provided an overload of Western content that was not necessarily relevant to critical application in the UAE. Conger (2013) describes three critical shortcomings that limit classroom experiences in leadership education and impede the facilitation and transfer of useful learning and its application to the day-to-day challenges that leaders face: (1) the reality gap, (2) the skill-intensive gap, and (3) the application gap. 'Many of our leadership constructs fail to identify leadership as a process that is highly contingent and multidirectional; instead focusing on models or approaches that offer 'what ifs' versus actual action' (Conger 1992, p. 30).

Our pedagogical approach was based on a Habermasian perspective where it was important for the students to engage in critical conversations and discussions to compare and contrast ideas and to adapt them to their own leadership context. What was important was the nature of the dialogue or what Habermas (1984) termed 'communicative action' between the Western faculty and Emirati students that served to 'transmit and renew cultural knowledge in a process of achieving mutual understandings' (Besley and Peters 2011, p. 8). Dialogue alone is not sufficient for intercultural education; it needs to occur in an affective context where attitudes such as empathy, curiosity and respect are evident (Perry and Southwell 2011).

In the first instance, we designed the initial course in the programme, one that would lay the foundations of leadership theory that would infuse the other courses across a two-year period. We focused on two key aspects—the learning environment and the course content. As experienced educators, we understood the importance of the classroom environment to support learning and discourse. Here, we aligned with McLoughlin's (2001) view that 'culture pervades learning and in designing instructional environments there needs to be serious debate about issues concerning the social and cultural dimensions of task design, communication channels and structuring of information if the needs of culturally diverse learners are to be met' (p. 9). With regard to the social dimension, we used the term 'colleagues' rather than student to address our course participants as we viewed them as our professional school-based contemporaries. This established a classroom environment of relative equality and reciprocity.

For the course content, our aim was to have the graduates critically compare and contrast Western and Arab/Islamic theories of leadership. In doing so, we utilised a variety of themes and paired them, with one article from each cultural context. Examples of themes included teamwork (Al Rawi 2008; Barry 1991), servant leadership (Crippen 2005; Sarayrah 2004), ethics (Shah 2006; Starratt 1991), shared and distributed leadership (Al Hinai and Rutherford 2002; Oduro 2004) and teacher leadership (Stephenson et al. 2012; York-Barr and Duke 2004; Demir 2015). In addition, we asked course members to critically reflect on their own leadership philosophy and practice and to identify influences on these. Typically, the Emirati students discussed being influenced by leadership models from family, workplace, Emirati national leaders, and the Prophet Muhammad all of which are significant in their culture. This pedagogical approach allowed further opportunities to draw connections to leadership in other cultural contexts.

To lead change and advance educational outcomes, graduate students in the UAE require educational leadership courses that effectively prepare them for their transformational and transformative roles. As such leadership education necessarily values, and is inclusive of, both curricular and co-curricular educational contexts (Andenoro et al. 2013). Curricular content recommended for leadership development in postgraduate students prepares them with knowledge of leadership concepts, skills, dispositions and communication strategies needed for effective and ethical leadership. Experiential learning that is integrated with curricular content enhances the development of leadership and communication skills (Benner et al. 2010). The pedagogical approaches we used evolved from a social-constructivist perspective exemplified in Lave and Wenger's (1991) view of learning as a social phenomenon and characterised as 'active, constructive, collaborative, intentional, conversational, contextual and reflective' (Jonassen and Peck 1999, cited in McLoughlin 2001, p. 14). Students of educational leadership learn well in what Lave and Wenger (1991) term 'communities of practice' that provide relevant experiences, rich feedback, and opportunities for reflection, as well as social support (Berry 2011, p. 1).

The authors brought a significant level of intercultural competence (Deardorff 2009) to our work with graduates, having taught in an Arab/Emirati context for several years prior. Together with the graduate students, we created an exemplar community of practice, which represented the type of innovative learning environment that supports development of leadership competencies in aspirant and practicing educational leaders in the UAE. We took an interdisciplinary approach to leadership education (Jenkins and Dugan 2013), promoting application across contexts, exposure to multiple ideas, and the recognition of situational influences, such as what leadership looks like across disciplines and across different cultural contexts. We re-evaluated the time devoted to conveying and discussing information on leadership versus the time spent by students reflecting on their own situations and applying tools to help them successfully navigate those situations (Conger 2013). The students engaged in critical inquiry into their leadership experience and behaviours which provided a unique opportunity for them to learn to actualise their leadership practices. To support their learning experiences, we compiled knowledge resources and made epistemological decisions about the content of the leadership courses, choosing from textbooks, articles, and videos; websites; and workbooks (see Fink 2013). Through this process, we assembled the essential inputs required to facilitate educational leadership learning for graduate students in their UAE context.

According to Harvey and Jenkins (2014), knowledge, praxis, and reflection are the three critical elements in leadership programmes. A focus on knowledge provides opportunities for students to challenge assumptions, theories, models, and approaches. We encouraged discussion, analysis of case studies and problem-based learning, and critical reflection pedagogies to ensure an environment conducive to teaching and learning leadership in the UAE context. These salient strategies are practical ways for students to develop leadership knowledge, skills and dispositions. Discussion-based pedagogies are frequently used in leadership education (see Jenkins 2012, 2013). It was therefore critical that as leadership educators we facilitated discussions that were intentional and critical. According to Brookfield (2012), to make discussion critical, facilitators should: (a) focus on members identifying assumptions, (b) focus on the degree to which these assumptions are accurate and valid, (c) attempt to fix the contextual validity of assumptions, (d) uncover evidence for generalisations, (e) keep a record of the links in an 'inferential chain,' (f) generate multiple perspectives and (g) be alert for groupthink. Additionally, criteria for evaluating whether a discussion is critical include: (a) structures that are in place to ensure inclusivity, (b) time limits, (c) mutual respect, (d) foci on similarities and differences that emerge, (e) a shared power differential and (f) active listening as the primary goal (Brookfield 2012). We used two broad approaches to discussion. Some occurred in face-to-face classes either with the whole group that allowed for wider sharing of ideas or in small group formats for more focused exchanges. The second format used an online asynchronous discussion forum. The class members individually contributed questions that were related to the course learning outcomes and to aspects of their own leadership role. They then analysed and grouped the questions into themes and for each forum the class was organised into small groups with a discussion leader and a set of protocols to carry it on over a week. The questions were based in their own school contexts, but they were expected to respond using references to both western and Arab/Islamic material from the course. Both types of discussion were grounded in a social-constructivist framework (Lave and Wenger 1991; McLoughlin 2001) that encouraged a critical analysis of intercultural perspectives. The analysis of western content was constantly underpinned by the question 'How does this "fit" in an Emirati educational context?'

Scholars have alluded to practicing critical reflection—a behaviour that integrates personal experiences with new learning and understanding—to engage and mobilise learners to act on new ideas and to challenge conventional thinking in both theory and practice (Jones et al. 2000; Reynolds 1999). We created opportunities for the graduates to practice critical reflection both individually and collectively to encourage and facilitate the important connection between critical thinking and leadership development (see also Guthrie and Jones 2012; Stedman 2009). Our experience resonated with the views of Brookfield (2012), Dewey (1933), Reynolds (1999) that engaging in critical reflection can create student discomfort and dissonance. Nonetheless, as Fink (2013) and others assert, discomfort often means learners are really thinking and consequently really learning. In leadership education, deep reflective learning requires learners to consider the underlying dynamics of power in the micro-politics of organisational contexts and to question basic assumptions and practices. For example, learners could be required to reassess the power they use in leadership situations to achieve their desired results (Jenkins and Cutchens 2011).

A further element in our pedagogical approach was the integration of technology in a blended face-to-face and online design through both synchronous and asynchronous sessions, drawing on Seimens' (2004) notion of 'connectivism' and its principles that nurturing and maintaining connections is needed to facilitate continuous learning, knowledge may reside in non-human appliances and that obtaining accurate up-to-date knowledge is the intent of connectivist learning activities (p. 5). During the synchronous online classes, faculty were aware of specific cultural beliefs about privacy that can impact the use of virtual classrooms; for example, the graduate students were working in their home environment where the women would not be covered with the traditional *shayla* (headscarf). Thus, to ensure their privacy, the webcam option was not used by the students but only by the faculty instructor. The synchronous online environment allowed for small group discussion similar to the face-to-face context with the added advantage that material could be recorded and used for further analysis or as a resource for coursework. In addition, it was regularly used to set up independent meeting times with groups of students to work collaboratively on class assignments. The faculty instructor could join these if requested to offer additional support. Evaluative data collected from the course participants suggested that the online model was effective, conducive to learning, enhanced student satisfaction and development and stimulated leadership learning.

Our intentional approach offered here is deeply rooted in graduate student leadership development, leadership education theories and pedagogical approaches, and it presents a process that demonstrates practices to empower and engage our emerging leaders. Further, the process supports a foundation for the creation of leadership learning in the UAE educational context.

The 'Fit' Between Theory and Practice

A review of our intercultural pedagogies in a graduate leadership programme identifies both successes and challenges. One of the main successes was the establishment of a classroom learning culture characterised by a community of practice (Lave and Wenger 1991) with our graduate colleagues. During our class sessions, they were confident to engage in the kind of Habermasian rational communication necessary for the sharing and exchange of ideas about leadership. The course participants varied from a small number who had recently graduated from university with fresh ideas, to experienced educational leaders with extensive professional practice and thus discussions were rich and productive. Occasionally, as in any critical learning environment, tensions could occur between members, but we encouraged them to view these as opportunity to use their leadership skills to find solutions.

The second key success was the level of engagement by course participants with the intercultural material. The readings, activities and assignments we used allowed graduates to draw strongly on their own cultural experience, both personal and professional, to examine their leadership beliefs and values from an Arab/Islamic perspective and then relate them to Western material to identify the 'fit' with their UAE educational context. Class members frequently went beyond the course material to find additional items to support their work. During communicative exchanges, learning occurred in reciprocal ways. An example of this arose during the analysis of an article which was about Islamic approaches to educational leadership but was set in a different cultural context. One of the class members explained to the others how in that particular context gender factors played out differently to those experienced in UAE educational leadership. This exposed the faculty instructor to new ideas also.

Coulby (2006) maintains that while it is probably impossible for most people to fully understand another culture in a pure sense, nevertheless it is necessary to make an attempt if 'gateways are to be made through the barriers of language and distance' (p. 252). This view resonates with the authors' experiences. A key challenge within the implementation of the graduate course was that of language. The majority of graduate participants spoke Arabic as their first language and while the faculty instructors spoke additional Middle Eastern languages other than their native English, they did not speak Arabic. Thus, an additional invisible barrier was inevitably in place that impacted the subtleties of intercultural discourse where imperceptible differences in meaning and context could impact understanding. We attempted to minimise this where possible by allowing the graduates to converse in Arabic during group discussion and to 'check' their understandings with the faculty instructors in front of the whole class. In addition, we would sometimes ask the class for the Arabic term for a key concept and thus allowed for some negotiation amongst the students themselves about the most appropriate term. In this sense, we were attempting to utilise a Habermasian notion of reciprocity and symmetry in dialogue. One of the successes of our approach was to first use both oral and written forms of communication to share, compare and contrast ideas across cultural perspectives and second, to allow for a more personal form of dialogue between instructor and student where the later engaged in individual reflection about content, including their emotional reactions to new ideas and course material. The dialogue in that instance occurs at a secondary asynchronous level where written feedback is given by the faculty instructor but at times was followed by face-to-face dialogue where any linguistic queries could be clarified.

The use of an online virtual classroom (first using Blackboard Collaborate software and then Adobe Connect) offered an alternative pedagogical strategy to engage graduate students in course content. However, it did present some communication challenges. First, for cultural and privacy reasons, the participants did not use their webcams, so the faculty instructor had to speak to a disembodied space and thus, the normal facial expression cues were absent and student reactions could not always be gauged. Second, there were occasional technical difficulties with microphone sound levels, or participants being 'dropped out' of the system that slowed the flow and comprehension of communication in a full-class context. The main challenges occurred during full-class presentation-type sessions, so these were used less often and the emphasis was moved to 'breakout sessions' where smaller groups could discuss and analyse content and where the faculty instructor could enter and join in discussion.

This approach allowed for a much higher level of student engagement in direct discussion. The participants were comfortable with the faculty member entering and participating in the small group sessions as a level of trust had been established in faculty–graduate relationships in the face-to-face classes. The trust component has been identified as a key factor in successful intercultural interactions in the information technology context (Zakaria et al. 2003; McLoughlin 2007) and the small group strategy also aligns with McLoughlin's (2007) advice to provide opportunities for students to 'engage in communication and reflection and develop a repertoire of cross-cultural skills and competencies' (p. 24).

While the majority of our graduate students were Emirati nationals, there were sometimes class members from other cultures including Western and other Gulf Cooperating Council (GCC) nations. In this sense, Habermas' notion of communicative rationality took on a more nuanced meaning. Individual values and social norms could impact on inter-student communication in sometimes unexpected ways. An instance of this happened in one class where tensions arose between two students, ostensibly about responsibility for shared group work, but which the faculty instructor realised were based on a subtler cultural issue related to religious perspectives, and one that she did not fully understand herself. Despite sensitive intervention, the tension was not resolved. There is a difference here between the ideal of rational communication and the reality of underlying psychological factors, values and beliefs (Hillier 2003).

The topic of cross- or intercultural communication has been extensively addressed in the literature, and the work of Trompenaars and Hampden-Turner (1998), extending Hofstede's (1983) seminal work on cultural dimensions, is an example of this. However, much of their work is about negotiation and interaction in business or commercial contexts and based predominantly on the experiences of males. The intercultural interaction between the authors and our mostly Emirati female students occurred in a collaborative rather than a transactional context and thus does not necessarily align with the dual-dimension typology of Trompenaars and Hampden-Turner (1998). In this case, it is potentially more useful to consider the views of Buda and Elsayed-Elkhouly (1998) who note that while a particular dimension of collectivism may be applied to Arabic societies, there may be tendencies towards individualism within those societies. Rather than dualities of culture, it may be better to think of a continuum with opposing dimensions clustered towards each end but along which groups and individuals may fit at differing points. In this respect, Trompenaars and Hampden-Turner (1998) suggest that cultures 'dance' from their preferred point to the opposite and back again in cross-cultural exchanges (1998, p. 27) thus allowing for reconciliation of seemingly opposing values. We saw evidence of this where course members explored similarities as well as differences between cultural explanations of leadership and its practice.

In more recent work, Trompenaars and Voerman (2009) have further explored the notion of values reconciliation using the concept of servant leadership as a vehicle for doing so, with its fundamental view that 'beneath all cultural differences, there is a common basis, namely, being human' (p. xiv). This perspective resonates strongly with our coursework where the graduate students compared and contrasted Western and Bedouin concepts of servant leadership and found a strong commonality between the two in terms of the espoused humanistic values and practices underpinning each. These include empathy, listening, awareness, building community, stewardship and commitment to the growth of others.

Fresh perspectives on the complexities of culture are seen in other contexts. As the fields of information systems, information management and information and communications technology have developed and penetrated globalised systems and virtual organisations the literature has focused more attention on intercultural issues within these spheres (e.g. Myers and Tan 2002; Karahanna et al. 2005; Srite and Karahanna 2006). Myers and Tan (2002) challenged the then prevailing notion of 'national' culture (Hofstede 1983; Trompenaars and Hamden-Turner 1998) to suggest that in the field of global information systems culture should be seen as 'contested, temporal and emergent' (p. 11) and that studies of a 'national' culture are too simplistic and suffer from theoretical and methodological flaws. This idea was further developed by Karahanna et al. (2005) who posit that workplaces have fundamentally changed through increased globalisation, increased immigration, the emergence of virtual organisations where members communicate via computer technology and the growth of sophisticated telecommunications systems (p. 1). They suggest that in any organisational context individuals operate within six interrelated levels of culture (individual, group, organisational, professional, national and supranational) and that their behaviour results from the dynamic interaction of these six levels. Karahanna et al. (2005) go on to argue that two key components in a culture are values and practices the former of which is mainly influenced by supranational (i.e. ethnic or religious) and national levels while practices are predominantly influenced by professional and organisational cultures (p. 7). Thus, in the context of our graduate programme that is concerned with leadership practice, the participants' interactions with the faculty and with each other would be influenced by professional organisational and group cultures, but within the framework of their broader Emirati and Islamic values (or other national cultures for non-Emirati participants). The initial theoretical framework developed by Karahanna et al. (2005) appears to provide a useful 'fit' to analysing the types of interactions we observed in our work with graduate leadership students.

Conclusion

Our aim in this chapter was to respond to the call of Mullen et al. (2013) for a 're-centering of the field towards orienting leadership practice ... around issues of pedagogy as opposed to those of management' (p. 183). In doing so, we have identified particular pedagogies for the teaching of educational leadership in an Arabic/Islamic context, grounded in both a Habermasian concept of 'communicative action', and a social-constructivist perspective that views learning as a social phenomenon enacted in a collaborative, intentional, active and reflective manner. As Western-educated faculty engaged in the preparation of educational leaders for mainly Emirati schools, we believed that it was essential to provide intercultural perspectives about leadership theory and practice that allowed course participants to critically discuss, compare and contrast material reflecting their own cultural context with that from a Western viewpoint so that they could adapt leadership practices that were an appropriate fit to their schools. In addition to suitable course content, we focused on the development of the kind of affective environment where participants were treated as colleagues and where they could freely engage in debate, critical reflection and exchange of ideas as they deepened their understanding of educational leadership. The establishment of this community of practice was a key success in our approach, together with the levels of engagement by course members with the intercultural material. We also faced challenges related to language and the use of technology. Our experience showed that, despite some occasional issues arising from student personal interactions, the underlying frameworks of communicative action and social constructivism provide a sound basis for the kinds of engagement we were aiming for. However, we found that the dual-dimensional view of culture espoused by Trompenaars and Hampden-Turner (1998) did not provide an adequate explanation for the intercultural exchanges occurring in our courses (although Trompenaars' more recent discussion about servant leadership did resonate). The more complex theoretical framework put forward by Karahanna et al. (2005) appeared to relate more closely to the nuances of interaction that we observed between ourselves and the students and between the students themselves.

Our commentary has provided a practical example of the development and implementation of an approach to leadership education in the Middle East in an attempt to examine the 'fit' between theory and practice. In doing so, it contributes to an understanding of the ways in which theory and practice are linked and opens opportunities for further examples of approaches to the realities and complexities of leadership education in Muslim countries.

References

Ahmed, A., & Abdalla Alfaki, I. M. (2013). Transforming the United Arab Emirates into a knowledge-based economy: The role of science, technology and innovation. *World Journal of Science, Technology and Sustainable Development, 10*(2), 84–102.

Al Hinai, H., & Rutherford, D. (2002). *Exploring the Alshura school leadership model in Oman.* Paper presented at the Annual Conference of the British Educational Leadership, Management and Administration Society (BELMAS), Birmingham, England, 20–22 September.

Al Rawi, K. (2008). Cohesiveness within teamwork: The relationship to performance effectiveness—Case study. *Education, Business and Society: Contemporary Middle Eastern Issues, 1*(2), 92–106.

Altbach, P. G., & Knight, J. (2007). The internationalization of higher education: Motivations and realities. *Journal of Studies in International Education, 11*(3–4), 290–305.

Andenoro, A. C., Allen, S. J., Haber-Curran, P., Jenkins, D. M., Sowcik, M., Dugan, J. P., et al. (2013). *National leadership education research agenda 2013–2018: Providing strategic direction for the field of leadership education.* Available http://leadershipeducators.org/ResearchAgenda.

Ashour, S., & Fatima, S. K. (2016). Factors favouring or impeding building a stronger higher education system in the United Arab Emirates. *Journal of Higher Education Policy and Management, 38*(5), 576–591.

Barry, D. (1991). Managing the bossless team. *Organizational Dynamics, 21*(1), 31–47.

Benner, P., Sutphen, M., Leonard, V., & Day, L. (2010). *Educating nurses: A call for radical transformation.* San Francisco, CA: Jossey-Bass.

Berry, L. E. (2011). Creating community: Strengthening education and practice partnerships through communities of practice. *International Journal of Nursing Scholarship, 8*(1), 1–18.

Besley, T., & Peters, M. A. (2011). Interculturalism, ethnocentrism and dialogue. *Policy Futures in Education, 9*(1), 1–12.

Besley, T., & Peters, M. A. (2015). *Interculturalism, education and dialogue.* New York: Peter Lang.

Bourdieu, P. (1998). A reasoned utopia and economic fatalism. *New Left Review, 227,* 125.

Bourdieu, P., & Wacquant, L. (1999). On the cunning of imperialist reason. *Theory, Culture & Society, 16*(1), 41–58.

Brookfield, S. (2012). *Teaching for critical thinking: Tools and techniques to help students question their assumptions.* San Francisco, CA: Jossey-Bass.

Buda, R., & Elsayed-Elkhouly, S. M. (1998). Cultural differences between Arabs and Americans: Individualism-collectivism revisited. *Journal of Cross-Cultural Psychology, 29*(3), 487–492.

Burden-Leahy, S. M. (2009). Globalisation and education in the postcolonial world: The conundrum of the higher education system of the United Arab Emirates. *Comparative Education, 45*(4), 525–544.

Conger, J. (1992). *Learning to lead.* San Francisco, CA: Jossey-Bass.

Conger, J. (2013). Mind the gaps: What limits the impact of leadership education. *Journal of Leadership Studies, 6*(4), 77–83.

Connell, R. (2013). The neoliberal cascade and education: An essay on the market agenda and its consequences. *Critical Studies in Education, 54*(2), 99–112.

Coulby, D. (2006). Intercultural education: Theory and practice. *Intercultural Education, 17*(3), 245–257.

Crippen, C. (2005). Servant-leadership as an effective model for educational leadership and management: First to serve, then to lead. *Management in Education, 18*(5), 11–16.

Deardorff, D. K. (Ed.). (2009). *The SAGE handbook of intercultural competence.* Thousand Oaks, CA: Sage.

Demir, K. (2015). The effect of organizational trust on the culture of teacher leadership in primary schools. *Educational Sciences: Theory and Practice, 15*(3), 621–634.

Dewey, J. (1933). *How we think. A restatement of the relation of reflective thinking on the educative practice.* Lexington, MA: Heath.

Dubai Online. (n.d.). Available https://www.dubai-online.com/essential/united-arab-emirates/. Accessed November 11, 2018.

Elyas, T., & Picard, M. (2013). Critiquing of higher education policy in Saudi Arabia: Towards a new neoliberalism. *Education, Business and Society: Contemporary Middle Eastern Issues, 6*(1), 31–41.

Fink, L. D. (2013). *Creating significant learning experiences: An integrated approach to designing College courses*. San Francisco, CA: Jossey-Bass.

Fox, W. H. (2007). The United Arab Emirates: Policy choices shaping the future of public higher education. Research & Occasional Paper Series: CSHE. 13.07. Berkeley, CA: Center for Studies in Higher Education.

Fullan, M. (2004). *Leading schools in a culture of change*. San Francisco, CA: Jossey-Bass.

Goodwin, S. M. (2006). Globalization, education and Emiratisation: A study of the United Arab Emirates. *The Electronic Journal of Information Systems in Developing Countries, 27*(1), 1–14.

Guthrie, K. L., & Jones, T. B. (2012). Teaching and learning: Using experiential learning and reflection for leadership education. *New Directions for Student Services, 2012*(140), 53–63.

Habermas, J. (1984). *The theory of communicative action: Reason and the rationalization of society* (Vol. 1). Boston, MA: Beacon Press.

Hamdan, A. K. (2014). The road to culturally relevant pedagogy: Expatriate teachers' pedagogical practices in the cultural context of Saudi Arabian higher education. *McGill Journal of Education, 49*(1), 201–226.

Harvey, D. (2007). *A brief history of neoliberalism*. New York: Oxford University Press.

Harvey, M., & Jenkins, D. M. (2014). Knowledge, praxis, and reflection: The three critical elements of effective leadership studies programs. *Journal of Leadership Studies, 7*(4), 76–85.

Hatherley-Green, P. (2012). Cultural border crossings in the UAE. (Policy paper No. 6). Ras Al Khaimah, UAE: Sheikh Saud Bin Saqr Al Qasimi Foundation for Policy Research.

Hillier, J. (2003). Agon'izing over consensus: Why Habermasian ideals cannot be 'real'. *Planning Theory, 2*(1), 37–59.

Hofstede, G. (1983). National cultures in four dimensions: A research-based theory of cultural differences among nations. *International Studies of Management & Organization, 13*(1–2), 46–74.

Jenkins, D. M. (2012). Exploring signature pedagogies in undergraduate leadership education. *Journal of Leadership Education., 11*(1), 1–27.

Jenkins, D. M. (2013). Exploring instructional strategies in student leadership development programming. *Journal of Leadership Studies, 6*(4), 48–62.

Jenkins, D. M., & Cutchens, A. B. (2011). Leading critically: A grounded theory of applied critical thinking in leadership studies. *Journal of Leadership Education, 10*(2), 1–21.

Jenkins, D. M., & Dugan, J. P. (2013). Context matters: An interdisciplinary studies interpretation of the National Leadership Research Agenda. *Journal of Leadership Education, 12*(3), 15–29.

Jiang, X. (2011). Why Interculturalism? A neo-Marxist approach to accommodate cultural diversity in higher education. *Educational Philosophy and Theory, 43*(4), 387–400.

Jonassen, D. H., & Peck, K. L. (1999). *Learning with technology: A constructivist perspective*. Upper Saddle River, NJ: Merrill.

Jones, M. E., Simonetti, J. L., & Vielhaber-Hermon, M. (2000). Building a stronger organization through leadership development at Parke-Davis Research. *Industrial and Commercial Training, 32*(2), 44–48.

Karahanna, E., Evaristo, J. R., & Srite, M. (2005). Levels of culture and individual behavior: An investigative perspective. *Journal of Global Information Management, 13*(2), 1–20.

Kirk, D. (2010). The development of higher education in the United Arab Emirates. *The Emirates Occasional Papers, 74,* 1–57.

Lave, J., & Wenger, E. (1991). *Situated learning: Legitimate peripheral participation*. Cambridge: Cambridge University Press.

Lingard, B. (2006). Globalisation, the research imagination and deparochialising the study of education. *Globalisation, Societies and Education, 4*(2), 287–302.

Lingard, B., Rawolle, S., & Taylor, S. (2005). Globalizing policy sociology in education: Working with Bourdieu. *Journal of Education Policy, 20*(6), 759–777.

Mansour, A. M. (2017). Has the United Arab Emirates government succeeded to transform its federal bureaucracy into a New Public Management system? *International Public Management Review, 18*(1), 116–134.

McLoughlin, C. (2001). Inclusivity and alignment: Principles of pedagogy, task and assessment design for effective cross-cultural online learning. *Distance Education, 22*(1), 7–29.

McLoughlin, C. (2007). Adapting e-learning across cultural boundaries: A framework for quality learning, pedagogy, and interaction. *Globalized e-learning cultural challenges* (pp. 223–238). Hershey, PA: IGI Global.

Ministry of Education. (n.d.). Strategic Plan 2017–2021. Available https://government.ae/en/about-the-uae/strategies-initiatives-and-awards/federal-governments-strategies-and-plans/ministry-of-education-strategic-plan-2017-2021. Accessed August 29, 2018.

Ministry of Higher Education and Scientific Research. (2004a). *Funding students first: Access to quality higher education programs in the United Arab Emirates.* Abu Dhabi: Office of Higher Education Policy and Planning.

Ministry of Higher Education and Scientific Research. (2004b). *Higher education and the future of the UAE.* Abu Dhabi: Office of Higher Education Policy and Planning.

Ministry of Higher Education and Scientific Research. (2007a). *The status of science and engineering education in the UAE.* Abu Dhabi: Office of Higher Education Policy and Planning.

Ministry of Higher Education and Scientific Research. (2007b). *Educating the next generation of Emiratis: A master plan for UAE higher education.* Abu Dhabi: Office of Higher Education Policy and Planning.

Mullen, C. A., English, F. W., Brindley, S., Ehrich, L., & Samier, E. A. (2013). Neoliberal issues in public education. *Interchange, 43,* 181–186.

Myers, M. D., & Tan, F. B. (2002). Beyond models of national culture in information systems research. In C. R. Snodgrass & E. J. Szewczak (Eds.), *Human factors in information systems* (pp. 1–19). Hershey, PA: IGI Global.

Nazzal, N. (2001, October 22). Call for change in UAE education policy. *Gulf News.* https://gulfnews.com/news/uae/general/call-for-change-in-uae-education-policy-1.427929. Accessed August 29, 2018.

Oduro, G. (2004). *'Distributed leadership' in schools: What English headteachers say about the 'pull' And 'push' factors.* Paper presented at the BERA Annual Conference UMIST, Manchester 14–18 September.

Perry, L. B., & Southwell, L. (2011). Developing intercultural understanding and skills: Models and approaches. *Intercultural Education, 22*(6), 453–466.

Reynolds, M. (1999). Critical reflection and management education: Rehabilitating less hierarchical approaches. *Journal of Management Education, 23*(5), 537–553.

Rowlands, J., & Rawolle, S. (2013). Neoliberalism is not a theory of everything: A Bourdieuian analysis of illusio in educational research. *Critical Studies in Education, 54*(3), 260–272.

Sarayrah, Y. K. (2004). Servant leadership in the Bedouin-Arab culture. *Global Virtue Ethics Review, 5*(3), 58–80.

Seimens, G. (2004). Connectivism: A learning theory for the digital age. *Elearnspace.*

Shah, S. (2006). Educational leadership: An Islamic perspective. *British Educational Research Journal, 32*(3), 363–385.

Shah, S. (2010). Re-thinking educational leadership: Exploring the impact of cultural and belief systems. *International Journal of Leadership in Education: Theory and Practice, 13*(1), 27–44.

Srite, M., & Karahanna, E. (2006). The role of espoused national cultural values in technology acceptance. *MIS Quarterly, 30*(3), 679–704.

Starrat, R. J. (1991). Building an ethical School: A theory for practice in educational leadership. *Educational Administration Quarterly, 27*(2), 185–202.

Stedman, N. L. (2009). Casting the net of critical thinking: A look into the collegiate leadership classroom. *Journal of Leadership Education, 7*(3), 201–218.

Stephenson, L., Dada, R., & Harold, B. (2012). Challenging the traditional idea of leadership in UAE schools. *On The Horizon—The Strategic Planning Resource for Education Professionals, 20*(1), 54–63.

Tienken, C. H. (2013). Neoliberalism, social Darwinism, and consumerism masquerading as school reform. *Interchange, 43*(4), 295–316.

Trompenaars, F., & Hampden-Turner, C. (1998). *Riding the waves of culture: Understanding diversity in global business.* New York, NY: McGraw Hill.

Trompenaars, F., & Voerman, E. (2009). *Servant leadership across cultures: Harnessing the strength of the world's most powerful leadership philosophy.* Oxford: Infinite Ideas.

Warner, R. S., & Burton, G. J. (2017). *A fertile oasis: The current state of education in the UAE.* Dubai: UAE Public Policy Forum, Mohammed Bin Rashid School of Government.

Wilkins, S. (2010). Higher education in the United Arab Emirates: An analysis of the outcomes of significant increases in supply and competition. *Journal of Higher Education Policy and Management, 32*(4), 389–400.

York-Barr, J., & Duke, K. (2004). What do we know about teacher leadership? Findings from two decades of scholarship. *Review of Educational Research, 74*(3), 255–316.

Zaatari, S. (2017). Education vital for switch to knowledge-based economy. *Gulf News,* 10 January. http://gulfnews.com/news/uae/education/education-vital-for-switch-to-knowledge-based-economy-1.1959679. Accessed August 31, 2018.

Zakaria, N., Stanton, J. M., & Sarkar-Barney, S. T. (2003). Designing and implementing culturally-sensitive IT applications: The interaction of culture values and privacy issues in the Middle East. *Information Technology & People, 16*(1), 49–75.

Barbara Harold is a Professor at Zayed University in the United Arab Emirates and currently Director of the Center for Educational Innovation. She is an experienced educator with a career that has spanned more than four decades from a primary teacher in New Zealand to a teacher educator in higher education. She holds a Ph.D. in Educational Leadership and Policy Development from the University of Waikato, New Zealand. Since joining Zayed University in 2001, she has held a range of leadership positions in the College of Education including Coordinator of Teaching Practicum, Director of Graduate Programs, Coordinator of Professional Development and Associate Dean. Her teaching, research and publication are in the fields of teacher education, educational leadership (including teacher leadership) and professional learning. She was part of the planning and implementation team for the COE graduate programme and has taught extensively in the educational leadership programme. In 2010, with Lauren Stephenson and a third colleague she led a university-wide 'Conversation on Leadership' project that culminated in a framework for leadership education in the ZU academic programme. She has also received the award of Outstanding Faculty of the Year during her time at ZU. Barbara has been involved in successful programmes of professional development for the Ministry of Education, public and private schools in the UAE and has presented at national, regional and international conferences in the US, UK, UAE, Saudi Arabia and Australia. She has participated in individual and team research projects at national and local levels in the UAE, including research into models of professional learning. Her current research interests include teacher leadership, narrative inquiry, and the use of digital technology in graduate leadership development.

Lauren Stephenson is currently the Dean of the School of Education, University of Notre Dame, Sydney Campus. She was formerly the Academic Lead for the Education and Arts National Professional Learning Hub, the Deputy Head Education NSW/ACT, Academic Lead for Sustainable Partnerships and Capacity Building and the National Coordinator, Educational Leadership, National School of Education, Faculty of Education and Arts at the Australian Catholic University. She has over 25 years of experience in a range of educational leadership roles and is an experienced educator with a combined 30 years in teacher education, educational leadership, and

English as an additional language/dialect (EAL/D). She has an extensive record of scholarly activities at national and international levels and has published in the areas of educational leadership, teacher education and professional learning, EAL/D, action research, autoethnography and narrative inquiry. She holds a PhD in Educational Leadership from the University of Sydney.

Part II
Current Controversies and Challenges

Chapter 5
The Knowledge Base on Educational Leadership and Management in Arab Countries: Its Current State and Its Implications for Leadership Development

Rima Karami-Akkary and Waheed Hammad

Abstract This chapter seeks to expose the challenges and promises faced by educational leadership and management (EDLM) scholars in Arab societies as they strive to establish an indigenous knowledge base that is connected to the global international scholarly discourse. We examine this issue and consider its implications for leadership development in the Arab context. Given the relative scarcity of Arab-related EDLM literature published internationally, our intention is to engage our international colleagues in the dialogue, hence responding to the multiple calls of international scholars to expand the cultural bases of the existing knowledge base in the field. In this chapter, we embrace a broad conception of leadership preparation that goes beyond initial preparation to encompass induction programmes and in-service training. The chapter engages with current international trends in educational leadership development and proposes future directions for research and practice in the Arab region.

Introduction

Over the past few decades, there has been a growing recognition among educational leadership and management scholars of the link between school leadership and school effectiveness. Evidence suggests that effective school leadership positively affects teachers' professional learning as well as student outcomes and that how school leaders are prepared makes a significant difference (Bush and Jackson 2002; McCarthy 2015; Murphy et al. 2008). This has given prominence to leadership preparation as a

---

R. Karami-Akkary (✉)
Educational Administration, Policy and Leadership, American University of Beirut, Beirut, Lebanon
e-mail: ra10@aub.edu.lb

W. Hammad
Educational Administration, College of Education, Sultan Qaboos University, Muscat, Oman
e-mail: waheedhammad@gmail.com

Damietta University, Damietta, Egypt

© Springer Nature Singapore Pte Ltd. 2019
E. A. Samier and E. S. ElKaleh (eds.), *Teaching Educational Leadership in Muslim Countries*, Educational Leadership Theory,
https://doi.org/10.1007/978-981-13-6818-9_5

promising area of research. A growing body of research has been conducted on the preparation and development of school leaders in different contexts (e.g. Asuga et al. 2015; Barnett 2004; Bates and Eacott 2008; Yan and Ehrich 2009; English 2006; Gurr and Drysdale 2015; Guerra and Pazey 2016; Orr 2006). Studies focused on the aims, content, and systems of delivery of leadership development programmes. Some of this research has focused on the context as it relates to leadership preparation, indicating that the use of imported frameworks in developing leadership can be problematic. Researchers are increasingly raising questions about the 'utility of knowledge across national contexts' (Hallinger 1995; Asuga et al. 2015), emphasising the need for a context-specific conceptualisation of educational leadership and management (Asuga et al. 2016; Beycioglu and Wildy 2015; Bush 2012; Lumby et al. 2009).

We argue that developing effective educational leadership programmes in Arab societies poses challenges that are shared with the rest of the international research community and yet requires additional considerations that are sensitive to cultural context and responsive to the priorities and needs of indigenous practitioners. At the root of these considerations is the development of a contextualised knowledge base to inform the pedagogical approaches to leadership development as well as the content knowledge and consequently the competencies that the prospective school leader ought to possess. We claim that aspiring educational leaders in Arab societies need to be also prepared to face the pressing demands of globalisation and concur with our international colleagues that educational leaders ought to be prepared to be part of 'global epistemic communities' (Crow et al. 2008 in Bush 2012) and that they need to have the ability to balance their commitment to be responsive to their local context with adopting global trends for conceptualising problems and designing solutions. This is particularly important in developing Arab societies, currently under sensitive sociopolitical conditions, where educators bear the responsibility to safeguard a national identity with a specific set of values and beliefs (Richardson 2004), values that are frequently misrepresented and undervalued on the global front.

The purpose of this chapter is to expose the challenges and promises faced by educational leadership and management (EDLM) scholars in Arab societies as they strive to establish an indigenous knowledge base that is connected to the global international scholarly discourse. We examine this issue and consider its implications for leadership development in the Arab region. While the issue is at the heart of educational scholars' concerns in the Arab region, we realise that the language barrier in the region will prevent many Arab scholars from accessing this work. Thus, our primary audience is international. We aim to engage our international colleagues in the dialogue, hence responding to the multiple calls of international scholars to expand the cultural bases of the existing knowledge base (Hallinger 1995; Hallinger and Leithwood 1996; Heck 1996; Bush 2012). Additionally, this chapter is based on a broad conception of leadership preparation that aligns with Bush's (2012) invitation to address leadership development as a continuum going beyond initial preparation, to encompass induction programmes and in-service training.

The first part of the chapter highlights current directions of research and practice found in the international literature. In the second part, we present the existing knowledge base available in the Arab educational leadership and management literature that is relevant to leadership preparation drawing upon recent reviews of this literature. In the last part, we present the implications of the local and global state of educational leadership development proposing future directions for research and practice.

Educational Leadership Development: The International Context

As a field of scholarship and research, educational management and leadership is still considered worldwide an emergent field characterised by continuous quest to overcome conceptual turmoil and build a knowledge base (Bridges 1982; Donmoyer 1999). It is often subjected to critique, especially on whether it provides actionable knowledge that can inform policy and practice (McCarthy 2015; Murphy et al. 2008). However, the impact of leadership on school effectiveness and the critical contribution of leadership preparation on achieving this effectiveness at all levels have become solidly established in the international literature (Bush 2012; Foster 1986; Heck and Hallinger 1999; McCarthy 2015, Murphy et al. 2008).

In the twenty-first century, the role of school leaders is expanding because of an increase in the complexity of schools as organisations and in the social and political demands placed on schools as socially impactful institutions. Consequently, educational leadership is broadly accepted as a 'specialist occupation which requires specific preparation' (Bush 2012, p. 665). For the most part, leadership development has been almost exclusively targeted at preparing individual educators to assume formal leadership roles in their institutions. In the West, it was historically focused on initial preparation of those individuals prior to their appointment to their position. Nowadays, leadership development is presented as a 'moral obligation', where development is conceived as a continuum that encompasses initial training, induction programmes, and in-service professional development (Bush 2012).

Though the practice of leadership has been part of the emergence of schools as social institutions, attempts at inducing it through knowledge acquisition and skill development in academic settings can only be tracked to the mid-twentieth century (Bush 2012; McCarthy 2015; Murphy 2002). In the USA, the first school management course was offered in 1881, but formal principal leadership preparation programmes started in the 1900s (Donmoyer 1999). The USA and few Western countries pioneered the efforts of establishing educational leadership as a field of graduate study in faculties of education, launching accreditation of preparation programmes for quality control, instituting licensure requirements as entry to the profession, and establishing professional and research associations to establish and promote a coherent knowledge base aimed at instilling effective leadership practices (McCarthy 2015; Murphy 2002; Murphy et al. 2008). Consequently, a growing knowledge base emerged and was documented in specialised journals, handbook of research, books and conference proceedings, mainly in English (Murphy 2002; Murphy et al. 2008). Countries around the world have been following suit offering researchers' programmatic commonalities as well as unique culturally contextualised practices (Bush 2012).

Within this trajectory of growth, the past three decades have witnessed an emerging trend in EDLM research characterised by concerted, more focused endeavours to diversify the global knowledge base in the field (Clarke and O'Donoghue 2017; Hallinger and Bryant 2013; Mertkan et al. 2017). This has led to a dramatic increase in EDLM scholarship from developing societies as indicative in the publication in 2008 of the first *International Handbook on the Preparation and Development of School Leaders* (McCarthy 2015) and the recent surge of reviews of EDLM research from Asia (Hallinger and Chen 2015), Africa (Hallinger 2018a), and Latin America (Castillo and Hallinger 2018). Much of this scholarship has been grounded in the limitations of 'Western' theories of educational leadership (Blunt and Jones 1997) and the need to examine and understand EDLM practices within the sociocultural, political, and economic context of the society (Clarke and O'Donoghue 2017; Hallinger 2018b; Mertkan et al. 2017).

Despite the noted turmoil and uneven growth of the field, EDLM scholars mark many recent developments as notable achievements. Examples of achievements are identified in leadership development programmes in the USA. These include a shift towards the following: a learner-centred mode of delivery; a move from presenting knowledge to be consumed by learners to collaboratively creating it (Bridges 2012); introductions of ethics courses; and an emphasis on addressing the cultural foundation and social justice (McCarthy 2015). Improvements are also noted in the delivery system as follows: establishing partnerships between district and school practitioners both in research and in teaching (McCarthy 2015), introducing field-based learning that permeates all offerings of the programme (Murphy et al. 2008), and adopting a cohort system (Barnett et al. 2000). Many US scholars have reported that underlying the above achievements is the establishment of the Interstate School Leaders Licensure Consortium (ISLLC) in the mid-1990s under the leadership of Joseph Murphy. This consortium currently comprises 45 state education agencies and 11 professional organisations committed to adopt or adapt the ISLLC standards in policy or statute, leading universities to align their initial licensure programmes with widely accepted standards (McCarthy 2015).

However, there is major criticism directed to these apparent achievements, mainly at how leadership development is conceived, researched, and practiced (Hess and Kelly 2007; Murphy 2002; Murphy et al. 2008; McCarthy 2015; Levine 2005). Many scholars questioned the coherence and rigour of leadership programmes as well as their overemphasis on theoretical knowledge at the expense of practice-based activities. Moreover, in a comprehensive review of initial leadership development programmes in the USA, McCarthy (2015) critically pointed at the limitations of using academic tests (like the GRE) as the sole determinant of leadership potential of applicants to the programmes. She also criticised the lack of alignment between the announced emphasis on leadership for learning and the existing curriculum content, noting that the latter remained unchanged with a dominance of discipline-based courses. A study by Hess and Kelly (2007) analysed in-depth course syllabi to determine what is chosen to be taught in principal preparation programmes. The study revealed that the category with the highest percentage was 'technical knowledge' which dealt with school laws, finances, etc., followed by 'managing for results' and 'course category which dealt with school-level program evaluation and implementation' (Hess and Kelly 2007, p. 11).

Researchers agree that despite various attempts to reform, the previous period is characterised by continuity (McCarthy 2015; Murphy 2002; Murphy et al. 2008). Upon examination of the reform initiative to rebuild programmes in 54 states in six states in the USA, Murphy et al. (2008) report that most reform attempts remained in the margin failing to make changes in the underlying values and professional beliefs. They explain that designers of new programmes lack imaginative capacity to innovate and are still operating within the confines of institutions that 'continue to approach program change as an administrative function to be accomplished with the least expenditure of time and resources' (p. 2186). Additionally, Murphy et al. (2008) suggest that programme designers lack an actionable theory about their work, defining actionable theory as lacking a 'set of generally well-tested propositions about relevant phenomena that can be applied in the school setting with confidence that the action will achieve some intended result' (p. 2187).

As she reviews research on educational leadership development, McCarthy (2015) expresses her frustration with the failed attempts at improvement and invites her colleagues to 'be open to different viewpoints, to take reasonable—and at times bold—risks, and to question deeply held values and assumptions' (p. 431). Similarly, Murphy (2002) proposes to 're-culture' the profession inviting colleagues to take risk and move away from traditional paradigms that he considered dysfunctional. Both stressed the need for a paradigmatic shift that challenges deeply rooted practices, especially in the academic circles of university preparation programmes. Murphy's (2002) call to 're-culture' the profession of educational leadership reflects his bold position for paradigmatic change. He advocates for a synthesising paradigm rooted in utilitarianism (Donmoyer 1999) where the emphasis favours valued aims over the narrow focus on technical knowledge and subject matter. Within this paradigm, he proposes three key concepts to anchor educational leadership as a profession: school improvement, democratic community, and social justice. The three concepts provide these valued aims for leadership development as well as for the educational leadership profession as a whole (Murphy 2002). Using the power of metaphors, he also advances a new definition of leadership that is aligned with the three concepts and builds on the accumulated knowledge base: leader as a steward, educator, and community builder (Murphy 2002). Against the backdrop of this proposed paradigmatic shift, we would like to conclude this overview by endorsing the recommendations that Murphy et al. (2008) advanced as holding promise to international reformers targeting the improvement of educational leadership development in their societies:

(1) working from an outcome-based paradigm; (2) creating a strong platform of actionable theory; (3) establishing a clear, coherent conceptual focus and foundation; (4) recruiting and selecting candidates through rigorous, value-based admissions; (5) grounding and integrating learning through practice- anchored learning experiences; (6) providing adequate support for technical and adaptive change; (7) replacing a culture of autonomy with a culture of

community; and (8) maintaining quality and continual improvement through outcome based accountability. (p. 2173)

Research on Educational Leadership and Management in Arab Societies

Despite apparent discrepancies, many scholars agree that since Arab societies share a common language, and several historical and sociocultural features that characterise them, we can address these societies as a distinct unit for study within existing international scholarship on educational administration (Hallinger and Hammad 2017; Karami-Akkary and El Saheb forthcoming). There are promising signals of rising interest in EDLM research in the region, with the volume of internationally published research sharply rising in the last two decades (Hallinger and Hammad 2017; Oplatka and Arar 2017). However, recent reviews of EDLM research conducted in the Arab region describe the existing literature as 'in its infancy', 'emerging', 'highly diffuse', 'decontextualised', 'lacking in programmatic inquiry', and falling short of addressing issues salient for policy and practice, which makes it far from the aim of building a knowledge base (Hallinger and Hammad 2017; Hammad and Hallinger 2017; Karami-Akkary and El Sahib forthcoming; Oplatka and Arar 2017).

A number of scholars point out that this emerging nature of existing Arab EDLM knowledge base in general, and one that is related to leadership preparation, has serious implications on practice in the region. One key implication is that most leadership development programmes have been strictly based on non-indigenous paradigms and modelled after existing programmes, mainly in the USA and Europe (Al-Dabbagh and Assaad 2010; Hallinger and Leithwood 1996; Kanan and Baker 2006; Romanowski 2017), thus paying little attention to local realities. Al-Dabbagh and Assaad (2010) explain that this persists even in the case of programmes that are being 'tailor made to the needs of the region' (p. 3).

The Knowledge Base in Educational Leadership in the Arab Context

Four recent reviews of existing EDLM scholarship reported a rising interest in research and practice within this field (Hallinger and Hammad 2017; Hammad and Hallinger 2017; Karami-Akkary and El Sahib forthcoming; Oplatka and Arar 2017). Oplatka and Arar's (2017) review synthesised results from 48 Arab-related EDLM articles published between 1990 and 2015 in international educational journals. Hallinger and Hammad's reviews covered 62 articles published in nine international EDLM journals between 2000 and 2016. Karami-Akkary and El Saheb's (forthcoming) reviewed 224 EDLM articles published in Arab journals between 2007 and

2016 that are accessible through 'Shamaa', a local database for Arab educational research. The studies aimed at understanding how the study of educational leadership is shaped within the social and cultural contexts prevalent in these countries while highlighting the challenge of building a knowledge base and the applicability of theories and concepts borrowed from the international literature. Findings revealed several common features. Generally, this literature was found to be relatively thin in scope, 'geographically dispersed' as many Arab countries were not covered in the studies identified (Hallinger and Hammad 2017; Oplatka and Arar 2017; Karami-Akkary and El Sahib forthcoming). In addition, the reviews highlighted other specific characteristics related to topical coverage as well as conceptual and methodological limitations. Topical coverage was found to be 'highly diffuse' as evidenced in the lack of connectedness among the studies (Hammad and Hallinger 2017). Karami-Akkary and El Sahib (forthcoming) reported that out of 224 full-text articles reviewed, they were able to extract only ten themes where more than three studies are addressing the same theme as a research focus. This diffusion limits the ability of reviewers to synthesise the results of research, hindering attempts at establishing a contextualised knowledge base.

The reviews also found that the Arab EDLM literature is characterised by a lack of conceptualisation of how EDLM practices are shaped by the social, cultural, and political characteristics observed in Arab societies. This is evidenced by the fact that many studies were found to be decontextualised (Hammad and Hallinger 2017; Karami-Akkary and El Sahib forthcoming; Oplatka and Arar 2017). Karami-Akkary and El Sahib (forthcoming) explain that Arab researchers seem to focus on applying methodologically complex statistical tools while keeping a distance from addressing critical problems of practice that are relevant to their contexts such as political instability, war-torn communities, economic deprivation and inequality, religious and ethnic tensions, colonialisation and corruption.

The reviews also revealed an uncritical reliance on Western conceptions while framing the research studies. Karami-Akkary and El Sahib (forthcoming) found that many studies adopted conceptions of educational leadership that are widely used in the international literature, like transformational leadership, learning organisations, and organisational culture. However, their review pointed at the absence of a cross-cultural perspective while adopting these international conceptions as theoretical lenses to interpret leadership practices in the Arab context.

While Oplatka and Arar's (2017) review concluded that there is limited capacity for EDLM knowledge production in this part of the world, Hallinger and Hammad (2017) emphasised the 'emerging' nature of the knowledge base, drawing attention to the similarities with the Western literature at earlier stages of its development. On the other hand, Karami-Akkary and El Sahib (forthcoming) conclude their review reporting the presence of what they deem to be 'promising' attempts at addressing issues in administration and leadership that reflect the priorities and concerns in the local context. They also consider the focused interest on certain topics, though limited, and the alignment with some key international trends as another promising move towards building a culturally grounded knowledge base.

Research on Leadership Preparation in the Arab Region

A number of researchers argue that research into leadership development in the Arab region has become particularly crucial, especially in recent times, characterised by a growing recognition of the importance of leadership development and the consequent rapid expansion of leadership programmes provided by public, private, and non-profit institutions across the Arab region (Kanan and Baker 2006; Al-Dabbagh and Assaad 2010). As suggested by Jiang et al. (2017), these studies 'not only contribute to the knowledge base but also will ensure that school leadership preparation and training is understood in more culturally and contextually appropriate ways' (p. 11).

Based on the literature we reviewed, most studies are evaluative in nature. Some focused on evaluating educational leadership degree programmes provided by Arab universities. These included a study of the educational leadership programme at Taibah University (KSA) from the point of view of the educational leaders enrolled (Abu Jamie 2015), a study of the master's programme in Educational Administration and Planning at the Faculty of Social Sciences at Imam Muhammad ibn Saud Islamic University in KSA (Al-Fantoukh 2015), a study of educational administration master's programmes offered by a Palestinian university from the perspective of a cohort of 23 graduates (Kanan and Baker 2006), and a study of the educational diploma programme in the College of Education at Umm Al Qura University (KSA) (Al-Omari 2012).

Other studies aimed at evaluating in-service leadership development programmes provided for practicing principals. For instance, Shehab (2009) explored the perceptions of primary school principals in Ninwa (Iraq) about their school leadership training programme. Alhouti and Male (2017) carried out a study to investigate the perceptions of Kuwaiti principals regarding their leadership preparation and in-service professional development needs. Hourani and Stringer's (2015) study explored the perceptions of school principals in Abu Dhabi regarding the benefits of their leadership development programmes at a time of educational reform.

In addition to research on principal preparation, a few more studies focused on preparation of higher-level educational leaders. These included Al-Humaidi's (2010) study of the preparation programme offered to candidates of the General Education Schools Agency in Taif (KSA), Ayesh et al.'s (2011) investigation of the preparation of supervisors at UNRWA centres in Jordan, Al-Shimari's (2012) study of the preparation of educational supervisors in Hail (KSA), and Kanan's (2005) exploration of the perceptions of superintendents and their supervisors about the roles and training needs of superintendents in Palestine.

The findings of these studies showed a variation in the attitudes towards leadership development programmes. Some were viewed positively (Hourani and Stringer 2015; Al-Humaidi 2010; Al-Omari 2012), others were perceived negatively (Alhouti and Male 2017), whereas Ayesh et al.'s (2011) study detected moderate positive attitudes towards the principal training programme. As for the studies related to evaluating the effectiveness of university preparation programmes, results showed that the master's of Educational Administration and Planning Programme at the Faculty of Social

Sciences at King Muhammad bin Saud Islamic University is 'poor' in general (Al-Fantoukh 2015). Kanan and Baker (2006) reported a lack of emphasis on important issues such as political leadership and educational policy analysis and concluded that the existing university programmes bore the features of similar ones in the West forty years ago. Some studies also identified impediments to advancement of leadership development in the region. They pointed at the highly centralised policies, the lack of economic resources, and the weak system of rewards and incentives adopted by universities as key constraints (Al Kadi 2013).

Directions for the Future

Developing effective, culturally relevant leadership development requires a solid, contextualised knowledge base that can inform both the competencies to be targeted and the pedagogical approaches suitable for preparing Arab educational leaders. Reviews of the existing Arab EDLM literature raise concerns about its ability to contribute to this goal. Interestingly, similar concerns are also felt by international scholars making them apply to the state of leadership development worldwide (Bush 2012; McCarthy 2015; Murphy et al. 2008). Consequently, Arab researchers carry a double burden as they are expected to navigate within the confines of both global and local challenges.

In the absence of an indigenous knowledge base, heavy reliance on Western leadership development methods and content pose a key challenge as to how to resolve 'the tension between dominant "Western" perspectives on leadership and "local" needs and realities' (Al-Dabbagh and Assaad 2010, p. 11). Hallinger and Leithwood (1996) stressed the importance of considering local cultures in the design of leadership preparation courses. Romanowski (2017) also warned against uncritical application of Western standards to develop or evaluate leadership preparation programmes in the Arab region, reasoning that these standards have different meanings and interpretations in different cultural contexts. Considering the above, we agree with Kanan and Baker (2006) that Arab countries must shift their focus to 'develop local paradigms of administrator preparation programs that spare them the exorbitant price of maintaining parody with western countries' (p. 167). We further assert that, with their knowledge base still in its infancy, Arab scholars have a unique opportunity to restore pride in their cultural heritage and acquire an in-depth understanding of how the prevailing sociocultural context shapes the demands and aspirations for developing educational leaders.

From that position, we would like to conclude this chapter by recommending some future directions that we think may contribute towards this end. A key starting point is achieving a paradigmatic shift. This requires a concerted effort at the national level where leadership development becomes a strategic goal for policy-makers and researchers alike. To anchor this paradigmatic shift, Arab policy-makers should push for adoption of national standards that capture the aspirations of their societies for effectiveness and ensure their readiness to be key players in the global economy. These standards should encompass a profile of Arab graduate, effective teacher, and educational leader, as well as characteristics of the effective school. As Murphy et al. (2008) recommend, we propose that these standards are grounded in a clear, coherent conceptual focus and foundation. This will require local reconstruction of internationally accepted conceptions like schools as learning organisations, distributive leadership, critically reflective practice and transformational change, and grounding them in the context as foundational components of these standards.

Recommendations for Research

On the research front, we recommend that researchers conduct additional, high-quality reviews of local studies focusing on topical domains that emerged from local and international reviews. We also invite researchers to examine these studies through a critical theorist lens that questions the moral imperatives of leadership and gives priority to addressing urgent issues of practice, especially those pertaining to social justice. With that, we suggest that Arab researchers remain abreast of international developments in the EDLM field, engaging in a critical dialogue with the international community and basing this engagement in a local agenda of research that seeks contextually relevant answers and avoids blindly following international trends in research and practice.

We also recommend that Arab researchers focus on understanding their context and explore the impact of societal and cultural factors on leadership practices in their societies. Contextualising leadership studies will be especially useful in determining the knowledge base to be taught in leadership preparation programmes (Hallinger and Leithwood 1996). EDLM researchers (Jiang et al. 2017; Qian and Walker 2014), particularly in the Arab context (Hammad and Hallinger 2017), have documented a lack of research studies exploring how leadership behaviours and practices are shaped by these factors. We believe that conducting more research to explore how these factors affect school leadership in Arab societies is crucial if we are to localise/contextualise leadership development and make it a better fit for the Arab local context.

Additional research is needed to understand the processes and skills for leading school-based improvement (Karami-Akkary 2014). Given the current educational changes and innovations taking place in many Arab countries, it is not clear how far the existing principal preparation/development programmes meet the requirements of Arab school principals to cope with and implement proposed changes. We also concur with Madsen's (2010) note that, 'timely research topics that have immediate practical applications for the implementation of leadership development programs are recommended' (p. 109). This means giving more attention from Arab EDLM researchers to exploring how Arab educators learn leadership. This is because designing effective leadership programmes that meet the developmental needs of learners depends to a large extent on understanding how they engage with their leadership learning experiences (Madsen 2010) and how these experiences are shaped by the values prevalent in their respective societies (Richardson 2004). Another area of enquiry is principals' training needs. Failure to identify these needs can be problematic in the context of increasing pressures on school principals to be more active in leading educational change at the school level (Jiang et al. 2017).

Recommendations for Designers of Leadership Development Programmes

On the other hand, and concerning leadership development practice, we recommend that designers of both pre-service and in-service leadership preparation provision anchor their programmes in nationally agreed-on standards while enforcing learner-centred approaches and adopting job-embedded strategies. We also call on leadership development designers to embed promoting a collaborative culture in their programmes' designs. This can be manifested through establishing a strong research and practice partnership between university scholars and school-based practitioners. Many researchers have argued that leadership development programmes should be designed and implemented in close collaboration with practitioners and should align with the professional vision of educational institutions as learning organisations with all members continuously drawing on theory and research to improve their practice (Bush and Jackson 2002). A collaborative culture is also reflected in building on the expertise of veteran educational leaders, supporting them to act as mentors and coaches to novice leaders.

We also encourage Arab countries to develop international collaborative initiatives in leadership preparation. Bush and Jackson (2002) suggested the establishment of 'an international network of leadership centers' (p. 427). These can be aimed at facilitating mutual learning in the field of leadership preparation (Murphy et al. 2008). It would be useful if Arab leadership preparation providers establish connections with existing centres and explore possibilities for collaboration. This would offer exposure to examples of good practice that would benefit existing leadership programmes in the Arab region such as employing external resources and facilitating exchange visits to widen leadership experience (Alhouti and Male 2017; Karami-Akkary and El Saheb forthcoming).

We offer additional recommendations that focus on the structure and content of the training programmes. These include: (1) alignment of the training programmes with the individual needs of principals and schools, which requires seeking participants' feedback on their future training requirements (Abu Jamie 2015; Amr and Awawda 2016; Hourani and Stringer 2015); (2) minimising the theoretical aspects of the training and reinforcing the practical ones through using a wider range of learning strategies such as study groups, 'virtual' provision using seminars and hands-on activities, incorporating mentoring and internship as important parts of principals' preparation programmes, employing external resources, and facilitating exchange visits among schools to widen leadership experiences (Alhouti and Male 2017; Al-Humaidi 2010; Amr and Awawda 2016; Ayesh et al. 2011; Bush and

Jackson 2002; Hourani and Stringer 2015; Kanan 2005; Murphy et al. 2008); (3) enriching courses with topics such as empowerment, creative problem-solving skills, team collaboration, and coordination (Al Kadi 2013); (4) raising the competencies of trainers and improving training activities (Amr and Awawda 2016; Hourani and Stringer 2015); (5) encouraging faculty to conduct collaborative action research maintaining quality and continual improvement through outcome-based accountability (Bush 2012; Murphy et al. 2008).

McCarthy (2015) concluded her reflections on the evolution and challenges of educational leadership preparation programmes in the USA admitting that despite decades of research and practice, scholars 'do not have all the answers' and yet assert that they 'cannot be paralysed by what we do not know'. According to her, 'we are ethically responsible to act on what we do know' (p. 431). Arab educational scholars must do just that. Despite the sociopolitical turmoil in the region, they have a unique opportunity for a fresh start informed by decades of international experiences, a heightened awareness of the added value of cultural diversity in the knowledge base, and a growing interconnected international community of researchers. There is a wealth of local and international experiences among researchers and practitioners alike that can be explored, examined, and synthesised to inform future directions of establishing a contextualised leadership development scholarship and practice.

Acknowledgement Special thanks to Nadia El Saheb for her assistance during the researching and writing of this chapter.

References

Abu Jamie, I. (2015). Evaluating the educational leadership program at Taiba University from the point of view of educational leaders. *Taiba University Journal of Educational Leadership, 10*(3), 389–403. (in Arabic).

Al Kadi, N. (2013). Levels of managerial training for the academic leaders of official universities in the Northern Province from their point of view. *Journal of the Faculty of Education for Girls, 24*(3), 670–688. (in Arabic).

Al-Dabbagh, M., & Assaad, C. (2010). *Taking stock and looking forward: Leadership development in the Arab world.* Dubai School of Government Working Paper. http://wagner.nyu.edu/files/leadership/LeadershipDevelopmentProgramsArabWorld. Accessed June 20, 2018.

Al-Fantoukh, A. (2015). Evaluation of the master's programme in management and educational planning in the Faculty of Social Sciences from the point of view of students. *Journal of the Association of Arab Universities for Research in Higher Education, 35*(1), 33–53. (in Arabic).

Alhouti, I., & Male, T. (2017). Kuwait principals: Preparation, induction and continuing development. *International Studies in Educational Administration, 45*(1), 89–105.

Al-Humaidi, M. (2010). *The contribution of the educational leadership training programmes for the candidates of the general education schools' assistant principalship in the Taif Governorate in developing their professional performance: An evaluative study* (Doctoral dissertation, Umm Al-Qura University). (in Arabic).

Al-Omari, M. S. (2012). *The suitability of the Educational Diploma Programme in the Faculty of Education at Umm Al-Qura University for the needs of female students* (Doctoral dissertation, Umm Al Qura University). (in Arabic).

5 The Knowledge Base on Educational Leadership and Management …

Al-Shimari, S. (2012). *The effect of a proposed training programme in the light of the European Excellence Model and Scottish quality management on the efficiency of educational strategic planning for female the educational supervisors* (Doctoral dissertation, Umm Al-Qura University). (in Arabic).

Amr, A., & Awawda, G. (2016). The effectiveness of in-service training programs of educational leaders in UNRWA Schools in Jordan: A field study. *Journal of Educational and Psychological Sciences, 17*(2), 563–598. (in Arabic).

Asuga, G., Eacott, S., & Scevak, J. (2015). School leadership preparation and development in Kenya: Evaluating performance impact and return on leadership development investment. *International Journal of Educational Management, 29*(3), 355–367.

Asuga, G. N., Scevak, J., & Eacott, S. (2016). Bringing a 'local' voice to a 'universal' discourse: School leadership preparation and development in Kenya. *International Studies in Educational Administration., 44*(1), 25–40.

Ayesh, A., Ayash, A., & Abbas, M. (2011). The effectiveness of an in-service training programme in developing the competencies of educational supervisors in UNRWA in Jordan from the point of view of educational supervisors. *Al-Najah University Journal for Research (Humanities), 25*(5), 1178–1212. (in Arabic).

Barnett, D. (2004). School leadership preparation programs: Are they preparing tomorrow's leaders? *Education, 125*(1), 121–129.

Barnett, B. G., Basom, M. R., Yerkes, D. M., & Norris, C. J. (2000). Cohorts in educational leadership programs: Benefits, difficulties, and the potential for developing school leaders. *Educational Administration Quarterly, 36*(2), 255–282.

Bates, R., & Eacott, S. (2008). Teaching educational leadership and administration in Australia. *Journal of Educational Administration and History, 40*(2), 149–160.

Beycioglu, K., & Wildy, H. (2015). Principal preparation: The case of novice principals in Turkey. In K. Beycioglu & P. Pashiardis (Eds.), *Multidimensional perspectives on principal leadership effectiveness* (pp. 1–17). Hershey, PA: IGI Global.

Blunt, P., & Jones, M. L. (1997). Exploring the limits of Western leadership theory in East Asia and Africa. *Personnel Review, 26*(1/2), 6–23.

Bridges, E. (1982). Research on the school administrator: The state of the art, 1967–1980. *Educational Administration Quarterly, 18*(3), 12–33.

Bridges, E. (2012). Administrator preparation: Looking backwards and forwards. *Journal of Educational Administration, 50*(4), 402–419.

Bush, T. (2012). International perspectives on leadership development: Making a difference. *Professional Development in Education, 38*(4), 663–678.

Bush, T., & Jackson, D. (2002). A preparation for school leadership: International perspectives. *Educational Management & Administration, 30*(4), 417–429.

Castillo, F. A., & Hallinger, P. (2018). Systematic review of research on educational leadership and management in Latin America, 1991–2017. *Educational Management Administration & Leadership, 46*(2), 207–225.

Clarke, S., & O'Donoghue, T. (2017). Educational leadership and context: A rendering of an inseparable relationship. *British Journal of Educational Studies, 65*(2), 165–182.

Crow, G., Lumby, J., & Pashiardis, P. (2008). Introduction: Why an international handbook on the preparation and development of school leaders? In J. Lumby, G. Crow, & P. Pashiardis (Eds.), *International handbook on the preparation and development of school leaders* (pp. 1–17). New York: Routledge.

Donmoyer, R. (1999). The continuing quest for a knowledge base: 1976–1998. In J. Murphy & K. Seashore-Lewis (Eds.), *Handbook of research in educational administration* (pp. 25–43). San Francisco: Jossey-Bass.

English, F. W. (2006). The unintended consequences of a standardized knowledge base in advancing educational leadership preparation. *Educational Administration Quarterly, 42*(3), 461–472.

Foster, W. (1986). *Paradigms and promises: New approaches to educational administration*. New York: Prometheus.

Guerra, P. L., & Pazey, B. L. (2016). Transforming educational leadership preparation: Starting with ourselves. *The Qualitative Report, 21*(10), 1751–1784.

Gurr, D., & Drysdale, L. (2015). An Australian perspective on school leadership preparation and development: Credentials or self-management? *Asia Pacific Journal of Education, 35*(3), 377–391.

Hallinger, P. (1995). Culture and leadership: Developing an international perspective in educational administration. *UCEA Review, 36*(1), 3–7.

Hallinger, P. (2018a). Surfacing a hidden literature: A systematic review of research on educational leadership and management in Africa. *Educational Management Administration & Leadership, 46*(3), 362–384.

Hallinger, P. (2018b). Bringing context out of the shadows of leadership. *Educational Management Administration and Leadership, 46*(1), 5–24.

Hallinger, P., & Bryant, D. A. (2013). Accelerating knowledge production on educational leadership and management in East Asia: A strategic analysis. *School Leadership and Management, 33*(3), 202–223.

Hallinger, P., & Chen, J. (2015). Review of research on educational leadership and management in Asia: A comparative analysis of research topics and methods, 1995–2012. *Educational Management Administration & Leadership, 43*(1), 5–27.

Hallinger, P., & Hammad, W. (2017). Knowledge production on educational leadership and management in Arab societies: a systematic review of research. *Educational Management Administration & Leadership*. https://doi.org/10.1177/1741143217717280.

Hallinger, P., & Leithwood, K. (1996). Culture and educational administration: A case of finding out what you don't know you don't know. *Journal of Educational Administration, 34*(5), 98–116.

Hammad, W., & Hallinger, P. (2017). A systematic review of conceptual models and methods used in research on educational leadership and management in Arab societies. *School Leadership & Management, 37*(5), 434–456.

Heck, R. (1996). Leadership and culture: Conceptual and methodological issues in comparing models across cultural settings. *Journal of Educational Administration, 34*(5), 74–97.

Heck, R. H., & Hallinger, P. (1999). Next generation methods for the study of leadership and school improvement. In J. Murphy & K. Louis (Eds.), *Handbook of research on educational administration* (pp. 141–162). San Francisco: Jossey-Bass.

Hess, F., & Kelly, A. (2007). Learning to lead? What gets taught in principal preparation programs. *Teachers College Records, 109*(1), 244–274.

Hourani, R. B., & Stringer, P. (2015). Professional development: Perceptions of benefits for principals. *International Journal of Leadership in Education, 18*(3), 305–339.

Jiang, N., Sumintono, B., Perera, C. J., Harris, A., & Jones, M. S. (2017). Training preparation and the professional development of principals in Henan Province, China: Formal and informal learning. *Asia Pacific Education Review, 19*(1), 1–11.

Kanan, H. M. (2005). Assessing the roles and training needs of educational superintendents in Palestine. *Journal of Educational Administration, 43*(2), 154–169.

Kanan, H. M., & Baker, A. M. (2006). Student satisfaction with an educational administration preparation program: A comparative perspective. *Journal of Educational Administration, 44*(2), 159–169.

Karami-Akkary, R. (2014). Facing the challenges of educational reform: Lessons from the Arab world. *Journal of Educational Change, 15*(2), 179–202.

Karami-Akkary, R., & El Sahib, N. (forthcoming). A review of studies on educational administration in Arab countries, Idafat (Shamaa Database 2007–2017). (in Arabic).

Levine, A. (2005). *Educating school leaders*. Washington, DC: The Education Schools Project.

Lumby, J., Walker, A., Bryant, M., Bush, T., & Björk, L. (2009). Research on leadership preparation in a global context. In M. D. Young, M. G. Crow, J. Murphy, & R. T. Ogawa (Eds.), *Handbook of research on the education of school leaders* (pp. 157–194). New York: Routledge.

Madsen, S. R. (2010). Leadership development in the United Arab Emirates: The transformational learning experiences of women. *Journal of Leadership & Organizational Studies, 17*(1), 100–110.

McCarthy, M. (2015). Reflections on the evolution of educational leadership preparation programs in the United States and challenges ahead. *Journal of Educational Administration, 53*(3), 416–438.

Mertkan, S., Arsan, N., Inal Cavlan, G., & Onurkan Aliusta, G. (2017). Diversity and equality in academic publishing: The case of educational leadership. *Compare: A Journal of Comparative and International Education, 47*(1), 46–61.

Murphy, J. (2002). Re-culturing the profession of educational leadership: New blueprints. *Educational Administration Quarterly, 38*(2), 176–191.

Murphy, J., Moorman, H., & McCarthy, M. (2008). A framework for rebuilding initial certification and preparation programs in educational leadership: Lessons from whole-state reform initiatives. *Teachers College Record, 110*(10), 2172–2203.

Oplatka, I., & Arar, K. H. (2017). The research on educational leadership and management in the Arab world since the 1990s: A systematic review. *Review of Education, 5*(3), 267–307.

Orr, M. T. (2006). Mapping innovation in leadership preparation in our nation's schools of education. *Phi Delta Kappan, 87*(7), 492–499.

Qian, H., & Walker, A. (2014). Principalship in China: Emerging propositions. *Leading and Managing, 20*(2), 60–74.

Richardson, P. M. (2004). Possible influences of Arabic-Islamic culture on the reflective practices proposed for an education degree at the Higher Colleges of Technology in the United Arab Emirates. *International Journal of Educational Development, 24*(4), 429–436.

Romanowski, M. H. (2017). Neoliberalism and Western accreditation in the Middle East: A critical discourse analysis of Educational Leadership Constituent Council standards. *Journal of Educational Administration, 55*(1), 70–84.

Shehab, S. H. (2009). The effect of a developmental programme in enhancing administrative and educational leadership skills for principals of primary schools in the Governorate of Ninwa. *Educational Studies, 2*(8), 7–48. (in Arabic).

Yan, W., & Ehrich, C. (2009). Principal preparation and training: A look at China and its issues. *International Journal of Educational Management, 22*(1), 51–64.

Rima Karami-Akkary is Associate Professor of Educational Administration, Policy and Leadership in the Department of Education at the American University of Beirut and Programme Advisor for the Educational Management and Leadership Programme. She holds a bachelor in science, diploma for teaching science at the secondary level, a master of arts in science education from the American University of Beirut (AUB), and a doctorate in education from Portland State University with a specialty in [K-12] Educational Administration and Supervision with a focus on school principalship, organisational change, and educational policy. She is Director and Co-principal Investigator of the TAMAM project—a joint project of the Arab Thought Foundation and the American University of Beirut to initiate and research school-based reform. The project has currently 47 participating schools around Lebanon, Jordan, Saudi Arabia, Egypt, Oman, Sudan, and Qatar. She is also Director of the TAMAM Lebanon Hub a research and development project which examines how to build leadership capacity for sustainable school-based improvement in Lebanese Public Schools. In addition, she has designed and conducted many professional development activities for school principals and supervisors, both independently and as part of large-scale reform initiatives. She has published in international and local journals on the principal role, approaches to professional development, programme and organisational level evaluation, and models for school-based reform.

Waheed Hammad is Assistant Professor of Educational Administration in the College of Education at Sultan Qaboos University, Oman, and Damietta University, Egypt. He previously held a lecturing position in King Faisal University, Saudi Arabia. He holds a bachelor in arts and education (French), and special diploma and master's in educational foundations from Mansoura University, Egypt. He received his Ph.D. from the University of East Anglia, UK. The focus of his Ph.D.

research was on institutional and cultural barriers to shared decision-making in Egyptian schools. Upon completion of his Ph.D., he was offered a postdoctoral visiting fellowship at the same institution. During this fellowship, he had the opportunity to work as a member of the tutoring team on the Egyptian Educators Programme from October 2009 to July 2010. He was assigned to deliver the academic writing component, in addition to providing pastoral and academic support to the educators. He is Member of the British Educational Leadership, Management and Administration Society (BELMAS) and the Gulf Comparative Education Society (GCES). He has published in international and local journals on a variety of research topics including school decision-making, school leadership challenges, decentralisation, and professional development. His recent publications include two systematic reviews of research on educational leadership and management in Arab societies in collaboration with Professor Philip Hallinger. His international publication outlets include educational administration quarterly, educational management, administration and leadership, compare, and school leadership and management. He presented several papers at international and regional conferences in the UK, France, Greece, Turkey, Oman, Lebanon, Kuwait, and UAE. His current research interests include educational leadership and management, instructional supervision, and teachers and principals' professional development.

Chapter 6
Educational Administration and Leadership Curricula for Modern Nation-Building in Muslim Countries: Modernisation, National Identity and the Preservation of Values and Culture

Eugenie A. Samier and Eman S. ElKaleh

Abstract Despite the dominance of neoliberal ideology aimed at economic advancement, two of the main purposes of educational systems still is the cultivation of national identity and the preservation and continued development of social, cultural and political traditions that shape and sustain national identity and the distinctiveness of a society. While some argue that Islam and modernisation are incompatible and to modernise Islamic countries, Islam as a religion, doctrine and political ideology should be eliminated, it is argued here that there are no inherent conflicts or contradictions between Islam and modernisation and that the Anglo-American approach is not the only path for modern societies. Muslim countries can find their own path to modernisation using Islamic principles and *Shura* as a political ideology. Through the application of multiple modernities, we suggest that teaching educational leadership can be effectively internationalised and modified to serve cultural and social heritage and goals of Muslim countries. Finally, we discuss the characteristics of educational leaders required for nation-building in Muslim countries, arguing that nation-building efforts should involve an extensive use of historical events, traditional narratives and literature that aim to explain and convey cultural values and national ideologies to the new generations. One approach is through hybrid curricula where international literature can be combined with material reflecting the nature and character of Muslim countries, particularly if presenting the field in an interpretive and critical manner and taking into account the collective nature of Muslim societies.

E. A. Samier (✉)
University of Strathclyde, Glasgow, UK
e-mail: eugenie.samier@gmail.com

E. S. ElKaleh
Zayed University, Dubai, United Arab Emirates
e-mail: eman.salah2@gmail.com

© Springer Nature Singapore Pte Ltd. 2019
E. A. Samier and E. S. ElKaleh (eds.), *Teaching Educational Leadership in Muslim Countries*, Educational Leadership Theory,
https://doi.org/10.1007/978-981-13-6818-9_6

Introduction

Many Muslim countries are undergoing postcolonial and development conditions, some relatively new nation states, including the establishment and improvement in educational systems, and some having to rebuild from recent wars and invasions. The purpose of this chapter is to determine what kind of teaching in educational leadership is necessary to these modernisation and (re-)nation-building efforts that are able to preserve national identity, traditions of distinctive social institutions and culture in an educational globalisation context consisting heavily of imported curriculum, instructors and branch universities from the West that many believe imperil their values, identities and organisations and the knowledge upon which they rest (e.g., Stewart-Harawira 2005; Stiglitz 2002). The proliferation of branch campuses in Arab states (Miller-Idriss and Hanauer 2011) and programmes delivering a predominantly foreign curriculum, it is argued in this chapter, do not meet the needs of many countries where social institutions are distinctively different resulting in educational administration and leadership failing to contribute to nation-building (see Kanan and Baker 2006), if not undermining the process in many cases. The chapter will use the case of the United Arab Emirates as an example of a Muslim country that is going through rapid development and nation-building processes with a strongly globalised Anglo-American curriculum.

A number of disciplines foundational to educational administration and leadership have produced more inclusive literature that recognises the legitimacy of other patterns of national development and interaction as well as conditions prevalent internationally. This includes, for example, Berry et al. (1997) three volume *Handbook of Cross-Cultural Psychology*, Cohen and Kennedy's (2013) *Global Sociology* and Seth's (2013) *Postcolonial Theory and International Relations* and other political science texts that have begun to include postcolonial perspectives (e.g., Baylis et al. 2014), Farazmand and Pinkowski's (2006) *Handbook of Globalization, Governance and Public Administration*, and security studies (Barkawi and Laffey 2006) as well as in the general management and leadership fields like organisation studies (Silverthorne 2005). The extensive studies in cross-cultural management are not only about global conditions, but are being increasingly written from the perspectives of non-Western countries (e.g., Branine 2011; Madhavan 2011) including postcolonialism (Gavin and Westwood 2010; Machal and Prasad 2003). These recent literatures also challenge the widespread bias that assumes that Western, especially Anglo-American, practices are superior and should be imitated, driven in part by Western accreditation bodies (Altbach 2003; Noori and Anderson 2013), heavily driven by neoliberal values (Romanowski 2017).

Educational administration and leadership as it is conceived in a few states or one part of the world can no longer claim to be necessarily relevant to others or to prepare people professionally for the organisations they will be working in, be inclusive of diversity, or even avoid disrupting or damaging nation-building process by challenging values and norms that can occur through educational colonisation (Suarez-Orozco and Qin-Hilliard 2004). The inadequacy of exported curriculum that bears little relevance culturally, or even constitutionally and legally, has been noted for some time (e.g., Hallinger and Leithwood 1996) and has appeared more recently (Romanowski 2013). However, there is, as Brooks and Mutohar (2018) claim, a dearth of research and literature on educational leadership in non-western countries, including very little on the administration and leadership of Muslim schools required to address their individual and societal needs.

To address this problem, this chapter is organised into two main sections. The first examines the requirements for modernised nation-building in Muslim contexts and how the recent theory of multiple modernities contributes to the administration and leadership of their higher education organisations. The second examines the requirements of national identity and the preservation of culture that can serve as a goal in teaching that forms and sustains national social institutions. The conclusion draws implications and conclusions for establishing foundational principles in curriculum and pedagogy that serve the qualities and skills required of Muslims in meeting the needs of their own countries in fulfilling an administrative and leadership roles in education that contribute appropriately to economic development, social cohesion, cultural appropriateness and national solidarity in modernising and nation-building states.

Nation-Building and the Modernisation Debate

The debate over modernisation based on Western models is associated with a broad range of economic, political and cultural changes that have tended towards 'Westernising' influences that suppress indigenous knowledge, skills and styles of social institutions, significantly affected nation-building efforts. A number of postcolonial authors have explored the negative effects that a colonising globalisation using an Anglo-American style of modernisation, including education, has on national identity. The major critiques include Thiong'o's (1986) on the colonisation of mind, Spivak's (1987) subaltern identity and Memmi (2003) on the destruction of spirit that affects social relations and social institutions as well as the uncritical adoption of Western curricula and education systems (Foskett and Maringe 2010; Giroux 2002), and more recently 'epistemicide' in South American jurisdictions (Hall and Tandon 2017). There has also been a growing body of literature on this critique in the Middle East, notably by Said (1978, 1993) in his Orientalism thesis and concerns about globalised education in the region (e.g., Fox et al. 2006) as well as critiques by Habermas (1979, 1984) through his concept of colonisation that can be extended internationally and Bourdieu (2013) from a critical theory perspective. The literature now also presents some examples of modernisation in non-Western societies such as Malaysia, Turkey and the UAE where leaders of those countries were able to advance economic development without sacrificing national identity (Hefner and Horvatich 1997).

The consequences for educational administration and leadership is that the values, roles, and professional identities are fashioned on a foreign literature and knowledge that do not take into account the structure of a different type of society, its social institutions, including constitution and laws, social and cultural structures and processes, national aims and goals, styles of decision-making, or policy and organisational patterns. The result for individuals, is that their sense of self, valuational orientations, determinants of right and good, styles of social interaction, and professional practices become modelled on foreign practices that for a Muslim country introduces secularity, materialism and English as the main medium of expression—in effect, as Khelifa (2010) has found in looking at the UAE case, that women in Westernised programmes are increasingly changing their behaviour, attitudes and value orientation. Sánchez (2010) claims that globalisation has negatively affected social structures and identity referents that provided meaning for individuals and communities, producing a dislocation that disrupts identity formation. The argument of this chapter is not that Western material should not be taught, after all, in any graduate professional programme, students need to master the field internationally, but that a neglect or exclusion of Islamic and national curricular content in effect acculturates those with administrative and leadership responsibilities in a way that distances them from their own countries. In much the same way that the exclusion of women from various professional fields both devalues women and does not provide them with the role modelling necessary to successful participation, Islamic and national traditions are devalued and no longer serve as suitable goals and values denying students valuable social and intellectual capital. The hidden curriculum can serve to turn locals into the instruments of Westernisation. These approaches fulfil at least part of 'Orientalism'—that knowledge, expertise and professionalism comes from elsewhere, and the rich, complex Islamic intellectual tradition which historically served as a foundation for much European/Western development (Morgan 2007; Saliba 2007) does not exist.

This applies also to conceptions of modernisation, which is generally taken to mean imitating a Western, usually American or British approach and hegemony, quite often taken to be an inevitable development internationally (e.g., Luhmann 1991; Parsons 1966; Wallerstein 1974). However, the extent to which forms of modernisation and Islam are compatible culturally to allow for the preservation of national integrity of identity and cultural practices (Habermas 1987; Habermas and Ben-Habib 1981; Mignolo 2011; Zaidi 2011) depends in part on the degree to which secular and materialistic values are promoted. More recently a multiple modernities thesis (e.g., Eisenstadt 2005) has emerged through which cultural and religious values and identities can be preserved while modernising society. Part of this new literature is Islamic modernisation studies (e.g., Abdurrahman 2009) that provide a contrast to conventional modernisation theories and models. For example, Jung (2017) argues that Islamic modernities are empirically substantiated cases that serve as refutations of secular models of modernisation and the socio-cultural 'convergence' globally that they predicted. Different models of modernisation, particularly in the Islamic world has a strong historical precedent, since many of the features of modernisation, the development of technology, professional fields like medicine and engineering as well as major advances in primary disciplines were made during the early centuries of Islam when the intellectual golden age formed that both preserved classical Greco-Roman and other knowledge while building on these foundations to put into place many of the foundations, including education and its humanistic philosophy, upon which modernisation came to rest (Al-Khalili 2010; Lombard 2004; Nasr 2001; Saliba 2007). In other words, Islam is not antithetical to many aspects of modernisation. For teaching educational administration, this means identifying features of modernisation and their culturally appropriate use that are in harmony with Islamic spiritual values concerned with the collective well-being of the society and which can help fulfil national aims and the development of the research and education sectors.

For the purposes of this chapter, the word 'nation' is taken to refer to a community or group of people who follow the same law and share common cultural values, heritage, history, language and geographic space. Through cultural values, practices and traditions, members of the nation are emotionally connected (Zajda 2009). Therefore, nation-building efforts should involve an extensive use of historical events, traditional narratives and literature that aim to explain and convey cultural values and national ideologies to the new generations. 'Nation-building', therefore, in general terms means the building of the social institutions of a nation and gaining their legitimacy as in state-building, including its history, culture and identity (Jones and Chandran 2008; Paris and Sisk 2009) aiming at peace, stability and sovereignty, but towards the sustaining of a national identity (Fritz and Menocal 2007; Lotz 2010), taken to mean forging a common national identity quite often constructed to replace multiple identities (Jones and Chandran 2008). This chapter extends these meanings to focus on institutions, culture and identity as sovereign and constructions to be protected and maintained, although in modified form, during modernisation. One challenge for authentic and sovereign nation-building is the effect that Western-style—often American style—modernisation has on a global level on the economy, politics, culture and social institutions (e.g., Beck et al. 2003).

The multiple modernities movement arising in sociology and political science argue for forms that do not have this degree of foreign disruptive effects (Sachsenmaier et al. 2002). The concept of 'multiple modernities' proposed initially by Eisenstadt (2000) has been investigated in political science (Bowman 2015), as the 'varieties of capitalism' in the new political economy (e.g., Streeck and Yamamura 2001) which lends itself to Islamic financing and banking practices, and sociology (Kohnert 2008), in some cases as 'varieties of modernity' (e.g., Schmidt 2006). However, the implications of multiple conceptions of modernisation have not yet been investigated to any large extent in educational fields, although authors like Doherty and Singh (2007) have begun exploring other forms of modernity in higher education relevant to the internationalisation of higher education curriculum and pedagogy cross-culturally to help sustain cultural and social diversity.

The disputes about the definition of modernisation involve decades of critique, outlined by Inglehart and Baker (2000) from an evaluation of Marxist theory that informed modernisation thinking to a critical analysis of the post-World War II dichotomy of American-led capitalist systems of Western and Communist modes of development affecting many Western and non-Western countries, to postcolonial critiques of neo-imperialism. More recently, diverging models of modernisation in

East Asia have challenged an American-centric notion of this kind of success with some East Asian countries achieving the highest rates of economic growth. The American-centric model consists of industrialisation and related changes such as higher education levels, changing gender roles, the nuclear family, secularisation and (American style) democratisation, with an explicit assumption that traditional values will be replaced—in fact, traditional values tended to be used to classify societies as 'backward'. In addition, according to Inglehart and Baker (2000), this form of modernisation theory ignored factors like colonialism, imperialism and new forms of economic and political domination. What has happened, though, in the contemporary historical record, is that societies follow different modernisation trajectories even with the same economic development, to a large extent confirming Weber's (1930) contention that factors of cultural heritage like religion have at least as large an influence on social institutions.

The conclusion from Inglehart and Baker's (2000) large-scale international study includes five modifications of modernisation theory, all incorporated to varying degrees in the multiple modernities literature: (1) modernisation takes a variable rather than linear path; (2) the role of an accompanying secularisation is greatly over-simplified; (3) the path dependency of religious foundation in the society, whether Christian, Confucian or Islamic, for example, have an enduring effect on developing social institutions; (4) while some of the dominating conceptions of modernisation are ethnocentrically American, the cultural changes occurring in many parts of the world are quite different, resulting in the USA being a 'deviant' case internationally; and (5) the process is far more complex than economic development, with many other historical and cultural factors have strong and even competing influences, therefore is 'probabilistic' rather than 'deterministic' (p. 49).

The historical argument for Islam's relationship with modernisation belies viewing Islam as a barrier, where politics and culture may be much more a barrier than religion. For centuries during the medieval period, Muslims were at the forefront of human civilisation, having powerful economy, military services and sciences while other parts of the world like Europe were not developing as rapidly. At that time, Muslim scholars and scientists made remarkable contributions to all aspects of knowledge (Lewis 2003), particularly those we associate with medicine, navigation, engineering and management, in line with knowledge principles in the Qur'an (Rosenthal 2007). Rather than impeding modernisation, one could argue that Islam was a driving force for developing a remarkable civilisation and knowledge base in the past upon which much that we associate with modernisation is based as the knowledge developed by Muslim scholars improved sciences and other fields, and institutionalised doubt (Lewis 2003; Sahide 2012) and scientific inquiry, absorbed elsewhere.

What is important to note here is that this work was conducted within an Islamic societal framework. However, the case in many Muslim countries currently consuming Western knowledge is doing so through an uncritical and unmodified application of Western curricula to their societies instead of contributing and adding to this knowledge (Noori and Anderson 2013) and making the adaptations necessary to preserve culture and maintain Islamic values. Hammad and Hallinger's (2017) recent survey article of educational leadership and management studies in Arab societies demonstrates the pervasive effect of exported Anglo-American style higher education: it generally focusses on the literature reviews and theoretical frameworks from Western societies, a lack of socio-cultural and political Arab contexts, usually decontextualised, and, implicitly, a lack of Arab intellectual heritage and contemporary scholarship in addition to research methodology reflecting Western practices and conditions. To a large extent, at least in the UAE, this is a consequence of decisions made to heavily rely in imported programmes and staff (Kirk and Napier 2009), which involves a hidden agenda of secular theories and models, consumerist values and leadership and administration conceptions that reflect Western societies' constitutions, legal systems, and institutional arrangements.

One of the critical factors that hindered modernisation in Muslim countries for nation-building through governance and administrative practices in the modern historical period is the ongoing and longstanding debate between fundamentalists and liberal intellectuals about secularisation, capitalism, gender equality and democracy and their compatibility with Muslim values, instead of focusing on education, scientific discovery and economic development, due mainly to the Western model that assumes secularisation, and particularly forms of capitalism and democracy as prerequisites. For example, conservative Muslims argue that Islam is incompatible with democracy because Islamic law *Shari'a* was defined in the *Qur'an* as the word of God and therefore cannot be changed by elected parliaments. On the other hand, a number of contemporary scholars argue that 'democracy is the spirit of the Islamic governmental system' contending that the role of democracy is to establish justice and ensure people's participation in determining their destiny, which are core principles in Islamic government and clearly provide a strong evidence of its compatibility with democratic practices (Voll 2007, p. 173).

Islam has a different approach to democratic practices, known as *Shura* (consultation), a critical component of leadership and government, which means seeking insight and advice from followers who are intellectually competent and knowledgeable about the topic under investigation. The *Qur'an* describes Muslims as those who conduct their affairs through the practice of *Shura* 'whose affair is [determined by] consultation among themselves' (*Qur'an* 42: 38) and for which leaders need to 'consult them [followers] in the matter' (*Qur'an* 3: 159), therefore, the Prophet Muhammad used public fora to seek advice from his companions. Ramadan (2007) describes how he used critical pedagogies to develop his companions' intellectual capabilities required for *Shura* by asking them questions or by making controversial statements that encouraged them to engage actively in discussion. For example, he once said, 'Help your brother, whether he is just or unjust!' This statement made his followers wonder and question how this could happen. After giving them time to discuss this among themselves, he answered 'prevent him from acting unjustly!' (p. 102). Ramadan argues that this critical pedagogy developed followers' intellectual capacity, arguing that in order to give useful advice, one needs to be intellectually competent and knowledgeable. It can also be a means to strengthen one's leadership capabilities. According to Jabnoun (2012), Umar ibn Al Khatab, the second successor of the Prophet Muhammad, well known for his strong character, effective leadership, and justice, did not send senior companions as his governors in other countries; he instead wanted them close to him for advice and to correct him when he made mistakes.

This discussion demonstrates the main differences between *Shura* and many forms of democracy. First, in Western democratic practices the leader accepts the decision of the majority while in *Shura* the leader is responsible for making the final decision after seeking genuine advice from followers. Second, in democratic practices everyone (in theory) has an equal opportunity to influence the decision whether having the knowledge and expertise or not, while in *Shura* knowledge and intellectual competency is a prerequisite for conducting effective *Shura* (Ramadan 2007; Saleh 2002). Muslim leaders should seek advice from everyone but eventually will be more influenced by those who are experts in the field. Hence, it could be concluded that democracy is not inconsistent with Islamic principles and beliefs as the *Qur'an* did not specify which type of political government to follow (Asad 1980; El Fadl 2003; Kelsay 2002). It was left to Muslims to select the leader and the political system they wanted to implement provided that it follows the fundamental principles of Islam, including the genuine practice of *Shura*.

Since democracy may take many different contradictory forms and models (Voll 2007), it is argued here that a Western model of democracy may not be the best approach to adopt in Muslim countries because *Shura* would be a more relevant approach that is consistent with Islamic law. Although, many practices and organisational structures that are not in inconsistent with Islamic principles can be adopted through policy transfer that makes adequate modifications. Through the genuine application of *Shura*, Muslim countries can create their own model of democracy and political government that distinguish them from Western patterns and models. Finally, democracy is not a prerequisite to modernisation. Some advocates of modernisation theory argue that there is one common path to democracy 'which begins with socio-economic modernisation and ends with political modernisation,' so the starting point for Muslim countries could be to generate scientific and economic development because citizens who value and appreciate democratic practices 'emerge as a by-product' of this developmental process (Ciftci 2010, p. 1444).

Some scholars portray Islam as an 'antithesis of capitalism, democracy, rationalism and reason', consequently, they argue that Islam and modernisation are incompatible and in order to modernise Islamic countries, Islam as a religion, doctrine and political ideology should be eliminated, partly because they see only the Western model as the path to modernisation. They consider any alternative form of modernisation as non-modern because it 'deviated from the ideal-typical Western outline' (Kamali 2006, pp. 32–37). Unfortunately, proponents of this view ignore other models and traditions of modernisation, including quite often many European models, and are at odds with newer developments in sociology and political science. According to Eisentadt (2000), the Western project of modernisation, while enjoying a historical precedence and being a point of reference, is not the only path to follow. The term 'multiple modernities' challenges the classical theories of modernisation which assume that the cultural patterns of modernity developed by European countries would be the only models that should be followed by other countries. Many of the modernisation movements in non-Western countries followed a different anti-Western path and 'yet all were distinctively modern' (p. 2). Consequently, Muslim countries can find their own path to modernisation, one that is based on Islamic principles and *Shura* as a political ideology.

National Identity and the Preservation of Culture

Despite the dominance of neoliberal ideology aimed at economic performance, one can still argue that two of the main purposes of educational systems is the cultivation of national identity and the preservation and continued development of social, cultural and political traditions that shape and sustain national identity and the distinctiveness of a society. From this identity perspective, the roles of educational and related leadership at the governmental and governance levels carry a heavy responsibility for ensuring that educational organisations operate in ways that help shape and support the formation of national identity, as well as use a curriculum and pedagogy that meets these aims.

Identity studies with a broader diverse and international scope have developed in a number of fields in the last twenty years ranging from professional role and national to the cosmopolitan and transcultural, particularly in interdisciplinary psycho-social and cultural studies. Some of the most significant, for example, are Côté and Levine's (2002) *Identity Formation, Agency, and Culture*, Weinreich and Saunderson's (2005) *Analysing Identity: Cross-cultural, Societal and Clinical Contexts*, De Anca's (2012) *Beyond Tribalism: Managing Identity in a Diverse World*, Kendall et al. (2009) *The Sociology of Cosmopolitanism: Globalization, Identity, Culture and Government*, and Nordin et al. (2016) *Transcultural Identity Constructions in a Changing World*. These fields are becoming increasingly important for the considerations they raise across disciplines and are critically important in the internationalisation of educational administration that can inform policy-making, pedagogy, curriculum development and research design.

In the context of the Middle East and Arab minorities, studies are appearing that focus on Arab identity and its implications for a number of fields and societal sectors. There are several important factors identified in this literature that need to be considered for educational administration and leadership, among which are the following:

1. Arab countries, like many others, have a stronger collective than individual identity (Chhokar et al. 2007; Findlow 2005), which in the UAE context means that educating and training people should support the collective social structures and institutional practices such as the extended family and tribal identities that both inform national identity and at times also competes with it;
2. A majority of Arabs are Muslim, for whom Islam is a central feature of their concept of self, values and their identity formation as well as the foundation for

legal and ethical systems. Islam has a long history of highly developed principles and practices aimed at the good of society that should play a strong role in any curriculum (Lee 2014);

3. The diversity of Arab cultures has to be recognised and included in the development of curriculum in order to present accurately differences in social institutions (e.g., Arar et al. 2017; Lee 2014);

4. Islam and the Arab world have a long and highly developed intellectual tradition, much of which informed the development of higher education and disciplines in Europe, that has long been ignored (Morgan 2007) but which is an important feature in the formation of national identity that should reflect the knowledge traditions as part of the historical memory that is generally the responsibility of a public education system (Smith 1991) and for administrative and leadership training should apply to any form of professional development since acculturation and socialisation are necessary dimensions of these roles;

5. The Middle East has a very long history of administrative and leadership development that one can trace back 5000 years that included many features associated with modern administration in structure and function, including law codes that included very early on highly developed mediation and arbitration guidelines and were more highly developed in the Muslim caliphates (Liverani 2006);

6. An educational administration and leadership curriculum should address postcolonial issues through a critical perspective and reflection, both from former colonial periods and in the neocolonisation through globalised education since not all foreign influences are benign or serve national and cultural goals (Arar et al. 2017; Rhea 2015; Samier 2017);

7. Because leadership identity as a part of national identity is a social construction, not only as an organisational process but in educational development where curriculum and pedagogy are critical parts of the active reflection that shapes identity (Wertsch 2012) as well as through dialogic social interaction examined in critical discourse analysis (Wodak et al. 2009).

One aspect of identity in the Middle East for a majority of people is Arab cultural identity, a highly complex and multi-levelled construct. To some extent, it is supranational, united to some extent by language (Carmichael 1969) yet takes different forms in each nation and tribal and cultural grouping making it a highly contested, yet identifiable, concept (Phillips 2013). It would be more accurate to refer to 'Arabisms', since the construction for identity purposes varies across individuals and groups, to varying degrees attached to a transnational concept, for some a more national identity, and for others a strong tribal affiliation. There are also issues of Arab identity reformation among those who are minorities in Western states, for example, in the USA (Haddad 2011) and the UK (Aly 2015), where hybrid identities form. For Suleiman (2011), part of Arab identity is how the Arabic language acquires symbolic value, particularly in symbolic violence in conflict situations (large-scale and micro-levels in everyday life) where the boundaries of identity and group affiliation are established (Bernstein 2000).

6 Educational Administration and Leadership Curricula for Modern … 103

Important also to Arab identity, for a majority is an Islamic identity, which, however, varies in cultural expression producing a diversity in how Islam is understood and practised (Hughes 2013), affecting the construction and expression of Arab identities. Critical to an Islamic identity is character development that meets the characteristics identified in the *Qur'an* and *Sunnah* that are expected of all people, but which is even more important for those working in education, and particularly those who have power and influence—those in administrative and leadership positions. There is an increasing number of sources now on the requirements and qualifications of those in administration and management (Ali 2005), in leadership (Beekun and Badawi 2009), and recently several sources in educational administration (e.g., Arar and Haj-Yehia 2018; ElKaleh and Samier 2013; Brooks and Mutohar 2018; Shah 2015).

The most important characteristics for educational leaders in this literature are the following: (1) *Tafakkur*, or using critical reflection that measures actions against higher-order values or foundational principles and which is necessary in setting a vision and a pragmatic plan that can be implemented; (2) *Ikhlas*, sometimes defined as sincere conduct that can be taken as reliability and an indication of integrity; (3) *Nasiha* good counsel, in the sense of accurate and principled rather than out of self-interest; (4) the use of *Shura* or consultation that requires collaboration and cooperation; (5) *Ikhtilaf*, or dissent in the sense of considering a range of differing opinions and judgments and necessary to the process of *Shura*; (6) *Maslaha*, or acting in the common public interest or the good of society; (7) *Amr bi'l ma'ruf wa al nahi an al munkar*, or the responsibilities to encourage right behaviour and discourage the wrong which is partly achieved through acting as a role model (*Qudwa Hasana*); (8) *Hisba*, or accountability to the community and society, while also encouraging collective responsibility; (9) *Adle*, or justice, sometimes interpreted as *Insaf* in the sense of fairness and equality; (10) *Amana*, or honesty and the avoidance of deceit; (11) *Ihsan*, being kind; (12) *Tafawut* or tolerance, particularly of other belief systems; (13) *Taeataf*, exhibiting a cluster of characteristics associated often with humanism, compassion and empathy; and (14) *Sabar*, or patience. Also stressed in the Islamic tradition is humility and modesty (*Tawadae*). And, of course, belief, which is intended to underpin all of these characteristics as they develop in the individual and their role constructions, and all future thought and action for which they are answerable to Allah and which are critically important in times of hardship or distress.

There are implications for research methods in educational administration and leadership of Arab and Muslim identity. Some forms are more conducive to research participants expressing the subjectivity of their sense of identity through autobiographical forms especially in ways that reflect a number of its manifestations 'as an ideological concept, a national affiliation, a cultural belonging, and a political entity' (Anishchenkova 2014, p. 2). Since the Arab Spring increasing identity clashes have surfaced over local and foreign identity conceptions from autocratic regimes, democracy movements, as well as through the renewed Western influence in much of the Middle East. There are many changes in the Middle East that create contextual conditions that need to be addressed in designing research studies, including geopolitical changes since the end of the Cold War, modernisation effects, invasion, and civil war that cause changes for identity on macro- and micro-levels due to changes in culture, social organisation and institutions, political systems, and economic structures and practices (Mutua and Sunal 2004).

Conclusion: Curricular Requirements for Leadership Roles in Islamic Contexts

There are a number of implications from the above discussion and conclusions one can draw about teaching educational administration and leadership in Muslim contexts. First, there are no inherent conflicts or contradictions in teaching the field for modernising states, as long as one is not tied to a particular form of Western modernisation theory. If one accepts multiple modernities, including those that are not secular or materialist, teaching educational leadership can be effectively internationalised and modified to serve the cultural and social heritages and goals of Muslim countries. One possible approach to this is through hybrid curriculum where international literature can be combined with material in the field reflecting the nature and character of other countries, particularly if one is presenting the field in an interpretive and critical manner.

Secondly, the field needs to develop and expand into foundational principles that include culturally appropriate practices that take into account to a much higher degree contextualisation (Miller 2017). Education administration, like other fields, has been challenged to modify its approaches or develop new ones that are grounded in a contextual understanding of historical and indigenous character (see Bourdieu 2013). Such advances have been made recently in this direction, by Dimmock and Walker (2005) and Reagan (2005), for example, on principles of international and comparative educational administration that recognise national and cultural differences. A small body of literature in English has emerged discussing those character and personality traits, as well as expertise and skills, needed for nation-building and modernisation in Muslim countries that derive from Islamic and international knowledge that contributes appropriately to economic development (including Islamic financing), social cohesion, national solidarity, and a promotion of culture (e.g., Ali 2005; Beekun and Badawi 2009; Elkaleh and Samier 2013; Green 1997; Shah 2015). The focus for many countries is the leadership qualities and skills that allow for effective ways to meet the nation-building and modernisation challenges while preserving social institutions. This necessitates educational administration and leadership programmes that are informed by historical narratives and contextual experiences as well as global and cross-cultural knowledge and practices (Kymlicka 2000; Moorosi and Bush 2011; Parolin 2010; Zajda et al. 2009). Curriculum and teaching have to take into account culture and other aspects of the context (Ayman 1993) as well as different approaches to leadership required internationally taking into account language, belief system and values, and social organisation in the society (Dorfman et al. 1997). Teaching methods and pedagogies should also recognise and support the collective nature of Muslim students. This requires developing the curricula towards more structured and supportive learning environments that encourage and promote group learning and team assignments and provide more intellectual and emotional support for students. These approaches also allow for the practice of shura within the class context, and opportunities for students to acquire or strengthen their leadership skills.

Thirdly, to achieve successfully these goals, a much greater attention needs to be paid to the impact of curricular content in the field on identity formation. Curriculum and pedagogy are not neutral or benign; they have a profound impact on how postgraduate students construct their leadership identities, assume what qualifies as good or preferable practices that affect the professional decisions they will make, and on a more macro-level shape what is considered to be good policy and governance. An underlying principle here is that of Bourdieu and Passeron's (1990) reproduction thesis: if one teaches people a foreign model with its shaping of values, identity, etc., it will be reproduced to at least some extent. Any form of teaching carries with it a hidden curriculum unless one practices a critical level of self-reflection and knowledge of the context and promotes this in the curriculum one designs and the pedagogical practices one performs. In other words, teaching as an expatriate in a foreign culture requires knowledge and understanding of the culture one is going into and perhaps should require a qualification.

What stands out starkly in terms of identity formation in the teaching of many expatriates in the Middle East, and the teaching and supervision of Arab Muslim graduate students in Western countries (who return to their countries to work in a professional capacity influencing the shaping of their social institutions, especially in Anglo-American contexts), is the almost exclusive use of a leadership canon that is primarily Anglo-American with occasional sources from Europe and other parts of the world. Teaching is a performativity that carries within it embodied values and conceptions (Alexander et al. 2005), itself a possible carrier of a hidden curriculum, particularly important in administration and leadership studies, where it is not only the curricular content one is conveying but the manner in which one does it that affects others' identity formation. Since, as Bardhan and Orbe (2012) claim, identity is also found in communicative interaction. The teaching of educational leadership in a wholly English language, with content that is predominantly Anglo-American, will have an effect on how identity, particularly leadership identity will form and assumptions made about education and knowledge.

Teaching administration and leadership to those in another cultural tradition, Michie (2014) argues, requires that some form of formal or informal acculturation needs to take place in order to teach what is necessary and relevant to those who professionally need to work in their own countries. Otherwise, one's activity contributes to a power imbalance related to what Said discusses in his Orientalism critique—that there is a hierarchy of knowledge and learning that is prejudicial. Teaching attitudes can take many forms on the part of expatriates, often held unconsciously and usually without sufficient critical self-reflection, falling into three main categories for Samier

(2014): public servant to the country one is teaching for; cultural diplomat, covering more than one tradition; and intellectual imperialist.

The frequent borrowing of educational administration and leadership from Western countries does not take constructive approaches since quite often constitutional and legal systems are ignored and other organisations and social institutions are not taken account of, whether through teaching or consultancy. However, there are ways in which this can be done in a culturally sensitive manner through policy and curriculum transfer by building on Islamic foundations and then drawing from the West where appropriate. One of the major current problems is that not all countries the neoliberal ideology and market-based aims informing much of Anglo-American education. National identity for leadership consists of values for both end goals, types of social relation and interaction, ways of thinking and acting, knowledge in the field, and conceptions of authority, obligation and responsibilities that go into constructing a leadership role.

References

Abdurrahman, T. (2009). *The spirit of modernity: An introduction to establishing the Islamic modernity*. Casablanca: Arabic Cultural Center.

Alexander, B., Anderson, G., & Gallegos, B. (Eds.). (2005). *Performance theories in education: Power, pedagogy, and the politics of identity*. Mahwah, NJ: Lawrence Erlbaum.

Ali, A. (2005). *Islamic perspectives on management and organization*. Cheltenham: Edward Elgar.

Al-Khalili, J. (2010). *The house of wisdom: How Arabic science saved ancient knowledge and gave us the Renaissance*. London: Penguin.

Altbach, P. (2003). American accreditation of foreign universities: Academic colonialism in action. *International Higher Education, 32*, 5–7.

Aly, M. (2015). *Becoming Arab in London: Performativity and the undoing of identity*. London: Pluto Press.

Anishchenkova, V. (2014). *Autobiographical identities in contemporary Arab cultures*. Edinburgh: Edinburgh University Press.

Arar, K., & Haj-Yehia, K. (2018). Perceptions of educational leadership in medieval Islamic thought: A contribution to multicultural contexts. *Journal of Educational Administration and History, 50*(2), 69–81.

Arar, K., Turan, S., Barakat, M., & Oplatka, I. (2017). The characteristics of educational leadership in the Middle East: A comparative analysis of three nation-states. In D. Waite & I. Bogotch (Eds.), *The Wiley international handbook of educational leadership* (pp. 355–374). Malden, MA: Wiley.

Asad, M. (1980). *The principles of state and government in Islam*. Kuala Lumpur: Islamic Book Trust.

Ayman, R. (1993). Leadership perception: The role of gender and culture. In M. M. Chemers & R. Ayman (Eds.), *Leadership theory and research* (pp. 137–166). San Diego: Academic Press.

Bardhan, N., & Orbe, M. (2012). *Identity research and communication: Intercultural reflections and future directions*. Plymouth: Lexington Books.

Barkawi, T., & Laffey, M. (2006). The postcolonial moment in security studies. *Review of International Studies, 32*(2), 329–352.

Baylis, J., Smith, S., & Owens, P. (Eds.). (2014). *The globalization of world politics*. Oxford: Oxford University Press.

Beck, U., Sznaider, N., & Winter, R. (Eds.). (2003). *Global America? The cultural consequences of globalization*. Liverpool: Liverpool University Press.

Beekun, R., & Badawi, J. (2009). *Leadership: An Islamic perspective* (3rd ed.). Maryland: Amana.
Bernstein, B. (2000). *Pedagogy, symbolic control, and identity*. Lanham, ML: Rowman & Littlefield.
Berry, J., Poortinga, Y., Pandey, J., Dasen, P., Saraswathi, T., Segall, M., Kagitçibasi, C. (Eds.). (1997). *Handbook of cross-cultural psychology* (Vol. 3). Boston: Allyn & Bacon.
Bourdieu, P. (2013). *Algerian sketches*. Cambridge: Polity.
Bourdieu, P., & Passeron, J.-C. (1990). *Reproduction in education, society and culture*. London: Sage.
Bowman, J. (2015). *Cosmoipolitan justice: The axial age, multiple modernities, and the postsecular turn*. New York: Springer.
Branine, M. (2011). *Managing Across cultures: Concepts, policies and practices*. Los Angeles: Sage.
Brooks, M., & Mutohar, A. (2018). Islamic school leadership: A conceptual framework. *Journal of Educational Administration and History, 50*(2), 54–68.
Carmichael, J. (1969). *The shaping of the Arabs: A study in ethnic identity*. Macmillan.
Chhokar, J., Brodbeck, F., & House, R. (Eds.). (2007). *Culture and leadership across the world: The globe book of in-depth studies of 25 societies*. Mahwah, NJ: Lawrence Erlbaum Associates.
Ciftci, S. (2010). Modernization, Islam, or social capital: What explains attitudes toward democracy in the Muslim world? *Comparative Political Studies, 43*(11), 1442–1470.
Cohen, R., & Kennedy, P. (2013). *Global sociology*. New York: Palgrave Macmillan.
Côté, J., & Levine, C. (2002). *Identity formation, agency, and culture: A social psychological synthesis*. Mahwah, NJ: Lawrence Erlbaum.
De Anca, C. (2012). *Beyond tribalism: Managing identity in a diverse world*. New York: Palgrave Macmillan.
Dimmock, C., & Walker, A. (2005). *Educational leadership: Culture and diversity*. London: Sage.
Doherty, C., & Singh, P. (2007). Mobile students, flexible identities and liquid modernity: Disrupting Western teachers' assumptions of the 'the Asian learner'. In D. Palfreyman & D. McBride (Eds.), *Learning and teaching across cultures in higher education* (pp. 114–132). Houndmills: Palgrave Macmillan.
Dorfman, P., Howell, J., Hibino, S., Lee, J., Tate, U., & Bautista, A. (1997). Leadership in Western and Asian countries: Commonalities and differences in effective leadership processes across cultures. *Leadership Quarterly, 8*(3), 233–274.
Eisenstadt, S. (2000). Multiple modernities. *Daedalus, 129*(1), 1–29.
Eisenstadt, S. (2005). *Multiple modernities*. New Brunswick, NJ: Transaction.
El Fadl, K. (2003). Islam and the challenge of democratic commitment. *Fordham International Law Journal, 27*(1), 4–71.
ElKaleh, E., & Samier, E. A. (2013). The ethics of Islamic leadership: A cross-cultural approach for public administration. *Administrative Culture, 14*(2), 188–211.
Farazmand, A., & Pinkowski, J. (2006). *Handbook of globalization, governance, and public administration*. Boca Raton: CRC Press.
Findlow, S. (2005). International networking in the United Arab Emirates higher education system: Global-local tensions. *Compare, 35*(3), 285–302.
Foskett, N., & Maringe, F. (2010). *Globalisation and internationalisation in higher education: Theoretical, strategic and management perspectives*. London: Bloomsbury.
Fox, J., Mourtada-Sabbah, N., Al-Mutawa, M. (Eds.). (2006). *Globalization and the Gulf*. London: Routledge.
Fritz, V., & Menocal, A. R. (2007). *Understanding state-building from a political economy perspective*. London: Overseas Development Institute.
Gavin, J., & Westwood, R. (2010). *International and cross-cultural management studies: A postcolonial reading*. Houndmills: Palgrave Macmillan.
Giroux, H. (2002). Neoliberalism, corporate culture, and the promise of higher education: The university as a democratic public sphere. *Harvard Educational Review, 72*(4), 425–464.
Green, A. (1997). *Education, globalization and the nation state*. Houndmills: Palgrave Macmillan.
Habermas, J. (1979). *Communication and the evolution of society*. Boston, MA: Beacon Press.

Habermas, J. (1984). *The theory of communicative action*. (Vol. 2) Boston: Beacon Press.

Habermas, J. (1987). *The philosophical discourse of modernity*. Cambridge: Polity Press.

Habermas, J., & Ben-Habib, S. (1981). Modernity versus postmodernity. *New German Critique, 22*, 3–14.

Haddad, Y. (2011). *Becoming American? The forging of Arab and Muslim identity in pluralist America*. Waco, TX: Baylor University Press.

Hall, B., & Tandon, R. (2017). Decolonization of knowledge, Epistemicide, participatory research and higher education. *Research for All, 1*(1), 6–19.

Hallinger, P., & Leithwood, K. (1996). Culture and educational administration: A case of finding out what you don't know. *Journal of Educational Administration, 34*, 98–116.

Hammad, W., & Halllinger, P. (2017). A systematic review of conceptual models and method used in research on educational leadership and management in Arab societies. *School Leadership & Management, 37*(5), 434–456.

Hefner, R. W., & Horvatich, P. (Eds.). (1997). *Islam in an Era of nation-states: Politics and religious renewal in Muslim Southeast Asia*. Honolulu: University of Hawaii Press.

Hughes, A. (2013). *Muslim identities: An introduction to Islam*. New York: Columbia University Press.

Inglehart, R. & Baker, W. E. (2000). Modernization, cultural change, and the persistence of traditional values. *American Sociological Review*, 19–51.

Jabnoun, N. (2012). *Islam and management: Your ultimate guide to running a business from an Islamic perspective*. Riyadh: International Islamic Publishing House.

Jones, B., & Chandran, R. (2008). *Concepts and dilemmas of state-building in fragile situations: From fragility to resilience*. Paris: OECD.

Jung, D. (2017). *Muslim history and social theory: A global sociology of modernity*. Cham: Palgrave Macmillan.

Kamali, M. (2006). *Multiple modernities, civil society and Islam: The case of Iran and Turkey*. Liverpool: Liverpool University Press.

Kanan, H., & Baker, A. (2006). Student satisfaction with an educational administration preparation program: A comparative perspective. *Journal of Educational Administration, 44*(2), 159–169.

Kelsay, J. (2002). Civil society and government in Islam. In H. Hashmi (Ed.), *Islamic political ethics: Civil society, pluralism and conflict*. Princeton, NJ: Princeton University Press.

Kendall, G., Woodward, I., & Skrbis, Z. (2009). *The sociology of cosmopolitanism: Globalization, identity, culture and government*. Basingstoke: Palgrave Macmillan.

Khelifa, M. (2010). Trading culture: Have Western-educated Emirati females gone Western? *OIDA International Journal of Sustainable Development, 1*, 19–29.

Kirk, D., & Napier, D. (2009). The transformation of higher education in the United Arab Emirates: Issues, implications, and intercultural dimensions. In J. Zajda, H. Daun, & L. Saha (Eds.), *Nation-building, identity and citizenship education* (pp. 131–142). Dordrecht: Springer.

Kohnert, D. (2008). Common roots, shared traits, joint prospects? On the articulation of multiple modernities in Benin and Haiti. In U. Schuerkens (Ed.), *Globalization and transformations of local socioeconomic practices* (pp. 151–173). New York: Routledge.

Kymlicka, W. (2000). Nation-building and minorities rights: Comparing West and East. *Journal of Ethnic and Migration Studies, 26*(2), 183–212.

Lee, R. (2014). *Religion and politics in the Middle East: Identity, ideology, institutions, and attitudes*. Boulder, CO: Westview.

Lewis, B. (2003). *What went wrong: The clash between Islam and modernity in the Middle East*. New York: Perennial.

Liverani, M. (2006). *Uruk: The first city*. London: Equinox.

Lombard, M. (2004). *The golden age of Islam*. Princeton, NJ: Markus Wiener.

Lotz, C. (2010). International norms in statebuilding: Finding a pragmatic approach. *Global Governance, 16*, 219–236.

Luhmann, N. (Ed.). (1991). *Soziologische Aufklärung*. Opladen: Westdeutscher Verlag.

Machal, G., & Prasad, A. (Eds.). (2003). *Postcolonial theory and organizational analysis*. New York: Palgrave Macmillan.

Madhavan, S. (2011). *Cross-cultural management: Concepts and cases*. Oxford: Oxford University Press.

Memmi, A. (2003). *The colonizer and the colonized*. London: Earthscan Publications.

Michie, M. (2014). *Working cross-culturally: Identity learning, border crossing and culture brokering*. Rotterdam: Sense.

Mignolo, W. (2011). *The darker side of Western modernity: Global futures, decolonial options*. Durham, NC: Duke University Press.

Miller, P. (2017). Cultures of educational leadership: Researching and theorising common issues in different world contexts. In P. Miller (Ed.), *Cultures of educational leadership: Global and intercultural perspectives* (pp. 1–23). London: Palgrave Macmillan.

Miller-Idriss, C., & Hanauer, E. (2011). Transnational higher education: Offshore campuses in the Middle East. *Comparative Education, 47*(2), 181–207.

Moorosi, P., & Bush, T. (2011). School leadership development in Commonwealth countries: Learning across the boundaries. *International Studies in Educational Administration, 39*(3), 59–75.

Morgan, M. H. (2007). *Lost history: The enduring legacy of Muslim scientists, thinkers, and artists*. Washington, DC: National Geographic Society.

Mutua, K., & Sunal, C. S. (Eds.). (2004). *Research on education in Africa, the Caribbean, and the Middle East: An historic overview*. Charlotte, NC: Information Age Publishing.

Nasr, S. H. (2001). *Science and civilization in Islam*. Chicago, IL: ABC International Group.

Noori, N., & Anderson, P.-K. (2013). Globalization, governance, and the diffusion of the American model of education: Accreditation agencies and American-style universities in the Middle East. *International Journal of Politics, Culture and Society, 26,* 159–172.

Nordin, I., Edfeldt, C., Hu, L.-L., Jonsson, H., & Leblanc, A. (Eds.). (2016). *Transcultural identity constructions in a changing world*. Frankfurt am Main: Peter Lang.

Paris, R., & Sisk, T. (2009). Introduction: Understanding the contradictions of postwar statebuilding. In R. Paris & T. Sisk (Eds.), *The dilemmas of statebuilding: Confronting the contradictions of postwar peace operations*. Oxford: Routledge.

Parolin, G. P. (2010). *Citizenship in the Arab world: Kin, religion and nation-state*. Amsterdam University Press.

Parsons, T. (1966). *Societies: Evolutionary and comparative perspectives*. New York: Prentice-Hall.

Phillips, C. (2013). *Everyday Arab identity: The daily reproduction of the Arab world*. London: Routledge.

Ramadan, T. (2007). *In the footsteps of the Prophet: Lessons from the life of Muhammad*. New York: Oxford University Press.

Reagan, T. (2005). *Non-western educational traditions: Indigenous approaches to educational thought and practice*. London: Lawrence Erlbaum.

Rhea, Z. (2015). *Leading and managing indigenous education in the postcolonial world*. Abingdon: Routledge.

Romanowski, M. (2013). The Qatar national professional standards for school leaders: A critical discourse analysis using Habermas' theory of knowledge constitutive interests. *International Journal of Leadership in Education, 17*(2), 174–199.

Romanowski, M. (2017). Neoliberalism and Western accreditation in the Middle East: A critical discourse analysis of educational leadership constituent council standards. *Journal of Educational Administration, 55*(1), 70–84.

Rosenthal, F. (2007). *Knowledge triumphant: The concept of knowledge in medieval Islam*. Boston: Leiden.

Sachsenmaier, D., Riedel, J., & Eisenstadt, S. N. (Eds.). (2002). *Reflections on multiple modernities: European, Chinese and other interpretations*. Leiden: Brill.

Said, E. (1978). *Orientalism*. London: Vintage.

Said, E. (1993). *Culture and imperialism*. London: Vintage.

Sahide, A. (2012). Islam and the failure of modernization in the Middle East. *Al-Albab: Borneo Journal of Religious Studies, 1*(1), 49–59.

Saleh, A. (2002). *Educational administration: An Islamic perspective*. Kuala Lumpur: Noordeen.

Saliba, G. (2007). *Islamic science and the making of the European Renaissance*. Cambridge, MA: MIT Press.

Samier, E. A. (2014). Western doctoral programmes as public service, cultural diplomacy or intellectual imperialist? Expatriate educational leadership teaching in the United Arab Emirartes. In A. Taysum & S. Rayner (Eds.), *Investing in our education: Leading, learning, researching and the doctorate* (pp. 93–123). Scarborough: Emerald.

Samier, E. A. (2017). Towards a postcolonial and decolonising educational administration history. *Journal of Educational Administration and History, 49*(4), 264–282.

Sánchez, M. (2010). Globalisation and loss of identity. *International Forum of Psychoanalysis, 19*, 71–77.

Schmidt, V. (2006). Multiple modernities or varieties of modernity? *Current Sociology, 54*(1), 77–97.

Seth, S. (2013). *Postcolonial theory and international relations*. Abingdon: Routledge.

Shah, S. (2015). *Education, leadership and Islam*. London: Routledge.

Silverthorne, C. (2005). *Organizational psychology in cross-cultural perspective*. New York: New York University Press.

Smith, A. (1991). *National identity*. London: Penguin.

Spivak, G. (1987). *In other worlds: Essays in cultural politics*. New York: Methuen.

Stewart-Harawira, M. (2005). *The new imperial order: Indigenous responses to globalization*. London: Zed Books.

Stiglitz, J. (2002). *Globalization and its discontents*. New York: W. W. Norton.

Streeck, Wolfgang, & Yamamura, Kozo (Eds.). (2001). *The origins of nonliberal capitalism: Germany and Japan in comparison*. Ithaca, NY: Cornell University Press.

Suarez-Orozco, M., & Qin-Hilliard, D. (2004). *Globalization: Culture and education in the new millennium*. Berkeley, CA: University of California Press.

Suleiman, Y. (2011). *Arabic, self and identity: A study in conflict and displacement*. Oxford: Oxford University Press.

Thiong'o, N. (1986). *Decolonizing the mind: The politics of language in African literature*. Oxford: James Currey.

Voll, J. O. (2007). Islam and democracy: Is modernization a barrier? *Religion Compass, 1*(1), 170–178.

Wallerstein, I. (1974). *The modern world-system*. New York: Academic Press.

Weber, M. (1930). *The protestant ethic and the spirit of capitalism*. New York: Charles Scribner's Sons.

Weinreich, P., & Saunderson, W. (Eds.). (2005). *Analysing identity: Cross-cultural, societal and clinical contexts*. London: Routledge.

Wertsch, J. (2012). Narrative tools and the construction of identity. In M. Schultz, S. Maguire, & A. Langley (Eds.), *Constructing identity in and around organizations* (pp. 128–146). Oxford: Oxford University Press.

Wodak, R., de Cillia, R., Reisigl, M., & Liebhart, K. (2009). *The discursive construction of national identity*. Edinburgh: Edinburgh University Press.

Zaidi, A. (2011). *Islam, modernity, and the human sciences*. New York: Palgrave Macmillan.

Zajda, J. (2009). Globalisation, nation-building, and cultural identity: The role of intercultural dialogue. In J. Zajda, H. Daun, & L. J. Saha (Eds.), *Nation-building, identity and citizenship education: Cross cultural perspectives* (pp. 15–24). Dordrecht: Springer.

Zajda, J., Daun, H., & Saha, L. J. (Eds.). (2009). *Nation-building, identity and citizenship education: Cross cultural perspectives*. Dordrecht: Springer.

Eugenie A. Samier is Reader in Educational Management and Leadership at the University of Strathclyde, Glasgow. Her research concentrates on administrative philosophy and theory, interdisciplinary foundations of administration, theories and models of educational leadership, and comparative educational administration. She has frequently been a Guest Researcher at the Humboldt University of Berlin, was Visiting Professor in the Department of Administrative Studies at the University of Tartu, Estonia (2003), a Visiting Fellow at Oxford Brookes University and has been a guest lecturer at universities and institutes in the USA, Germany, Estonia, Russia, Norway, Lithuania, Finland, Qatar, Bahrain and the UAE. Her publications include book chapters and articles on organisational culture and values, the new public management, the role of history and biography in educational administration, the role of humanities, aesthetics and literary analysis in administration, and Weberian foundations of administrative theory and ethics in a number of international book collections and many leading journals in the USA, Australia, the UK, Germany, the Baltic region, and Canada. She is a founding board member of *Administrative Culture* journal and is editor of several book collections with Routledge on ethics, aesthetics, politics, emotions, trust and betrayal, ideologies and maladministration in educational administration. She is also an associate editor of the four-volume Master Works *Educational Leadership and Administration* (Sage 2009), a contributor on authority, bureaucracy, critical theory to *Encyclopaedia of Education Law* (Sage 2008), on aesthetics and human agency to the *Handbook of Educational Leadership* (Sage 2011), aesthetics of leadership and bureaucratic theory to the *Handbook of Educational Theory* (Information Age Publishing 2013). She has also written a number of articles on topics like toxic leadership, passive evil, kitchification of educational leadership, the avant-garde, postcolonial educational administration, and Islamic ethics, social justice, global governance, administrative tradition, and educational change in the Middle East for several journals and book collections. She also worked as a management consultant in Canada to the public sector for a number of years on a broad variety of projects including legislation development, organisational reviews, board development, and government department restructuring and redesign.

Eman S. ElKaleh studied her M.B.A. at the University of Wollongong followed by a Ph.D. in Management, Leadership and Policy at the British University in Dubai in association with Birmingham University, UK. She received an Academic Excellence Award by Dubai International Academic City for her dissertation entitled 'Teaching Leadership in UAE Business and Education Programs: A Habermasean Analysis within an Islamic Context'. While Eman hails from Egypt, she has worked in the UAE at two major universities for nearly twenty years. Currently, she teaches business leadership at Zayed University's College of Business in addition to overseeing the Admission and Recruitment Unit. Understanding the need to develop leadership capacity in Gulf Region countries, she is actively developing programmes and workshops to help Muslim students as well as the faculty and staff with whom they interact gain a better understanding of leadership from an Islamic perspective. She has given guest lectures on Islamic leadership at a number of universities abroad such as University of Oxford Brookes, UK, the Humboldt University of Berlin, Germany, Qatar University and at the British University and Zayed University in the UAE. Eman was selected to serve as the Chair of Professional Development in the MENASA NASPA Advisory Board. She is also participating in a number of international research projects in leadership studies. Eman also has a solid experience in reviewing research studies and serves as a reviewer for a number of international and national peer-reviewed conferences and research awards. Tasked with developing a comprehensive programme for student success, Eman was recognised for her innovation in 2012 by receiving Zayed University's highest honour at a university-wide ceremony.

Chapter 7
Locality, Leadership and Pedagogies for Entrepreneurship Education

M. Evren Tok and Cristina D'Alessandro

Abstract Embeddedness and local cultures and contexts are key in the development of entrepreneurship. Embeddedness is cultural, territorial and networked. All these aspects have to appropriately translate into entrepreneurship education, training and curricula. Entrepreneurs must be able to understand and translate values and culture, as well as the knowledge of their territories, into their work and practices. After a literature review, this chapter showcases these principles through the example of Islam as a cultural foundation for Arab countries and societies. Leadership and policies may have a great role in encouraging these processes and designing appropriate policies and regulations sustaining entrepreneurship education in line with national needs and aspirations. The example of Qatar is presented in the chapter as a useful one to this extent. The Qatar National Vision 2030 indicated the path to follow with the need to diversify the economy through entrepreneurship development in the country. In a global world, entrepreneurs must be both embedded in local/national realities, capable to respond to social needs, but also able to integrate global markets and value chains and compete with other entrepreneurs. This is a challenge for which embedded values and moral behaviours may be useful in the end.

Introduction

This study concentrates on embeddedness and local context in the development of entrepreneurship. It argues that the nexus between entrepreneurial knowledge acquisition, behaviours and experiences of entrepreneurs, and the moral bases of a society (the impact of cultural traits, norms, and values) have been understudied. Therefore,

---

M. E. Tok (✉)
College of Islamic Studies, HBKU, Doha, Qatar
e-mail: etok@hbku.edu.qa

C. D'Alessandro
University of Ottawa, Ottawa, Canada
e-mail: cristina.dalessandro@wanadoo.fr

© Springer Nature Singapore Pte Ltd. 2019
E. A. Samier and E. S. ElKaleh (eds.), *Teaching Educational Leadership in Muslim Countries*, Educational Leadership Theory,
https://doi.org/10.1007/978-981-13-6818-9_7

the paper aims at fulfilling the following. First, it explores the modalities, scope and gaps of raising home-grown leaders via entrepreneurship education within the Qatari ecosystem. Secondly, it aims to incorporate local social, moral, traditional, cultural and sustainability aspects of entrepreneurship in building the next generation of entrepreneurs. Studies suggest that encouraging the leadership training in entrepreneurship promotion and entrepreneurship education in Qatar will stimulate the mindsets and skills of students, school leavers, women, adult learners as well as those already engaged in entrepreneurship activities by helping them understand the real benefits and opportunities in entrepreneurship.

The discussion revolves around the premise that entrepreneurship (and its education) is an embedded process. Although an 'entrepreneur' is inherently an 'individual', educators and the providers of entrepreneurship should be cognisant of the forms of sociality, spatiality, community as well as various norms, codes and symbols that define cultural traits. A second aim is to share some recent initiatives from Qatar's dynamic entrepreneurship ecosystem and its evolution that illustrates the importance of bringing 'context' to entrepreneurship education. 'Entrepreneurship education' (EE) entered the mainstream literature decades ago and has captured the attention of policy-makers and members of the private sector in many countries. Starting with the comprehensive report of the UNESCO World Conference in 1998, EE has become a pillar of national economic development strategies (Greene et al. 2014). Nonetheless, the existing literature suggests the lack of a global definition for it, and its scope differs according to the needs and standards of each country, territory or the population it serves. In this sense, this paper coins the terms 'localising entrepreneurship education' for the first time as a novel, creative and innovative contribution in a transformative manner. It is transformative because 'localised' versions of EE would supplement 'off-the-shelf' types of models and help different stakeholders, entrepreneurs and end users in the entrepreneurship ecosystem.

The impact of culture on entrepreneurship has been a rather understudied area with existing studies often looked into the perceptions towards business, attitudes towards work and wealth, and leadership (Chell and Karataş-Özkan 2014). This study focuses on an often-underestimated factor in defining the entrepreneurial nature of a society, which is culture and the ways within which economic behaviours are embedded in various cultural and social institutions, codes, scripts and structures. Entrepreneurship, viewed as one of the main dynamic economic factors in a country, is affected by underlying cultural traits of societies. More importantly, this enhances the existing ways and pedagogies of delivering EE by diagnosing the specific scope and types, shaped by its unique culture and traditions.

As such, the growing interest in entrepreneurship can be harnessed as a catalyst for economic diversification efforts and its education. In this study, the growing interest and its impact will be analysed in a locally sensitive and informed manner by highlighting the characteristics of entrepreneurial leadership qualities and formations that work best in the Qatari and the Gulf context. By studying these qualities, localised versions of EE that are provided in tandem with traditional/conventional values and ways can be developed. In order to pursue these goals, an initial step is to explore the qualities of EE and its practices that have been yielding fruitful results and the instances in which the results have been negative.

Research Methodology

This study employs an exploratory analysis of cases of leadership and EE. The analysis of the current literature on locality, leadership and pedagogies for entrepreneurship provided broad perspectives for the conceptual and theoretical frameworks for EE in Qatar. The literature employed was used in gathering important facts in regard to the management and development of EE both internally and externally. Semi-structured in-depth interviews were used to determine the relevant trends of what the present situation reveals and what has happened in the past. Selected appropriate literature was used as a foundation for this study. As such, the activity involved the use of periodicals, bulletins, journals and any other possible source of secondary information.

Background

Entrepreneurship pushes people to seek opportunities beyond what they can control; hence, its management requires the capacity to influence and motivate others, culture, processes and systems. Entrepreneurial leaders have to have visionary skills that can enable them to engage with teams in identifying, developing and taking advantage of opportunities so as to gain competitive advantage.

Entrepreneurship leadership calls for an education that should offer courage, social interaction skills, experiential and reflective methods that inspire business capability (Roomi and Harrison 2011). Other skills offered include risk-taking, strategic initiative establishment, proper decision-making and problem-solving (Roomi and Harrison 2011). In their study, Roomi and Harrison (2011) establish that corporate entrepreneurship, which is properly incorporated with leadership education, permits accessibility to entrepreneurial aspects that students are less inclined to encounter hence offer creativity, innovation entrepreneurial culture, teamwork and organisation skills among others. Entrepreneurship has turned out to be a definitive aspect of business around the world. Currently, women have become part and parcel of entrepreneurship even in the Muslim context. According to social capital and suitable sociocultural theory, it offers a significant contribution towards the growth of sales and employment rates in organisations. Nonetheless, features such as personality, behaviour and attitude are important for growth. Within Islamic societies when women-owned businesses grow, it must be critical that EE is offered to people so that socio-economic values and related factors are integrated (Roomi 2011). Pistrui and Fahed-Sreih (2010) opine that in the Gulf, economic development and entrepreneurship have led to the need to learn about entrepreneurship hence making EE essential.

EE began in the 1990s in its first phase when the questioning of trait theories became necessary. By the end of the 1990s and the onset of 2000s, there was an in-depth evaluation of entrepreneurship learning as the second phase. The third phase came in 2005 when the methodologies and approaches of teaching entrepreneurship were perceived as important. Afterwards, it was necessary to establish who the entrepreneurial teacher is and the kind of setting that could facilitate entrepreneurial behaviour before Phase Five of EE could begin (Hägg and Kurczewska 2016). As Phase Five occurred, there was a need to determine how entrepreneurial identity development happens, the ethics within it, and how to have a sustainable entrepreneurship situation. As such, there are two different approaches to EE: the first approach to entrepreneurship is European, while the second is more generally Anglo-American where ontology, epistemology and axiology are used and related learning paradigms look into the theories of teaching and learning, didactics and pedagogy as well as learning and teaching practices with explicit versus implicit focus, respectively. In the teaching of entrepreneurship, the philosophical view based on contextual and cultural foundations is what provide the root of behaviour. According to Hägg and Kurczewska (2016), there should be consciousness, utilisation of present learning theories and attributes derived from the context in which entrepreneurship and the objectives of EE will operate. In addition, the content, methods, and setting must be entrepreneurial. What is important is that the past and present must be integrated in order for EE to be successful and be consciously connected to reality. It is important to note that ethical issues are focal in EE because they guide educators to make conscious and knowledgeable decisions (Hägg and Kurczewska 2016).

An evaluation of European EE shows that there has been a global significance in the long-term learning process. The universities have been major agents (Volkmann and Audretsch 2017) by considering the advancement of entrepreneurial knowledge, attitudes and techniques, which can empower learners and allow them to think and act entrepreneurially so as to realise opportunities and substantively apply learned knowledge. Therefore, innovative teaching processes in various countries have been used to shape and design business programmes and spin-off activities. Besides, government support is vital in offering entrepreneurship programmes. The exploration of entrepreneurship programmes in Europe served in the adoption of Sustainable Development Goals within the Nation's 2030 agenda, and it stressed a focus on quality dimensions instead of simplistic quantitative approaches. The EU strategy targets lifelong learning, in which entrepreneurship is preferred as both a start-up practice and training where more knowledge is offered to individuals (Volkmann and Audretsch 2017).

According to Volkmann and Audretsch (2017), the use of external stakeholders, having the required resources, and addressing institutional issues offer a quality education. Besides, learning of many lessons and regional educational networking impacts on EE because it offers intent and knowledge. The consideration of curricular, extracurricular teaching and suggestion of entrepreneurship formats is essential in targeting various groups within the EE packages (Volkmann and Audretsch 2017). An evaluation of innovative, thematically wide teaching, broadly geographically inclusive, transferability based and diverse higher education institutes serve as the best study samples for any study. In Volkmann and Audretsch's (2017) study, such cases demonstrated that state policy, external support, and the nature of education influences entrepreneurship. Furthermore, when university settings have room for students to become involved in entrepreneurship, then their skills are action-oriented. Furthermore, the programmes tend to be more effective when they priorise the meeting of real entrepreneurs, and stress success, trust, courage, testing ideas, as well as learning which is multidisciplinary and practical (Volkmann and Audretsch 2017). By embedding entrepreneurship within the regional context, Lund University developed consistently transformational educational strategies that consistently reflected teaching activities (Volkmann and Audretsch 2017). In embedded EE, government strategies become important, and so, the funding and continuous structuring of it offer worthwhile training that is often innovative, organised and intensive targeting various groups of people (Volkmann and Audretsch 2017). Consideration of locations, timing, formal evaluation, and informal evaluation as well as the use of both experienced teachers and mentors assists in the proper teaching of EE.

In the Middle East, which is just getting into free market systems, EE has become an essential tool of the successful transformation process, but religion is the driving force for business performance and entrepreneurship. The economic, geopolitical and cultural aspects of Islamic societies influence entrepreneurship and private enterprise growth through values that define gender and family participation in entrepreneurship and appropriate practices.

In entrepreneurial situations, moral issues are common. Generally, entrepreneurs face such issues while making a choice between the pursuit of self-interest and maintenance of normative entrepreneurship ethics. In essence, some of them even perform very poorly, especially when faced with some ethical challenges (Gangi 2017). Furthermore, some never consider at all the moral aspects, which emerge in these kinds of situations. As such, they lack moral awareness. Moral issues erupt in entrepreneurship when people pursue self-interests and forget about the sustenance of normative business ethics. Such a conflict results in wrong decision-making and poor moral judgment that cannot permit self-regulation (Byrant 2009). When one has moral reasoning, decisions are made through moral consideration; hence, information collection and ethical choices become the amplifying and dynamic process through which personal pursuits and organisational information processing are conducted. Meanwhile, a lack of such awareness has an important significance in the sense that such individuals would unlikely consider the moral aspects in deliberating and making decisions. Therefore, moral awareness serves as the foundation of moral reasoning and ethical decision-making.

Presently, moral awareness has been relatively neglected in the entrepreneurial literature. Instead, scholars have placed the focus on the processes within moral reasoning by business people such as moral judgment and making of decisions. According to Bryant (2009), the level of an individual's self-efficacy will have an impact on the manner in which an individual reacts to different aspects of entrepreneurship situations. An individual who has strong entrepreneurship self-efficacy might have higher chances of being confident and having an obligation in entrepreneurship circumstances, together with a strong sense of moral identity and great determination in upholding moral principles and proximal self-direction. Therefore, such a person may attend more strongly to damage within entrepreneurial states. On the other hand, an individual with weak entrepreneurial self-efficacy might display a weak sense of moral identity through lack of commitment and confidence in such conditions. Still, such individuals might still have a higher concentration on the social values and digital self-guidance, depicting the admiration for ethical compliance in entrepreneur conditions (Bryant 2009). As such, the roles of business people are instances of a decision to become an entrepreneur. While the cognitive representation and data are presented to an economic controller in the foundation for deciding, such a person is located within a social context which has an impact on the depiction and educational processes. Besides, entrepreneurship results from the creativity, drive, and commitment of individuals. That way, the business environment can influence the nature and behaviour of entrepreneurs.

Entrepreneurship plays a great role in a country's process of economic growth. Generally, it creates employment opportunities, enhances the level of technological innovativeness and stimulates development. Based on the dynamic perspective, entrepreneurs serve as agents of change. Since entrepreneurship relates to the start of new businesses, it enables people to experiment with new techniques, introduce new products or even create new marketplaces (Periz-Otiz and Merigó-Lindahl 2015). In Qatar, entrepreneurship advancement is one of the areas that has been incorporated by the government to assist in the diversification of its economy. In this case, entrepreneurial training and education programmes have been initiated as policy instruments to nurture novelty and enhance entrepreneurship progress. This implementation is founded on the trust that entrepreneurship edification and knowledge preparation could assist in constructing a solid individual character while equipping learners with the correct set of skills and knowledge for starting their own business, thereby contributing to jobs for persons in diverse sectors of the economy. However, despite such a programme existing in Qatar for several years, very minimal research has been done on this topic and the number of available studies is quite a few. In spite of many nations having analysed and explored the context globally, there is a limited literature that concerns these topics in the Qatari context (Periz-Otiz and Merigó-Lindahl 2015). Even the ones that exist do not take into consideration the connection between the knowledge of its economy and EE. As such, the gap in the literature is obvious and there is an unquestionable requisite for research to cover the gap.

The aim of this study is to build on this initial research by delving into the experience of training and EE in Qatar. This examination will assist in identifying the experience of Qatar while providing a glimpse into its drawbacks and strengths if they are available. The importance of this research stems from the need for a mutual comprehension on the significance of EE and preparation of techniques for the Qatar economy and its function in fulfilling the needs of the country and the intent to develop a diversified and knowledge-based economy (Gangi 2017).

Theoretical Framework

The theoretical lens of this paper is built on the concept of embeddedness. Communitarianism is an articulated social form, and the link between commodified capitalist class processes and non-commodified production is, in turn, embedded in other economic and cultural practices. In embedding economic actions, both the social and cultural are operational. According to DiMaggio (1994), culture as shared collective understandings can be constitutive and regulative. It becomes constitutive through the 'categories, scripts and conceptions of agency' (Swedberg 2003, p. 42) that shape the way 'we conceive, define, and rationalise decisions' (Hess 2004, p. 166), and regulative through the 'norms, values, and routines' (Swedberg 2003, p. 42) that govern our decisions and action. In short, the categories, values and norms that emerge from culture shape the actions and decisions of agents.

Communitarianism varies across localities, but in general involves three types of embeddings (Hess 2004):

- Societal embeddedness: This type of embeddedness highlights the importance of an actor's provenance. It is related to the social structures that influence and shape the actions of individuals and collective actors within their respective societies. Social embeddedness involves cultural embeddedness, which relates to the role of historically established societal power relations, cultural imprints and heritage. Societal embeddedness refers mostly to the power of prominent local tribes/families who have built the city's economic infrastructure and have helped to build communitarian efforts and influence spatial practices. These actors can give life to their cities and can use their hegemony over other urban residents. Thus, it is not surprising that the social coalitions produced through the active leadership of these locally hegemonic families generate controversy as they often involve significant pressure on the local population.
- Territorial embeddedness: This type of embeddedness refers to the extent to which an actor is anchored in a particular territory or place. In Anatolia, this type of embeddedness manifests as strong 'city identities'. Many of the businessmen surveyed by Hess noted that their primary motivation was to improve their city. Economic actors become embedded in the city in which they live and work and, in some cases, become constrained by the economic activities and social dynamics that already exist in those places. When the attachment to the locality is strong, it can increase the efficiency of cooperation and coordination among business people and help to mobilise their philanthropic agendas.
- Network embeddedness: This type of embeddedness describes networks of formal and informal actors and includes the institutional and organisational capacities. Network embeddedness can be seen as the product of a process of trust-building between network agents that is central to successful and stable relationships. Network embeddedness is related to societal embeddedness with regard to the role of, for example, religion and sect establishments, as businesses often benefit from connections based on Islam. These bond and trust mechanisms can reach beyond cities and the urban scale, especially when local entrepreneurs target connections abroad.

Literature Review

Entrepreneurship as an Embedded Process

In addition to its economic base, entrepreneurship is a social process that is embedded in multiple non-economic realms. For instance, a common depiction of entrepreneurship rests on individual behaviour. Is the individual the only agent undertaking the entrepreneurship process? The answer to this question is both 'yes' and 'no'. The 'yes' part is quite obvious, as the entrepreneur is usually the individual seeking out opportunities. Entrepreneurial process entails a cognitive dimension before ideas are put into action. Entrepreneurial initiatives are preceded by intense preparatory stages that are mentally demanding. Obviously, the 'individual' is theoretically at the centre of this process; however, as this process evolves, the individual endeavour starts to connect with other structures. It is this phase in which the transformative power of entrepreneurship is disguised in its collective nature.

The collective nature could be understood in diverse ways and methods. Cox and Mair (1988, p. 307) have identified an integral characteristic of place-based actors in their discussion of 'local dependence', a concept that refers to the dependence of various actors (such as entrepreneurs) on the reproduction of certain social relations within a particular territory. Cox and Mair's local dependence make us think about the ways economic actors, such as entrepreneurs, build their ideas by capitalising on various forms of embeddedness in their local contexts. For instance, they benefit from 'societal embeddedness', which corresponds to the social structures that influence and shape the actions of individuals within their respective societies. Social embeddedness involves cultural embeddedness, which relates to the role of historically established societal, communal, tribal relations, cultural imprints and heritage. Societal embeddedness means that entrepreneurs need to be well informed about the realities and dynamics of societal structures. In a way, it is a rejection of the tendencies that individualise entrepreneurship. Entrepreneurs have social objectives in addition to economic ones. Mobilising societal resources and articulating them to economic resources is what entrepreneurs should do more and more. In order to preserve their attachment to their societal bonds and unleash more innovative and creative undertakings, entrepreneurs need to frame their mindsets by acknowledging societal embeddedness and balance social justice and economic profit. This balance does not mean that entrepreneurs are less successful; in contrast, community building and profit-making go hand in hand.

Another kind of embeddedness is related to the network. This type of embeddedness describes networks of actors and includes the institutional and organisational capacities that could be utilised by entrepreneurs. Entrepreneurs are embedded in different kinds of networks. In fact, this type has a significant intersection with the societal embeddedness, as some networks are already formed around societal bonds. The third kind of embeddedness pertains to the territory. This type of embeddedness refers to the extent to which an actor is anchored in a particular territory or place. For instance, why would an entrepreneur choose to invest in his or her own 'land' despite having some other overseas entrepreneurship opportunities? The answer is not that easy. It is quite complex.

It is true that economic globalisation created a strong sense and perception of a 'deterritorialised' world and 'place' has been losing its importance, as the world becomes a 'global village'. This is, however, not the entire picture. To start with, the entrepreneur has a locality, a place and a sense of that place. Multiple belongings, identities, history and bonds coexist. In other words, 'territory' is not entirely lost when an entrepreneur performs its cognitive and practical actions. The answer to the question raised above is related to the territorial attachment or as Cox and Mair referred to as 'local dependency'. Local dependency should not be understood as an obstacle, but it can be an empowering mechanism. In fact, this is true for many kinds of embeddedness. They signify deviations from accounts of explaining entrepreneurial trajectories; however, their existence creates more opportunities than limitations if correctly and smartly diagnosed.

Implications of Embeddedness in Qatar

The need to study societal, network and territorial embeddedness for entrepreneurship and its education in Qatar has strong resonance with the Qatar National Vision 2030 and its development plans. The Qatar National Vision aims at 'transforming Qatar into an advanced country by 2030, capable of sustaining its own development and providing for a high standard of living for all of its people for generations to come' (QNV 2008: 2). One of the key challenges identified in this document pertains to modernisation and preservation of traditions. In many ways, QNV 2030 and its human, social, environmental and economic pillars make implicit and explicit connections to the importance of these forms of embeddedness. As clearly stated in the QNV 2030, it is crucial to balance modernisation with tradition. Searching for the moral basis of entrepreneurship in this regard could help identify new articulations between globalisation and localisation, religion and capitalism, culture and markets and, finally, between modernisation and tradition. Identification of these articulations is important to scaffold Qatar's transition to a diversified knowledge-based economy and to allow Qatar to attain global competitiveness through its rising entrepreneurial spirit, as we witness very closely Qatar's expanding and deepening entrepreneurship ecosystem.

Social capital is a successful export from sociology, because it facilitates attainment of goals among actors. There are social networks that receive opportunities of using the financial and human capital for defining the community perception. Through community structures, social control is built and a demand for complementary societal resources obtained. The environment within which business is operated too determines the culture values and strategic orientation of a business (Thornton 2011). In teaching EE, culture, human and social capitals have to be considered because they make entrepreneurship a whole. The social embeddedness view of economic and social behaviour argues that as civilisation moves further along its track of modernisation and development, economic transactions become more and more decoupled from kinship relations and are more accustomed to influential rationality. As such, it relates to the role of historically established societal, shared, tribal relations as well as cultural imprints and heritage (Tok and Kaminski 2018). In reference to Qatar, the societal embeddedness implies that entrepreneurs need to be well informed about the realities and dynamics of societal structures.

According to Tok (2017), societal embeddedness in Qatar corresponds to the social arrangements that impact and shape the actions of personalities within their corresponding communities. As such, it involves cultural embeddedness, which relates to the role of historically established societal, shared, ethnic relations and cultural heritage. Meanwhile, entrepreneurs ought to be well informed about the truth and changes in societal frameworks. So as to preserve their attachment to their societal ties and unleash more inventive and creative undertakings, entrepreneurs will gain from decision-making mindsets thus conceding societal embeddedness by matching social justice with monetary income.

Ramadani et al. (2017) opine that Islamic entrepreneurship and management are now essential in EE because Islam as a religion is now highlighting the significance of business activities which is improving the society at large with restrictions aiming to reduce harm to society. They also argue that the incorporation of the social, economic, ethical and environmental aspects is important and must be parallel to the Islamic law. Further, arguments indicate that a consideration of cultural uniqueness of Islamic markets is increasing since many people desire to be involved in business and interdisciplinary perspectives have to be considered for the right processes to be utilised in business. Islamic knowledge carries ethical values that one must learn if undertaking entrepreneurship so as to manage business well. Besides, with the internationalisation of Islam to the global market, every entrepreneur has to learn how to accommodate Islamic laws and requirements for social economic development (Ramadani et al. 2017). However, the context of a entrepreneurship is important because it offers sense, meaning and action orientation in the process (Bråten 2013).

Bråten (2013) discusses how social networks, collective obligations and demands of home communities are the influencers of economic spheres and value conversion. While the Chinese are willing to engage in business in other worlds through self-experience, the Indians are unwilling to let others on their premises and they guard business secrets because of low trust in strangers. That makes them visible in the local market than global. Local communities offer shares, comic, material space and social life that is shared in a manner that gender-age or class-specific ideas are applied in business. Similarly, wage work and flexibility are based on the readiness of local people to hire others or be hired.

A brief look at the Amish people shows that they are a humility-based entrepreneur. According to Dana (2007), Protestantism encourages self-restraint and accumulation of assets in capitalism, while Buddhists consider privatised ownership of industry and business hence favouring competition unlike Hindus, Christians and Muslims. For example, Islam teaches comprehensive holistic global development. Amish people of Pennsylvania owner partial universes where mutual accommodation, cooperation and tolerance hence resist modernisation. With the value for economic development, the

7 Locality, Leadership and Pedagogies for Entrepreneurship …

Amish have managed to maximise monetary profits in tobacco farming. However, the Amish reject government support and consider family operation; hence, they export buggies and quilts through middlemen.

Territories and Networks Territories as Tools of Embeddedness in Qatar

A different type of embeddedness relates to network affiliations in Qatar. Basically, this describes networked players and comprises the organisational and institutional capabilities that could be exploited by entrepreneurs (Tok 2017). In fact, this concept of networks has a substantial connection with that of societal embeddedness; it is obvious that some networks are formed around social bonds. In terms of territorial embeddedness, this refers to the extent to which a player is anchored in a specific place or territory. While it is obvious that economic globalisation has created a perception and a strong sense of a deterritorialised world and place, this has been losing its importance in Qatar.

To enhance young people's knowledge and their contribution to the economy, the organisation introduces learners to critical thinking, innovation and new business ideas. This gives other business organisations a chance to shape their impending workforce (Ennis 2013). To realise these objectives, INJAZ offers free training programmes that cover work readiness, entrepreneurship and financial literacy to youths in Qatar. As the largest educational partnering organisation of local business community in Qatar, INJAZ provides entrepreneurship education programmes, services, programmes in preparatory schools, high schools, universities and at youth centres across Qatar. It is increasingly recognised that leadership and entrepreneurship play an essential role in economic and social development. As a result, policy-makers, educators' researchers and practitioners have shown a specific interest in comprehending these phenomena. Leadership and entrepreneurship study have covered different aspects such as behaviours, traits, personality, skills and knowledge. Apparently, these elements are shaped by the sociocultural setting. Qatar Development Bank as the largest financial entity set up by an Emiri Decree supports SMEs in Qatar. Qatar Development Bank also provides support to entrepreneurs in starting up businesses and offers various Islamic financial products.

Qatar Business Incubation Center focuses on incubation and helps entrepreneurs in various ways to start up their business, provide supplementary services and orient towards obstacles to grow initiatives and survive in the market on a long-term basis, whereas the Qatar Finance and Business Academy aims to raise the qualities of the business environment in Qatar by offering various tailored programmes to individual and organisations. Silatech as Member of Qatar Foundation promotes job creation and economic opportunities in the MENA region. Silatech as a regional organisation emphasises innovative enterprise development with an extremely large network of organisations in the Arab world and will be contributing immensely to the communication of research findings as well as dissemination of findings to larger audiences in the Arab world. Similar ecosystems also exist in the rest of the world.

In Europe, for example, there is a rich diversity of teaching methods, approaches and strategies for delivering and managing entrepreneurship training in higher education. In the past year, entrepreneurship education has gained global significance as a lifelong learning process. At universities, the main focus of entrepreneurship education is primarily on the development of entrepreneurial skills, knowledge and attitudes that enable learners to think and act in an entrepreneurial manner by potentially realising those opportunities. In one study within the industry of tourism, Morrison (2006) found that organisational context motivates the survival of an entrepreneurship activity because it builds the structure that is instrumental in the operation and intensification of business. Moreover, the managerial capacity, emotional attachment, financial ability and potential growth are determined by organisational behaviour, the available resources and how they impact on entrepreneurial outcomes (Morrison 2006). On the other hand, Fayolle (2007) purports that there have been changes and demands in an entrepreneur's techniques and skills such that innovative and modern methods of teaching entrepreneurship are necessary. Within the cultural context, EE must intervene in the culture of various societies and how they enhance or limit business. In the institutional context, Fayolle (2007) argues that a multifaceted teaching of various paradigms that determine entrepreneurial goals and successful business ventures has to be facilitated. He also argues that the national context too ought to highlight what happens in an entire state business while the political contest trains on massive public investment and evaluation of decision-making, such as in the context of Brazil where classic economic theory has served in offering a radical change in entrepreneurship with individual and collective dreams turning into business activities and learning. The use of consultants, technicians and evaluations has fostered economic development. Furthermore, a research on women and entrepreneurship globally has emphasised on past experiences, role modelling, social learning and stereotypes that are culturally defendant so as to prevent financial stagnation. In academic institutions, both business and non-business students are now being taught entrepreneurship educations somehow.

Contemporary leaders and global agenda call for ethics because it is an aspect of great significance in economic activity and overall business practices. Be it small- or medium-sized entrepreneurship as a form of business activity that serves the social phenomenon of individuals, private and social lives of people are supported through its commercial activities (Staniewski et al. 2015). Entrepreneurship is the backbone through which many nations build the economy because employment is advanced in it. Besides, the living standards of many people are improved through entrepreneurship such that levels of social unity are promoted and the social marginalisation situation prevented. Through entrepreneurship market competition is changing and revived as more new technologies are changed, fresh products and services are created and enterprises are built. In this case, entrepreneur ethics serve in the management of the SMEs and shaping the reputation of these business activities while shaping the satisfaction, comfort and suitable setting for people working in business firms. The treatment of business structures as human organisations, the protection of the interests of the stakeholders through the defence of their respect and the provision of morally permissible aspects are imperative in offering fair play in business (Staniewski et al. 2015). Within business ethics, entrepreneurial values serve as professional assets since it is functional in operating business. Professional ethics require reflection on the standards and norms of behaviour and practice in the business profession. Entrepreneurs have particular behaviour that they exhibit towards business when they make decisions. Since business activity often requires creativity, valuing time, effort, anticipated reward, as well as risks that are involved in it (Staniewski et al. 2015). The ethical dependency aims at the constructive thought that maintains human dignity and builds honour. In the present time, people are engaging in business to grow rich; hence, their thoughts skip religious ideology with creative efforts pursued to ensure there is a generation of more money. Economics and theorists have reached a consensus that growing rich is part of the morally correct behaviour, yet it has to be constrained within particular limits of social and economic reality so as not to build negative consequences in life (Staniewski et al. 2015).

In a free market, there are democratic systems that offer rules about how business has to be conducted. However, there is no freedom to do what can harm others; hence, morally correct practices and behaviour become the keynote of a free market for it gives direction to how business people can cooperate and conduct entrepreneurship in a just manner (Staniewski et al. 2015). This aspect has resulted in making business people understand that their activities should not only be confined to making profit since safety is necessary and that makes every business entrepreneur an agent of social responsibility through which the negative effects against human well-being have to be controlled so that discrimination of social groups, destruction of the natural environment, social costs and negative effect of a business are prevented (Staniewski et al. 2015). Entrepreneurial ethics encourages the reflection of several special issues.

Based on various cultural beliefs and religious values, entrepreneurship could be perceived as illegitimate and unnatural hence not worth taking part in it. Such values share the entrepreneurial environment because it might provide or withhold resources. The legitimisation and illegitimisation also happen based on the cultural beliefs (Dana 2009). There is a belief that value orientation is a determiner of the success of entrepreneurship, and it relies on the religious or cultural norms of a society (Dana 2009). Given that religions are depositories of values and wisdom, because of the cultural foundations within them, causal relationships exist as an influencing factor that entrepreneurs can pursue. Methodists, for example, accept the differences between poor and rich people and consider trade as part and parcel of worship. There are different levels at which religious values are integrated into entrepreneurship through religions; there are value differences and specialisation on how they shape and consider entrepreneurship. Furthermore, the co-religionists' information, credit, employment and supply networks affect entrepreneurship. Through religions, entrepreneurship can have opportunities or have the entrepreneur spirit hampered due to its built-in approaches for value perpetuation. Structural functionalism considers society as interrelating and balancing its various sectors through collective norms and values. For instance, change results in an imbalance of the community and business operations.

Similarly, in reference to Thomas and Znaniecki's social perspective (Thomas et al. 1984), value must acquire social meaning and the society's overall way of life as it implicitly and distinctively influences an individual or a particular group about the possible methods, means and ends of action (Thomas et al. 1984). Among influential values are terminal and instrumental values: terminal values meaning desirable states of existence, whereas instrumental values are a means of attaining the desired objectives. Value emerges from the enduring belief that a specific way of behaviour or end-state of existence is socially or personally preferred compared to an opposite way of behaving and end of state conduct. Culture is often an integrated system of learned partners, products and behaviour or ideas on the society, and they are key towards individual achievement, power, self-direction, hedonism, conformity and tradition. Such values do determine the nature and the way social responsibility is conducted in teaching, curricula and subsequently entrepreneurship.

Different religions value entrepreneurship differently, and this translates into teaching and curricula. Among the religions that value religions, there are the Jews, Mormons, Jains and Mennonites because they encourage an economic transition. Buddhism and Christianity favour capitalism, while Islam does not because they are against competition, private property and qualifying for incentives (Dana 2009). Islam looks at the notion of development holistically, yet it never negates material development. It is therefore suited to develop a modern and knowledge-based economy where entrepreneurship must use its knowledge to pursue business.

Moreover, varied religions yield varied patterns of entrepreneurship. For example, in Europe, the Jews are said to have brought about the development of trade, and other products because the Europeans were prohibited from holding the land (Dana 2009). Since they had been discriminated against, entrepreneurship became a source of building livelihoods. On the other hand, Indian business communities evolved within particular castes and religions and followed the strictures of profit-making but treat money as neutral. Thus, their merchants have contradictory objectives of creating wealth yet frugality with religious practices, which serve in enhancing market reputation (Dana 2009). Moreover, specialisation along religious lines shapes business entrepreneurship. In certain situations, given that religious groups do specialise in particular economic sectors. When religion preaches given values, then certain products are manufactured and sold more than others in a way that business entrepreneurship is shaped in that form. In other situations, when given religious affiliation prefers a given type of business, it then picks up in the entire nation. In Morocco, it has been realised that the Muslims did silver smiting, while the Jews were practicing supplies and peddling of gold (Dana 2009).

Correspondingly, credit, information, supply and employment networks are related to marriage alliances and particular interpretations of such situations: teaching and pedagogical structures and training do need to take it into account. Thus, the network of merchants for a particular group does offer pedagogy in given finance processes among the co-religionists. Muslims in Morocco, too, conduct merchandise business and require mutual trust between peddler and supplier meaning that such co-independence services in a co-religionist financing context (Dana 2009). As for employment networks, entrepreneurship tends to hire workers from their immediate circles. On the other hand, there are entrepreneurs who prefer strangers and immigrants. Within the information networks, co-religionist groups offer credit or preferential treatment of the workforce through it. In some cases, the information is larger and is attached to family loyalty which supports both rural and urban economies. This is commonly seen in livestock merchandise where a broker is involved in the communication (Dana 2009). In London, Muslim entrepreneurs use religion and seek advice that enhances entrepreneurship. The supply networks, on the other hand, exist through the co-ethnic suppliers who offer access to low wholesale costs and retail costs enhancing competitiveness. At the end of it, there is an established intra-enclave business activity where ethnic identification serves in the entire entrepreneurship community. It is obvious that religious values and religions offer prospects for entrepreneurship because it can create needs and entrepreneurship opportunities based on the definition of when to transact business, how to produce it, what levels of profits to yield and which foodstuffs to take.

Religious beliefs do hamper entrepreneurial desire, because they are the social and cultural backbone of the people. This has to be considered when building curricula for entrepreneurs. There are religions that preach against unsatisfied desire, and this happens to come with entrepreneurship meaning material wealth could be of less importance among people from such communities whether employed or given leadership roles (Dana 2009). Somehow the Muslim is a barrier towards capital access because it does not allow payment of interest and that makes business people like Indians merchants fail in countries that are domineered by Muslims. A leader within an organisation must check on the cultural beliefs of the society and how it hampers or fosters business.

There are cases, however, where religious use built-in approaches to perpetuate values because they have co-religionists who match make or propagate certain norms. They ensure a girl is married to a man who shares a language, a dietary description, language and holidays. In such a situation, entrepreneurship is moulded in a particular way that leaders of organisations must study so as to manage business correctly (Dana 2009).

On the other hand, Zeffane (2014) argues that personality traits serve greatly in influencing entrepreneurial behaviours among which intentions and potentials fall: curricula have to properly take these elements into account. Entrepreneurs with different psychological characters might exhibit varying levels of entrepreneurial behaviours. Since the entrepreneurial process is highly 'individualistic', there has been a view that through individuals and their behaviours, a business activity can nourish or perish. This means that leaders can determine how well a company can grow or decline. On the other hand, countries in the Gulf consider collective decision-making as significant in the growth of entrepreneurial initiatives.

Collectivism and individualism make cultural dimensions through which entrepreneur processes are moulded and built. Both situational and self-efficacy attributes contribute towards social behaviour, and that is why, they impact on business development. Even though some people see entrepreneurship as synonymous with individualism, the truth is that venturing into business or having a successful business idea could be both an individualistic and/or collective process. In the individualistic situation, entrepreneurship spirit, the pursuit of business opportunities and reaction to events can be taken by one person as his or her full responsibility. Even though external aspects block success, the individual puts the 'me' or 'I' as a consideration here, but in the Arab culture one has to consider others (family, community and society). Nevertheless, corporate entrepreneurship could be built through connection with others so that they help in making the best decision, gathering better ideas and putting them into practice (Zeffane 2014).

Islamic economics has been basically part and parcel of the universal social and moral philosophy of Islam for a while. However, after the Second World War, the economic development assumed the shape of a discrete discipline reflecting on alternative approaches of post-colonial social companies, especially those that were in line with the Islamic ethos. The Islamic Ethos developed by Chapra (1970) calls upon business people to engage in business activities where moral values, socio-economic justice and human brotherhood are fostered and not Marxist or capitalist concepts that depend on the market for visualisation. This ethos depends on the integral roles of norms and organisations, families, society, market and the state to make sure that there is *Falah*, the well-being of everyone. Great emphasis focuses on social change through reformation of individuals and the society, without which the market and the nation might cause inequalities (Hassan and Lewis 2014). An evolution of the Islamic economies is associated with the Mecca economies and the importance of appreciating the market workings. The Holy Qur'an, therefore, laid down standards that were necessary for contracting. Prophet Mohammed did prohibit *riba* which is an extra charge, gambling (*maysir*) and uncertainty (*Gharar*) where an entrepreneur hides some information or creates an open space for extra charges or losses to the buyer in the contract. Besides, the *Shariah* was built as a guideline to economic life, the utilisation of analogy reasoning (*Qiyas*) and the collection of *hadith* which form the traditions (*Sunnah*) (Hassan and Lewis 2014).

For a Muslim, there is utility maximisation where revelation serves to offer knowledge on metaphysical aspects, ethics and justice. As economic theories make a person an assortment of preferences like law, actions, taste and attitudes that adjust to the cost and resource benefit changes for maximum utility, Islam sees a human being as a servant and vice-agent of God on earth, hence must have both spiritual and material focus. Thus, the concept of utility in Islamic economics covers satisfaction in which both material and spiritual utility must be realised. Furthermore, there is the extension of utility from life on earth to eternity and then the explicit recognition where communal duties and that well-being can never be attained in any real sense without worrying about the welfare of others. A faithful being has to pursue personal interests within the constraint of communal expectations and rely on moral forces of brotherhood, affection, altruism, fraternity and mutual respect, which prevent lust for riches and selfishness. Thus, for anyone taking part in an economic activity within Islamic economies, there should be a religious responsibility through which he or she pursues personal goals while complying totally with the norms and values of the community to make sure they have a privilege to similar freedoms. *Shariah* as a guideline serves the achievement of the application of human endeavours and economic resources in seeking satisfaction for both financial and social benefits (Hassan and

7 Locality, Leadership and Pedagogies for Entrepreneurship ...

Lewis 2014). Teaching needs to include all of this and have students take into account the implications of this for their own entrepreneurial practices. In consideration of the mainstreams foundations such as maximisation of gains, scarcity of resources and the pursuit of self-interest, Islam economies are built upon the views that resources as a property of God which cannot be exhausted. Likewise, even though self-interest is acceptable in Islam economies, it must remain within the social and moral Islamic boundaries so that selfishness is not the driving force. Further arguments indicate that in maximisation there should be valid methods of evaluation for efficient use of scarce resources (Hassan and Lewis 2014). The Islam honours accountability to both the community and God because it contributes towards responsibility which should reflect in the attitudes towards corruption, accounting principles, business ethics and corporate governance. All these values and cultural believes should be translated in Arab contexts as part of education of entrepreneurs.

Conclusion

To summarise, the thematic focus of the above-mentioned excursion makes a direct reference to the embeddedness of economic behaviour and invites various leading intellectuals from a wide range of fields to discuss the moral bases of entrepreneurship for a fairer world. Qatar's National Vision 2030 already identified the importance of these embedding processes. There is now a need to conduct more interdisciplinary and applied research on how these could translate into entrepreneurship education curriculum, teaching materials and other pedagogies to be used in the process. The inclusion of non-economic variables that embed economic behaviour necessitates a deconstructing and reconstructing of the relationship between moral values and the role of the community, social institutions, economy, markets and entrepreneurship.

There is a great need to study the societal, networked and territorial embeddedness in Qatar so as to develop a sustainable future for the impending generations. Given that Qatar is increasingly becoming more entrenched in the global capitalist system, there is an urgent need for the country to become more cognisant of local forms and connections between the societies and the markets. As such social entrepreneurship as a form of social embeddedness has a strong significance with Qatar National Vision 2030 and its development strategies. In essence, this vision statement together with its economic, social, human and its environmental pillars makes explicit and implicit connections to the importance of these forms of embeddedness linking traditions with modernity. While social embeddedness is based on connected individuals experiencing a common environmental reality, it is important to understand that societies and their communal subgroups exist through interaction. It is through this that different individual's experiences are shared and communal life is maintained. Given that entrepreneurs are closely tied through a diversity of social relationships to a broader network of actors, entrepreneurship has proved a fertile field in which the concept of embeddedness has taken hold and flourished. EE may be a unique opportunity to transpose these values into teaching and curricula and to implement them more effectively into entrepreneurial principles and practices.

Acknowledgement This publication was made possible in part by NPRP grant #10-1203-160007 from the Qatar National Research Fund (a member of Qatar Foundation).

References

Bråten, E. (2013). *Social sciences in Asia*. Boston: Koninklijke Brill.

Bryant, P. (2009). Self-regulation and awareness among entrepreneurs. *Journal of Business Venturing, 24*(5), 505–518.

Chapra, M. U. (1970). The economic system of Islam: A discussion of its goals and nature: Part I. *Islamic Quarterly, 14*(3), 3–18.

Chell, E., & Karataş-Özkan, M. (2014). *Handbook of research on small business and entrepreneurship*. Cheltenham: Edward Elgar.

Cox, K., & Mair, A. (1988). Locality and community in the politics of local economic Development. *Annals of the Association of American Geographers, 78*(2), 307–325.

Dana, L. (2007). A humility-based enterprising community: The Amish people in Lancaster County. *Journal of Enterprising Communities: People and Places in the Global Economy, 1*(2), 142–154.

Dana, L. (2009). Introduction: Religion as an explanatory variable for entrepreneurship and innovation. *International Journal of Entrepreneurship and Innovation, 10*(2), 1–24.

DiMaggio, P. (1994). Culture and economy. In N. Smelser & R. Swedberg (Eds.), *The handbook of economic sociology* (pp. 27–57). Princeton: Princeton University Press.

Ennis, C. (2013). Rentier 2.0: *Entrepreneurship promotion and the (re) imagination of political economy in the Gulf cooperation council countries*. Doctoral thesis, University of Waterloo, Canada.

Fayolle, A. (Ed.). (2007). *Handbook of research in entrepreneurship education: Contextual perspectives*. Cheltenham, UK: Edward Elgar.

Gangi, Y. (2017). The role of entrepreneurship education and training on creation of the knowledge economy: Qatar leap to the future. *World Journal of Entrepreneurshi, Management and Sustainable Development, 13*(4), 75–388.

Greene, P. G., Brush, C., Eisenman, E. J., Neck, H., & Perkins, S. (2014). *Entrepreneurship education: A global consideration from practice to policy around the world*. Wellesley, MA: Babson College.

Hassan, M. K., & Lewis, M. K. (2014). Islam, the economy and economic life. In M. K. Hassan & M. K. Lewis (Eds.), *Handbook on Islam and economic life* (pp. 1–18). Cheltenham: Edward Elgar.

Hägg, G., & Kurczewska, A. (2016). Connecting the dots: A discussion on key concepts in contemporary entrepreneurship education. *Education & Training, 58*(7/8), 700–714.

Hess, M. (2004). Spatial relationships: Towards a re-conceptualization of embeddedness. *Progress in Human Geography, 28*(2), 165–186.

Morrison, A. (2006). A contextualization of entrepreneurship. *International Journal of Entrepreneurial Behaviour & Research, 12*(1), 192–209.

Periz-Otiz, M., & Merigó-Lindahl, J. M. (2015). *Entrepreneurship, regional development, and culture: An institutional perspective*. New York: Springer International.

Pistrui, D., & Fahed-Sreih, J. (2010). Islam, entrepreneurship and business values in the Middle East. *Journal of Entrepreneurship and Innovation Management, 12*(1), 107–120.

Ramadani, V., Dana, L., Geurguri-Rashiti, S., & Ratten, V. (2017). *Entrepreneurship and management in an Islamic context*. Switzerland: Springer International.

Roomi, M. (2011). Entrepreneurial capital, social values and Islamic traditions: Exploring the growth of women-owned enterprises in Pakistan. *International Small Business Journal, 31*(2), 175–191.

Roomi, M., & Harrison, P. (2011). Entrepreneurial leadership: What is it and how should it be taught? *International Review of Entrepreneurship, 9*(3), 1–44.

Staniewski, M. W., Slomski, W., & Awruk, K. (2015). Ethical aspects of entrepreneurship. *Filosofija Sociologica, 26*(1), 37–45.

Swedberg, R. (2003). The case for economic sociology of law. *Theory and Society, 32*(1), 1–37.

Thomas, W. I., Znaniecki, F., & Strübing, J. (1984). *The polish peasant in Europe and America.* Urbana: University of Illinois Press.

Thornton, P. (2011). Socio-cultural and entrepreneurial activity: An overview. *International Small Business Journal, 29*(2), 105–118.

Tok, M. E. (2017). States, markets, and communities: Rethinking sustainability and cities. *Q Science Connect.* https://doi.org/10.5339/connect.2017.qgbc.7.

Tok, M.E., & Kaminski, J.J. (2018). Islam, entrepreneurship, and embeddedness. *Thunderbird International Business Review.* https://doi.org/10.1002/tie.21970.

Volkmann, C. K., & Audretsch, D. B. (Eds.). (2017). *Entrepreneurship education at universities: Learning from 20 European cases.* Bloomington: Springer International.

Zeffane, R. (2014). Does collectivism necessarily negate the spirit of entrepreneurship? *International Journal of Entrepreneurial Behavior & Research, 20*(3), 1–20.

M. Evren Tok received his MA and Ph.D. from Carleton University, Ottawa, Canada. His MA was in political economy, and his Ph.D. was a collaborative degree in public policy and political economy. He is currently Faculty Member in the Public Policy Programme in the Qatar Faculty of Islamic Studies and has been acting as Co-Lead Investigator in grants looking into various corporate social responsibility practices globally and in studying the entrepreneurship, ethics and values nexus. More recently, He organised a conference in Doha entitled Public Policy, Entrepreneurship and Education Nexus in February 2017. His most recent publication in collaboration with Leslie Pal and Lolwah Al Khater is an edited volume looking into the policy-making dynamics in Qatar, the first and only academic study bringing together Qatari perspectives by Qatari scholars in Qatar. He also teaches courses on ethics and entrepreneurship, and his courses had a social enterprise development requisite, through which have resulted in various entrepreneurship projects by his graduate students, many of which were showcased during the visit of the Higher Education Institute's visit to Qatar Faculty of Islamic Studies in May 2016.

Cristina D'Alessandro is Senior Fellow at the Centre on Governance of the University of Ottawa (Canada), Research Fellow at the Research Centre PRODIG (Université Paris 1 Panthéon Sorbonnne, CNRS), and Affiliate Associate Professor at Riara University in Nairobi, Kenya. She has more than twenty years teaching and research experience with qualifications in political, economics and public policy. She has been Guest Lecturer at the Paris School of International Affairs, the University Bordeaux Montaigne in France, Sciences-Politique Grenoble, the University of Bergamo, the University of Milan, and the University of Cyprus among others. With a strong academic and policy research background, she serves as an international consultant with various organisations and institutions, including the African Capacity Building Foundation, African Development Bank, UN Woman, the United Nations Economic Commission for Africa, the BMW Foundation, and the Qatar National Research Fund, delivering presentations, attending conferences, preparing policy documents and reports, and serves as an expert and advisor in Africa, Europe and the USA. Previously, she served as Scientific Manager at the French National Agency for Research, as Professor at the Paris School of International Affairs (Sciences Po, Paris, France), as Knowledge Expert at the African Capacity Building Foundation in Harare (Zimbabwe) and as Professor at the University Lumière Lyon 2. She serves on the boards of *Canadian Journal* *of Development Studies*, *L'Espace politique*, the *African Geographical Review* and the journal *EspacesTemps.net*. She has published books and papers extensively in French, English and Italian. Her work focuses on urban planning, management and transformation, natural resource and environmental governance, political, economic and territorial governance, institutional capacity building and leadership.

Part III
Country Cases

Chapter 8
The 'Westernised' Map of the Field of Educational Administration in Turkey and Dominant Perspectives in School Leadership Education

Kadir Beycioglu, Ali Çağatay Kılınç and Mahmut Polatcan

Abstract Although the development of educational administration has remained on the agenda for over a half century, it is apparent that the field has encountered a number of problems in Turkey. Strategies, legislative regulations, and various practices over school administrators' training and assignment have long been debated, and problems encountered in school administration as long-term policies on the training and assignment of school principals could not be developed. This study focuses on the historical development of school administrators' training and assignments in Turkey and on school administrators' behaviours from Hofstede's cultural perspective. Finally, a centralist approach in public administration and the understanding that teaching is the basis for being a school administrator which denotes that no formal in-service education is required for being appointed as a school administrator are two main factors that inhibit the development of school administration as a professional field in Turkey. Furthermore, the fact that school administrator practices have changed repeatedly in an inconsistent manner and that the common public opinion that exams for assignment of school administrators are far from objectivity come under criticism for a considerable amount of time in Turkey. On the other hand, in the context of Hofstede's culture dimensions, it is possible to argue that the schools accept a large degree of power distance and feel uncomfortable with uncertainty. It is also reasonable to suggest that school administrators build stronger and healthier ties with other staff in the dimensions of collectivity, femininity, and indulgence.

K. Beycioglu (✉)
Faculty of Education, Dokuz Eylul University, Buca, Izmir, Turkey
e-mail: beycioglu@gmail.com

A. Ç. Kılınç · M. Polatcan
Department of Educational Sciences,Faculty of Letters, Karabuk University, Karabuk, Turkey
e-mail: cagataykilinc@karabuk.edu.tr

M. Polatcan
e-mail: mpolatcan@karabuk.edu.tr

© Springer Nature Singapore Pte Ltd. 2019
E. A. Samier and E. S. ElKaleh (eds.), *Teaching Educational Leadership in Muslim Countries*, Educational Leadership Theory,
https://doi.org/10.1007/978-981-13-6818-9_8

Introduction

In the second half of the last century, educational administration became a scholarly field (Dimmock and Walker 1998a; Evers and Lakomski 1994; Gunter 2003). According to Hallinger and Leithwood (1996), recent years 'have been a time of questioning and introspection in the field of educational administration' (p. 98). As for Dimmock and Walker (1998b), the field 'as a field of research and practice has grown impressively over the last few decades.' (p. 379) and has been developing its theories and ethos.

While the field has been trying to construct a place for itself, there also have been different issues on the agenda of scholars in the field of educational administration. For example, English (2002), in his challenging article entitled 'The Point of Scientificity, the Fall of the Epistemological Dominos, and the End of the Field of Educational Administration', uses various symbols to refer to the issues in the field. Similarly, Maxcy (2001) points out that 'No one much cares about a science of educational administration anymore'. Besides, Leithwood and Duke (1999) report that the scholars of the field have remarkably concentrated extensively on leadership and school leaders. Of them, principal/leadership preparation is one of the most discussed issues among scholars in different contexts. Donmoyer (2001) and Beycioğlu (2012) speculated that some have been in search of a 'Holy Grail' to find a new way of leadership preparation or as Maxcy (2001, p. 575) explained, to find a 'solution to the errors of past theoretical systems'. In the end, we can claim that it is widely accepted that principal leadership is a key factor in schools and school effectiveness that begs the question of leadership preparation. The related literature provides us a summary of what is known about the preparation of principals from a range of educational settings, and educational researchers have emphasised that context matters in leadership preparation (Beycioğlu and Wildy 2015). As Middlewood (2010) argues, what principals can do depends on what they may do and this, in turn, is shaped by the educational system in which they work and by the local context (Huber and West 2002; Lumby et al. 2009; McCarthy 1999; Smylie and Bennett 2005).

In this chapter, we aim to provide a brief historical overview of the Turkish field, which is generally regarded as a field under the influences of Anglo-American perspectives, and the dominant leadership preparation approaches and practices in Turkey. We also aim to determine to what extent the culture and values of society affect the preparation of educational leaders based on Hofstede's (2001) cultural dimension theory that claims that cultures have various effects on organisations and individuals. By doing this, with the benefits of cross-cultural and cross-context studies of principal preparation in mind, the aim of this chapter is to contribute to the field from the perspective of the Turkish context as a Muslim and relatively a 'secular' country.

A Brief History of the Emergence and Development of Educational Administration in Turkey

It can be argued that the development levels of countries are related to the education systems they have as the quality of the education system of a country affects its economic growth, cultural development and political prestige in the international arena. As a matter of fact, most people base their countries' breakthroughs in different fields of education. The success of the economist who manages the economy or the politician who governs a country is directly proportional to the quality of education provided in this country. In this context, the improvement of the quality of education depends on the good administration of the system. The better the system is managed, the more the quality of education is expected to increase. In this regard, it can be said that although some advances have been made in the area of educational administration in Turkish Education System, the efforts on specialisation initiatives in the field are inadequate. It may be stated that the tendency can be summarised as 'being a teacher is the basis in the profession' restricts the development of the educational administration field.

Developments in the field of administrative studies have been reflected in the field of educational administration which is a sub-field and have led to the change of this field. Especially, with globalisation since the last quarter of the twentieth century, developments such as the information society, neoliberalism, multiculturalism, and standardisation have forced the field of educational administration to change. These developments have led to the creation of new expectations about the knowledge and skills of education and school leaders. This situation obliges the institutions training the education leaders to reorganise not only the curriculum but also the scope and methods of teaching (Balcı 2011). It can be stated that Turkey, which models the advanced Western countries in their founding philosophies, has also been affected by this development and change efforts. Moreover, it can be said that much research and many meetings for the development of educational administration are on the agenda. As stated in the literature, it is clear that some important decisions and practices taken by the authorities in the development process of educational administration are related to the results of such studies (Şimşek 2002; Üstüner and Cömert 2008).

There are debates as to whether or not educational administration will be an academic field (Balcı 2008; Örücü and Şimşek 2011). Balcı (2008) argues that educational administration is an academic field within the scope of the discussions in the literature. According to the author, the departments and the units of the field at universities, requiring expertise, conducting scholarly research, the presence of academic journals, and the organisations of members working in the field are indicative of educational administration as an academic field. However, Balcı points out that the discussion of whether educational administration in Turkey is a profession or an academic field is hidden in the historical roots of the field. As a matter of fact, the establishment of the Educational Administration Research and Development Association (EARDA), the Training Managers and Specialists Association (TMSA), the National Educational Administration Congresses (since 2001), and the National Council of

Professors of Educational Administration (NCPEA) meetings and reports can be evaluated as the indicators of the formation of an academic organisation in the field (Örücü and Şimşek 2011). According to Şimşek (2002) who categorises educational administration as a practice-oriented academic discipline, educational administration is a field of application of educational organisations' intended policies and decisions taken by using human and material resources effectively in accordance with the determined targets.

Policies and practices for the training of school administrators in Turkey have been the focus of a series of research projects (Acar 2002; Aksoy 2002; Ayral 2016; Balcı and Çınkır 2002; Balyer and Gündüz 2011; Işık 2002; Süngü 2012; Şimşek 2002; Şişman and Turan 2002). Research draws attention to the lack of continuity in the training and assignment policies of educational administrators in Turkey (Karabatak 2015). It can be clearly seen that concrete and coherent policies towards the training and assignment policies or practices of school administrators are not followed in other contexts either (Çelik 2002; Çınkır 2002; Özmen 2002; Şişman and Turan 2002). On the other hand, despite Turkey having a well-established management tradition of public administration, it is difficult to claim that it has a systematic structure for training and assignment of education/school administrators (Acar 2002; Balcı 2002; Şimşek 2002). Beycioğlu and Dönmez (2006) identified the problems that have been experienced in the field of educational administration in Turkey to be the lack of an effective consensus on the production of theoretical knowledge, of boundaries between the theories, of theories with practical applications, of sufficient theoretical resources, and of a disconnection between academicians. Most of the initiatives for training and assignment of school administrators are constantly being changed in line with the ideological aims of the dominant powers that hold enforcement. This finding verifies that although there are many different applied models for training and assignment of administrators in Turkey to the present time, there is not a national policy for the training of professional administrators (Baş and Şentürk 2017). As a matter of fact, the research conducted in this subject mostly refers to the training and assignment policies and practices of educational administrators in the developed countries (Balcı 2011; Pehlivan Aydın 2002; Çınkır 2002; Özmen 2002; Şişman and Turan 2002).

It can be reported that Turkey, which has 60 years of tradition for training and assignment policies of educational administrators, has prepared many legal texts (Beycioğlu and Wildy 2015) including advisory reports, regulations, and training programmes for educational administrators. With the establishment of the Republic of Turkey, one of the main focuses of Atatürk's era, who made great strides in terms of economic and political development, was education. Indeed, the first great revolution of the Founding President Atatürk who wants to adopt advanced Western educational practices in was Act no. 430 'Unification of the Educational System'. Later, the establishment of the 'Secondary Teacher Training School' (Gazi Education Faculty) in 1926 constituted a step in the specialisation period in education. In addition, Atatürk invited John Dewey, an important American educator, and requested him to prepare a comprehensive report about the Turkish education system. Some issues about the training of school administrators were addressed in this report which included several findings such as the budget of the education system, training practices, teacher training, and curriculum practices. In subsequent periods, an institution, the Public Administration Institute for Turkey and Middle East (PAITME), was founded in order to follow the developments in the field of public administration in Turkey and conduct research on the management of public institutions (Beycioğlu and Wildy 2015; Recepoğlu and Kılınç 2014). For example, the reports of PAITME's Central Government Organization Research Project (MEHTAP) and Public Administration Research Project (KAYA) produced decisions and proposed solutions in all areas of public administration (education, health, culture, etc.) which are among the important milestones on administrative issues in Turkey. In addition, there were some decisions made about training educational administrators during the IV National Education Council, an advisory authority that produces proposals for solving problems in the Turkish Education System. Decisions and revised practices concerning the training and assignment of educational administrators in legal texts are very important in revealing the state of educational administration. In this context, it is necessary to address these extensive studies and practices for the training and assignment of education/school administrators (KAYA 1991; MEHTAP 1963).

In Dewey's Education Report on the restructuring of the education system of the Republic of Turkey, there is not an enlightening explanation for the training of educational administrators. However, it was emphasised that requiring budgetary expenditure from the upper-level ministry units for record keeping, building/facility maintenance, and repair expenses under the school principals' responsibility rather than training the school administrators causes unnecessary time and wastes energy. Therefore, this situation prevents school principals from spending energy on teaching tasks. Meanwhile, in order to resolve this problem, the assignment of two different principals, one for education and the other for administrative duties, in the schools especially in large cities was recommended (Dewey 1939).

It is clear that some of the recommendations in the MEHTAP, an advisory report on the training of educational administrators in Turkey, have been put into practice. This report's findings regarding qualifications of educational administrators at various levels of the Ministry of National Education (MoNE) are remarkable. The report documents the majority of administrators who work for state schools and are professionally trained teachers. They are expected to play important roles because of a lack of expertise in educational administration, educational policies, and economic goals. Therefore, educational administrators who work in these positions need to be experts in the field. In this respect, it is not absolutely necessary for them to come from the teaching profession; however, it may be important to have teaching experience to be a school administrator at many levels of school. Ultimately, it was proposed that education faculties and departments in this area of expertise were opened to train educational administrators who would work in many positions of MoNE (MEHTAP 1963). Following the publication of this report, education faculties (Ankara University Faculty of Educational Sciences) and departments which train educational administrators (Hacettepe University, Department of Education) were opened (Eğitim-Bir-Sen 2017).

In the PAITME's KAYA report (1991) on the current status of the national education system, it was proposed that legal arrangements for the employment of experts and administrators working in teaching services were made. Accordingly, it is necessary to make arrangements for major branches (educational administration, educational psychology, educational planning, measurement and evaluation, curriculum development, etc.) which have arisen in the field. According to the report, these regulations will clarify the status, duties, and authorities in the field (1991). On the other hand, although there are various opinions on the training of the educational administrators in some national education, the training has become the main agenda item in the IV National Education Council (Eğitim-Bir-Sen 2017). In the council, it is proposed to increase the power of administrators and qualifications in educational administration, hierarchical progress, and promotion in the profession. In this context, it was decided that the cooperation with universities in the training of existing educational administrators and admission of the persons who have educational administration qualifications should be considered (Decisions of IV National Education Council 1993).

As a result, it can be said that educational administration in Turkey started with the MEHTAP report. Due to the report's recommendations, educational administration started to be established as an academic discipline at state universities. Undergraduate programme training students in Educational Administration, Supervision, Planning and Economics were closed in 1997 (Recepoğlu and Kılınç 2014; Üstüner and Cömert 2008). Şimşek (1997, 2002) indicates that the field in Turkey, which was created with great effort, cannot keep up with contemporary developments in the world, thereby remaining weak because of a centralised view of education, the traditional gap between theory and practice, and communication and cooperation problems between universities. Today, the field is represented by a course entitled 'The Turkish Education System and School Administration' given at the undergraduate level (Balcı 2011).

One Step Forward Two Steps Back: The Preparation and Appointment of School Leaders in Turkey

School organisations have to reform themselves according to the need for change that arises due to academic developments. Indeed, with the emergence of the concept of school effectiveness or improvement or achievement (keeping in mind that the meanings of concepts may differ from one culture to another and here we use effectiveness) traditional school understanding has given way to contemporary school approaches. Besides having good teachers, one of the other dominant factors, for many scholars, in the effectiveness of schools is the school administrator. In this respect, the fulfilment of expected roles and duties from school administrators depends on the quality of education they had. Within this scope, the training of education and school administrators in the context of educational administration expertise in the Turkish education system is ignored or not considered an important field by political makers (Balcı 2011). Because of this, the practices in selecting and assigning school principals have been a subject of constant debate. The relations between those who have been assigned as education/school administrators and the government have significant influences in the assignment process which results in poor management by non-specialist school administrators. However, contemporary education/school administration is a challenging field of study requiring expertise (Balcı 2008).

A number of solutions have been proposed for the training and appointment of school administrators in many studies conducted in Turkey. The suggestions in most of these have similar features: providing in-service training and graduate education programmes for school principals, curriculum development studies for the training of educational administrators, establishment of cooperation between academics and experienced managers in the training and assignment of administrators, developmental leadership after teaching experience, counselling, organisational structuring, effective organisation, implementation of curriculum in staff development areas, the inclusion of the candidates selected according to the results of written and oral examinations conducted by an academic committee in-service training programmes, an assignment system based on examination, the requirement of professional qualifications, and leadership traits and merit (Ezgün 2011; Aslanargun 2011; Altınay 2013; Aktepe 2014; Balcı and Çınkır 2002; Balyer and Gündüz 2011; Çelik 2002; Çetin and Yalçın 2002).

The training and assignment of school administrators have also been included in the legal regulations. The statement, 'Only the teachers and supervisors shall be assigned to the vocational services of the Ministry of National Education and school administrations' in the 18th article of the Act on the Organisation of the Ministry of National Education (1926) showed for the first time that school administration is not accepted as a profession, and those assigned to these positions are teachers or educators. This has been one of the obstacles to the professionalisation of educational administration in Turkey, hindering its development in the next periods, partly because educational administration has been perceived to be a temporary task (Eğitim-Bir-Sen 2017). The assignment of school administrators in the Turkish Education System has been determined by a number of regulations issued regularly from 1998 to 2018. Despite the criteria for determining the importance of knowledge, skill, and merit in their assignment, the general social tendency is that objectivity is ignored in the assignments.

In Turkey, the specialisation and examination practices to become an administrator in educational institutions came into force with the regulation on assignment and relocation of the administrators of educational institutions affiliated to the Ministry of National Education in 1998; in this context, objective evaluation criteria have been introduced in the assignment of school administrators requiring that teachers have at least five years of teaching experience to apply to the selection examination. Candidates who succeeded in the examination participated in a 120 h administrator training course which included theories of Westernised and/or Anglo-American perspectives on training school principals. On the other hand, according to the regulation, teachers who have at least five years of teaching experience and have graduated from the department of educational administration or PAITME public administration graduate programmes were exempted from the candidate selection test and taken directly into the courses. Candidates who succeeded in the assessment test after administrator training were entitled to be appointed as school administrators (Official Gazette 1998).

Vice principals who needed to be assigned according to the examinations and some career steps of school principals were determined as well. Regulation in Official Gazette (2004) stated that the duties of the administrators who have completed the four-year period of office cannot be administrator in the same educational institution with the same title for more than eight years. In the evaluation form appended to the regulation, there are seven different evaluators for the educational administrators, whose period of office will be extended, consisting of the district director of national education, department chief who is responsible for human resources in the directorship of national education, department chief who is responsible for the educational institution to be evaluated, the most senior teacher in the educational institution, the teacher who has the least seniority in the educational institution, two teachers to be selected by the teachers' council, the president and vice president of the parent–teacher association, and the president of the student council.

Official Gazette (2007) can be considered as one step back because with the arrangements, the examination process in the selection of the school principal was cancelled and completing the candidateship of the teachers was seen enough in order to be assigned as a school principal. With the amendments published in the Official Gazette (2008), the administrator evaluation form was redesigned governing the appointment of school principals. Official Gazette (2009) reinstated the examination process and required at least eight years of teaching experience as a condition for assignment as a school principal. With the amendment made in the previous regulations, the duration of an appointment was limited to eight years and the condition of compulsory relocation depended upon the decision of the principal (Official Gazette 2004, 2007, 2008, 2013).

In addition, in the regulation on the appointment and relocation of administrators working in educational institutions affiliated to the Ministry of National Education in 2014 it was required that administrative duty is carried out within the scope of laws no. 657 and no. 652. Some conditions were required for those assigned as administrators: graduation from higher education, working as a teacher in the Ministry's institutions, having the required qualifications to be assigned as a teacher at the date of appointment, and being not suspended from his administration duty as a result of a judicial or administrative investigation in the previous four years of the assignment date. Moreover, those who will be appointed are required to have at least one of these conditions: served as principal or principal chief assistant for at least two years; as a founding principal, principal chief assistant, assistant principal or teacher having principal authorisation for a total of three years in the same or multiple positions; as department chief apart from the Ministry's education and training services or superior positions; or as tenured teacher in the Ministry for at least eight years (Official Gazette 2014).

Differently from the previous regulation, by 2007 at least four years of teaching was required for the appointment of administrators working in educational institutions affiliated to the Ministry of National Education. It was aimed to appoint the principal candidates based on written–oral examinations and an administration evaluation form. Written examination weights in the regulation are listed as information about regulations, analytical thinking and ability to perform analysis, the level of representability and merit, reasoning power and understanding skill, communication skills, self-confidence and ability of persuasion, liberal education, Ataturk's principles and reforms. The minimum passing score in the oral assessment was set at 60. Finally, in the 2018 regulation, at least one year of experience as a principal, assistant principal, or teacher having principal authorisation or experience as a department chief or superior positions in the central organisation of the ministry was required (Official Gazette 2017, 2018).

As a result, the assignment of school principals and assistant principals was determined by the regulations in Turkey. The fact that these regulations have been frequently changed shows that the central government has not developed a healthy and sustainable policy in the training and appointment of administrators. The common point in the appointment of directors in all regulations is the requirement of being a teacher. This is an indication that the concept of 'being a teacher is the basis in the profession' is reflected in the regulations. However, there are ambiguities about the extent to which examinations measure the qualifications of contemporary school administrators. In addition, it cannot be said that the public is sufficiently satisfied with the criteria of the oral examinations and transparency.

Hofstede's Culture Dimensions and School Principalship in Turkey: A Quick Evaluation

Culture is expressed as the lifestyles of societies. According to Balcı (2007), it is a set of premises, beliefs, and values that are applied consciously, semi-consciously, or unconsciously in a society. Tezcan (1985) refers to culture as a combination of material and spiritual values that people have created to adapt to the environment they live in. Hofstede (1997) described culture as a conventional mental software, viewing it not as heritage, but as acquired later on in life. Culture is the whole set of meanings that are accepted in a society over a certain period of time. The reflections of culture are symbols, languages, faiths, rituals, and myths (Hoy and Miskel 2010).

Cultural models such as Schein and Geert Hofstede's dimensions of the national culture model have been developed in the organisational culture literature (Eren 2004; Erkmen 2011; Özkalp and Kırel 2000; Şişman 2007). In dimensions of the national culture model developed through a research carried out with more than 100,000 IBM employees in more than 40 countries, Hofstede argues that administrative practices and theories are inevitably tied to national culture since they affect the business environment. Hofstede used a number of dimension continua to classify national organisations: power distance, uncertainty avoidance, individualism versus collectivism, long-term orientation versus short-term normative orientation, indulgence versus restraint, and masculinity versus femininity (Hofstede 1997, 2001). Power distance is about whether the power between employees is distributed equally or not. Uncertainty avoidance measure shows individuals behave in cases of uncertainty. Countries with high uncertainty avoidance tend to maintain rigid rules and structures in order to provide control, whereas those with weak uncertainty avoidance are less concerned with the structure and they show a greater tolerance for risk taking. Individualism versus collectivism focuses on social needs, group belonging, and loyalty, whereas high individualism attaches importance to individuals with autonomy and self-confidence. Long-term orientation versus short-term normative orientation is concerned with the degree of accepting the cultural values of the society. In indulgence versus restraint dimension which is the fifth one, cultures are divided into two as indulgent and restrictive. Finally, in the context of masculinity versus femininity, males are overwhelmed in the administrative positions in the societies where the masculinity level is high.

Turkey's scores on the Hofstede index are high on power distance and uncertainty avoidance, moderate in indulgence, masculinity, and long-term orientation, and low on individualism (Hofstede 2018). One of the aims of education is to transfer the distinctive culture of the countries to its citizens. Therefore, education and in particular, training educational administrators should be consistent with the social structure and culture of the society even in a country that does not provide structured professional training programs for principals such as Turkey. Şahin et al. (2017) pointed out that there are cultural differences in the training and appointment of school leaders in their study about the school leadership research. The culture of the school, which is a subsystem of education, consists largely of unwritten rules of the school. The values, norms, traditions, beliefs, and symbols of the school are the basic elements that make up the school culture (Bursalıoğlu 2010). A strong school culture arises as a result of the unity of the administrators and teachers around common values, norms, and beliefs which can also prevent the formation of harmful subcultures. School administrators can lead school cultures consciously or unconsciously through their practices. A school administrator who knows the power of school cultures can show a more successful organisational culture as Hosftede index also classified the culture in Turkey as a collectivist one that may help principals to create a collaborative school culture. As culture arbiter, administrators should set a philosophy and vision that reflects the belief that all learners can learn in schools. This understanding should not be determined and expressed only by the administrator, it should be done in a discussion platform, and a compromise must be reached on it (Çelik 2009).

Hofstede relates the low level of power distance and uncertainty avoidance which are the dimensions of culture to high level of justice among stakeholders, participation in decision-making processes, and trust and cooperation among employees. It was found in a number of studies that school administrators are not fair at a high-level justice in many researches about the behaviours of school administrators in schools in Turkey (Ay and Koç 2014; Altınkurt and Yılmaz 2010; Baş and Şentürk 2017; Oğuz 2011; Yılmaz and Taşdan 2009); employees do not have a high level of confidence in their administrators (Ercan 2006; Gören and Özdemir 2015; Öksüzoğlu 2012; Öztürk and Aydın 2012; Taşdan 2012); the participation level of employees is not at a high level, and they do not go beyond the regulations (Can and Serençelik 2017; Demirtaş and Alanoğlu 2015; Özdoğru and Aydın 2012). This situation can be explained by school principals tending to exhibit the behaviours of traditional authoritarian school principals. However, it has been found that school principals show democratic leadership behaviours in many researches on leadership behaviours exhibited by school administrators (Bozdoğan and Sağnak 2011; Terzi and Çelik 2016). At this point, the contradictions between the results obtained in organisational culture research in Turkey have come to light. As a matter of fact, Hofstede (2001) argued that the low level of power distance and uncertainty avoidance is indicative of administrators demonstrating democratic leadership behaviours.

It can be concluded that school principals in Turkey give prominence to collective interest rather than individualism. In many studies, it has found that school principals exhibit value-based leadership and distributive leadership behaviours and share their responsibilities with teachers. These results support Hofstede's (1997, 2001) finding in analysing cultural dimensions that Turkish society is a collective society. Indeed, some studies report that school principals in Turkey share decisions, collaborate with each other, and establish a sincere relationship with their workmates; as a result, the findings point that educational institutions show characteristics of feminine culture (Baloğlu 2012; Korkmaz and Gündüz 2011; Yılmaz and Turan 2015). Çelikten (2004) investigated the small number of female school principals in Turkey and attributed the reasons to a lack of self-confidence of female principals, not being supported by the social environment, and an inability to choose between work and family.

Conclusion

In this conceptual paper, the historical development process of training and appointing school administrators and the behaviours of school administrators were discussed. In this context, a great deal of research has been done on the training and appointment of school principals in Turkey.

Although some have been done by the central government for the training of school administrators in Turkey, many have not been taken into consideration or have been delayed in the following periods. As a matter of fact, Dewey's suggestion for the training of school administrators remains superficial. However, in National Education Councils in the following periods and in the reports of MEHTAP and KAYA projects published by PAITME, it was demonstrated that school administration is a professional job and the individuals involved should be educated. Some school administrator training practices have been put into practice in line with the recommendations of these reports; however, in the following years, these practices were not maintained due to the understanding that 'school administration is not a profession'.

The selection and appointment of the persons who will be assigned as school principals and vice principals in Turkey are realised through regulations. The fact that these regulations are frequently changed shows that the central government cannot develop a policy for the training and appointment of administrators. The common point in all regulations in terms of the appointment of administrators is the requirement of being a teacher. This is an indication that the concept of 'being a teacher is the basis in the profession' is reflected in the regulations. However, it can be said that there are ambiguities about the extent to which examinations measure the qualifications of contemporary school administrators. In addition to this, it cannot be said that the public is sufficiently satisfied with the criteria of the oral examinations and the transparency of the process.

Finally, the assumption that leadership behaviours of school administrators in Turkey are influenced by the culture of the community is addressed in the context of the National Cultural Dimensions of Hofstede. No studies yet have been done on schools using Hofstede's dimensions of power distance, associated with justice, equality and trust, and uncertainty avoidance. In this regard, it can be said that the level of power distance and uncertainty avoidance is high in the relationship of school administrators in Turkey. However, many studies have found that school principals incorporate employees into decision-making, cooperate with each other, and establish a sincere relationship with their workmates. These results can be expressed in terms of collectivism, femininity, and indulgence from the dimensions Hofstede's model includes. When training education administrators is considered, it can be argued that programmes should be sensitive to cultural dimensions of the country context. As we previously indicated in this chapter, Turkish education system does not have a regular training programme for newly appointed educational administrators before service. They sometimes participate in local trainings that generally do not have core scopes of developing educational administrators. So, if any programme is provided in future, the above-debated issues could be considered in a possible curriculum.

References

Acar, H. (2002). 21. yüzyıla girerken Millî Eğitim Bakanlığı'nda eğitim yöneticilerinin yetiştirilmesi ve geliştirilmesinde yeni yaklaşımlar. In C. Elma & Ş. Çınkır (Eds.), 21. *Yüzyıl eğitim yöneticilerinin yetiştirilmesi sempozyumu bildirileri kitabı* (ss. 179–194). Ankara: Ankara Üniversitesi Eğitim Bilimleri Fakültesi Yayınları.

Aksoy, H. H. (2002). ABD 'de eğitim yöneticilerinin istihdamında aranan nitelikler, koşullar ve ücretleri. In C. Elma & Ş. Çınkır (Eds.), 21. *Yüzyıl eğitim yöneticilerinin yetiştirilmesi sempozyumu bildirileri kitabı* (ss. 255–274). Ankara: Ankara Üniversitesi Eğitim Bilimleri Fakültesi Yayınları.

Aktepe, V. (2014). Okul yöneticilerinin seçme ve yetiştirme uygulamalarına yönelik öğretmen ve yönetici görüşleri. *Turkish Studies, 9*(2), 89–105.

Altınay, E. (2013). *Okul yöneticileri ve öğretmenlerin eğitim kurumlarına yönetici atamaya ilişkin görüşlerinin incelenmesi (İzmir ili Çiğli ilçesi örneği)*. Okan Üniversitesi Sosyal Bilimler Enstitüsü, İstanbul: Yüksek Lisans Tezi.

8 The 'Westernised' Map of the Field of Educational ...

Altınkurt, Y., & Yılmaz, K. (2010). Examining the relationship between management by values and organizational justice by secondary school teachers perceptions. *Educational Administration: Theory and Practice, 16*(4), 463–485.

Aslanargun, E. (2011). Türkiye'de okul yönetimi ve atama yönetmelikleri. *E-Journal of New World Sciences Academy, 6*(4), 2646–2659.

Ay, G., & Koç, H. (2014). Determine the relation between perception of organizational justice and level of organizational commitment: study case of teachers. *Journal of Business Turk, 6*(2), 67–90.

Ayral, M. (2016). Okul müdürü yetiştirmede 2015: Sorunlar ve gelecek. In A. Aypay (Ed.), *Türkiye'de Eğitim Yöneticileri ve Maarif Müfettişleri Seçme, Atama ve Yetiştirme* (ss. 113–144). Ankara: Pegem Akademi.

Balcı, A. (2002). Türkiye 'de eğitim yöneticilerinin yetiştirilmesi. In C. Elma & Ş. Çınkır (Eds.), 21. *Yüzyıl eğitim yöneticilerinin yetiştirilmesi sempozyumu bildirileri kitabı* (ss. 327–330). Ankara: Ankara Üniversitesi Eğitim Bilimleri Fakültesi Yayınları.

Balcı, A. (2007). *Örgüt mecazları*. Ankara: Ekinoks Yayınları.

Balcı, A. (2008). Türkiye'de eğitim yönetiminin bilimleşme düzeyi. *Kuram ve Uygulamada Eğitim Yönetimi Dergisi, 14*(2), 181–209.

Balcı, A. (2011). The changing context of educational administration and its effects on educational administration postgraduate programmes. *Education and Science, 36*(162), 197–208.

Balcı, A., & Çınkır, Ş. (2002). Türkiye'de eğitim yöneticilerinin yetiştirilmesi. In C. Elma & Ş. Çınkır (Eds.), 21. *yüzyıl eğitim yöneticilerinin yetiştirilmesi sempozyumu bildirileri kitabı* (ss. 211–236). Ankara: Ankara Üniversitesi Eğitim Bilimleri Fakültesi Yayınları.

Baloğlu, N. (2012). Relations between value-based leadership and distributed leadership a casual research on school principles' behaviors. *Educational Sciences: Theory & Practice, 12*(2), 1367–1378.

Balyer, A., & Gündüz, Y. (2011). Training school principals in different countries: A new model proposal for the Turkish Educational System. *Journal of Theoretical Educational Sciences, 4*(2), 182–197.

Baş, E. A., & Şentürk, İ. (2017). The viewpoints of school administrators about the regulation for the assignment of principals in education institution associated with the ministry of education released. *Ondokuzmayis University Journal of Education, 36*(2), 119–143.

Beycioğlu, K. (2012). Will evers and Lakomski be able to find leadership's Holy Grail. *KEDI Journal of Educational Policy, 9*(2), 349–362.

Beycioğlu, K., & Dönmez, B. (2006). Issues in theory development and practice in educational administration. *Educational Administration: Theory and Practice, 47*(47), 317–342.

Beycioğlu, K., & Wildy, H. (2015). Principal preparation: The case of novice principals in Turkey. In K. Beycioğlu & P. Pashiardis (Eds.), *Multidimensional perspectives on principal leadership effectiveness* (pp. 1–17). Hershey: IGI Global.

Bozdoğan, K., & Sağnak, M. (2011). The relationship between leadership behaviors of elementary school principals and learning climate. *Abant İzzet Baysal University Journal of Educational Faculty, 11*(1), 137–145.

Bursalıoğlu, Z. (2010). *Okul yönetiminde yeni yapı ve davranış (15. baskı)*. Ankara: Pegem Akademi.

Can, E., & Serençelik, G. (2017). The investigation of pre-school education teachers' participations in the school management. *Dicle University Journal of Ziya Gokalp Education Faculty, 30*, 525–542. https://doi.org/10.14582/DUZGEF.791.

Çelik, V. (2002). Eğitim yöneticisi yetiştirme politikasına yön veren temel eğilimler. In C. Elma & Ş. Çınkır (Eds.), 21. *Yüzyıl eğitim yöneticilerinin yetiştirilmesi sempozyumu bildirileri kitabı* (ss. 3–12). Ankara: Ankara Üniversitesi Eğitim Bilimleri Fakültesi Yayınları.

Çelik, V. (2009). *Okul kültürü ve yönetimi (4. baskı)*. Ankara: Pegem Akademi.

Çelikten, M. (2004). Okul müdürü koltuğundaki kadınlar: Kayseri ili örneği. *Erciyes Üniversitesi Sosyal Bilimler Enstitüsü Dergisi, 1*(17), 91–118.

Çetin, K., & Yalçın, M. (2002). MEB yönetici eğitim programlarının değerlendirilmesi. In C. Elma & Ş. Çınkır (Eds.), 21. *Yüzyıl eğitim yöneticilerinin yetiştirilmesi sempozyumu bildirileri kitabı* (ss. 49–57). Ankara: Ankara Üniversitesi Eğitim Bilimleri Fakültesi Yayınları.

Çınkır, Ş. (2002). İngiltere'de okul müdürlerinin yetiştirilmesi: okul müdürleri için ulusal mesleki standartlar programı. In C. Elma & Ş. Çınkır (Eds.), 21. *Yüzyıl eğitim yöneticilerinin yetiştirilmesi sempozyumu bildirileri kitabı* (ss. 275–292). Ankara: Ankara Üniversitesi Eğitim Bilimleri Fakültesi Yayınları.

Decisions of IV National Education Council (1993). IV. Millî Eğitim Şurası Kararları. https://ttkb. meb.gov.tr/meb_iys_dosyalar/2017_09/29164715_4_sura.pdf. Accessed 09 June, 2018.

Demirtaş, Z., & Alanoğlu, M. (2015). The relationship between participation in decision-making of teachers and job satisfaction. *Journal of Kirsehir Education Faculty, 16*(2), 83–100.

Dewey, J. (1939). Dewey Education Report. https://www.tbmm. gov.tr/eyayin/gazeteler/web/kutuphanedebulunandıjıtalkaynaklar/kıtaplar/ dıgeryayınlar/197000571turkıyemaarıfıhakkındarapor(johndewey)/0000_ 0000turkıyemaarıfıhakkındarapor(johndewey).pdf Accesed 09 June, 2018.

Dimmock, C., & Walker, A. (1998a). Towards comparative educational administration: Building the case for a cross-cultural school-based approach. *Journal of Educational Administration, 36*(4), 379–401.

Dimmock, C., & Walker, A. (1998b). Comparative educational administration: Developing a cross-cultural conceptual framework. *Educational Administration Quarterly, 34*(4), 558–595.

Donmoyer, R. (2001). Evers and Lakomski's search for leadership's Holy Grail (and the intriguing ideas they encountered along the way). *Journal of Educational Administration, 39*(6), 554–572.

Eğitim-Bir-Sen. (2017). *Eğitim yönetiminde liyakat ve kariyer_sistemi raporu.* http://www.ebs.org. tr/ebs_files/files/yayinlarimiz/egitim_yonetiminde_liyakat_kariyer_sistemi.pdf. Accessed 09 June, 2018.

English, F. W. (2002). The point of scientificity, the fall of the epistemological dominos, and the end of the field of educational administration. *Studies in Philosophy and Education, 21*(2), 109–136.

Ercan, Y. (2006). Okullardaki örgütsel güven düzeyinin bazı değişkenler açısından incelenmesi. *Selçuk Üniversitesi Sosyal Bilimler Enstitüsü Dergisi, 16,* 739–756.

Eren, E. (2004). *Örgütsel davranış ve yönetim psikolojisi (7. Baskı).* İstanbul: Beta Basım Yayın Dağıtım.

Erkmen, T. (2011). *Örgüt kültürü.* İstanbul: Beta Basım Yayın Dağıtım.

Evers, C. W., & Lakomski, G. (1994). Three dogmas: A rejoinder. *Journal of Educational Administration, 32*(4), 28–37.

Ezgün, C. (2011). *Cumhuriyetten günümüze ilk ve orta dereceli okullarda müdür atamalarının mevzuata göre değerlendirilmesi.* Yeditepe Üniversitesi Sosyal Bilimler Enstitüsü, İstanbul: Yüksek Lisans Tezi.

Gören, S. Ç., & Özdemir, M. (2015). Examination of secondary school teachers' perceptions of organizational trust in terms of various variables. *Mersin University Journal of the Faculty of Education, 11*(3), 793–801.

Gunter, H. (2003). Intellectual histories in the field of educational management in the UK. *International Journal of Leadership in Education, 6*(4), 335–349.

Hallinger, P., & Leithwood, K. (1996). Culture and educational administration: A case of finding out what you don't know you don't know. *Journal of Educational Administration, 34*(5), 98–116.

Hofstede, G. (1997). *Cultures and organizations* (2nd ed.). New York: McGraw-Hill.

Hofstede, G. (2001). *Culture's consequences: comparing values, behaviors, institutions, and organizations across nations* (2nd ed.). Thousand Oaks, CA: Sage.

Hofstede, G. (2018). Hofstede Insights. www.hofstede-insights.com. Accessed 9 June, 2018.

Hoy, W. K., & Miskel, C.G. (2010). *Educational administration: Theory, research and Practice* (S. Turan, Trans.). Ankara: Nobel Yayıncılık.

8 The 'Westernised' Map of the Field of Educational ...   149

Huber, S. G., & West, M. (2002). Developing school leaders: A critical review of current practices, approaches and issues, and some directions for the future. In K. Leithwood & P. Hallinger (Eds.), *Second International handbook of educational leadership and administration* (pp. 1071–1102). Dordrecht: Kluwer Academic.

Işık, H. (2002). Okul müdürlüğü formasyon programları ve okul müdürlerinin yetiştirilmesi. In C. Elma & Ş. Çınkır (Eds.), 21. *Yüzyıl eğitim yöneticilerinin yetiştirilmesi sempozyumu bildirileri kitabı* (ss. 25–36). Ankara: Ankara Üniversitesi Eğitim Bilimleri Fakültesi Yayınları.

Karabatak, S. (2015). Training of school administrators in Turkey and investigation of the model. *Turkish Journal of Educational Studies, 2*(3), 79–107.

KAYA (1991). *Kamu yönetimi araştırması raporu.* http://www.todaie.edu.tr//resimler/ekler/185a8f8def383a8_ek.pdf. Accesed 09 June, 2018.

Korkmaz, E., & Gündüz, H. B. (2011). Indexing levels of distributive leadership behaviours of primary school principals. *Kalem International Journal of Education and Human Sciences, 1*(1), 123–153.

Leithwood, K., & Duke, D. L. (1999). A century's quest to understand school leadership. In J. Murphy & K. S. Seashore (Eds.), *Handbook of research on educational administration* (pp. 45–72). San Francisco: Jossey-Bass.

Lumby, J., Walker, A., Bryant, M., Bush, T., & Björk, L. G. (2009). Research on leadership preparation in a global context. In M. D. Young, G. M. Crow, J. Murphy, & R. T. Ogawa (Eds.), *Handbook of research on the education of school leaders* (pp. 157–194). New York: Routledge.

Maxcy, S. J. (2001). Educational leadership and management of knowing: The aesthetics of coherentism. *Journal of Educational Administration, 39*(6), 573–578.

McCarthy, M. M. (1999). The evolution of educational leadership preparation programs. In J. Murphy & S. K. Louis (Eds.), *Handbook of research on educational administration* (pp. 17–35). San Francisco: Jossey-Bass.

MEHTAP (1963). *Merkezi hükümet teşkilatı araştırma projesi raporu.* http://www.todaie.edu.tr//resimler/ekler/bdfe5e3cddec94c_ek.pdf. Accessed 09 June, 2018.

Middlewood, D. (2010). Managing people and performance. In T. Bush, L. Bell, & D. Middlewood (Eds.), *The principles of educational leadership and management* (pp. 135–150). London: Sage.

Oğuz, E. (2011). The relationship between teachers' perceptions of organizational justice and administrators' leadership styles. *Inonu University Journal of the Faculty of Education, 12*(1), 45–65.

Öksüzoğlu, M. (2012). Organizational trust in educational management: A Case study of a high school in North Cyprus. *Eurasian Journal of Educational Research, 49,* 121–140.

Örücü, D., & Şimşek, H. (2011). The state of educational administration scholarship in Turkey from the scholars' perspectives: A qualitative analysis. *Educational Administration: Theory and Practice, 17*(2), 167–197.

Özdoğru, M., & Aydın, B. (2012). The relationship among elementary school teachers' participation in decision-making, their desire and motivation levels. *Abant İzzet Baysal University Journal of Educational Faculty, 12*(1), 357–367.

Özkalp, E., & Kırel, Ç. (2000). *Örgütsel davranış.* Eskişehir: Anadolu Üniversitesi Yayınları.

Öztürk, Ç., & Aydın, B. (2012). High school teachers' perceptions of trust in organization. *Gaziantep University Journal of Social Sciences, 11*(2), 485–504.

Pehlivan Aydın, İ. (2002). Amerika Birleşik Devletleri'nde eğitim yöneticilerinin yetiştirilmesi ve yönetici geliştirme akademisi örneği. In C. Elma & Ş. Çınkır (Eds.), 21. *Yüzyıl eğitim yöneticilerinin yetiştirilmesi sempozyumu bildirileri kitabı* (ss. 293–306). Ankara: Ankara Üniversitesi Eğitim Bilimleri Fakültesi Yayınları.

Official Gazette. (1998). Millî Eğitim Bakanlığı eğitim kurumları yöneticilerinin atama ve yer değiştirme yönetmeliği. Sayı: 23472 ve Tarih: 23.09.1998. http://mevzuat.meb.gov.tr/html/23472_0.html. Accessed 11 June, 2018.

Official Gazette. (2004). Millî Eğitim Bakanlığı eğitim kurumları yöneticilerinin atama ve yer değiştirme yönetmeliği. Sayı: 25343 ve Tarih: 11.01.2004. http://mevzuat.meb.gov.tr/html/egikuryon_1/egikuryon_1.html. Accessed 11 June, 2018.

150 K. Beycioglu et al.

Official Gazette. (2007). Millî Eğitim Bakanlığı eğitim kurumları yöneticilerinin atama yönetmeliği. Sayı: 26492 ve Tarih: 16.05.2007. http://mevzuat.meb.gov.tr/html/26492_0.html. Accessed 11 June, 2018.

Official Gazette. (2008). Millî Eğitim Bakanlığı eğitim kurumları yöneticilerinin atama yönetmeliği. Sayı: 26856 ve Tarih: 15.10.2008. http://mevzuat.meb.gov.tr/html/26856_0.html. Accessed 11 June, 2018.

Official Gazette. (2009). Millî Eğitim Bakanlığı eğitim kurumları yöneticilerinin atama ve yer değiştirmelerine ilişkin yönetmelik. Sayı: 27318 ve Tarih: 13.08.2009. http://mevzuat.meb.gov.tr/html/egikuryon_1/egikuryon_1.html. Accessed 11 June, 2018.

Official Gazette. (2013). Millî Eğitim Bakanlığı eğitim kurumları yöneticilerinin atama ve yer değiştirmelerine ilişkin yönetmelik. Sayı: 28573 ve Tarih: 28.02.2013. http://www.resmigazete.gov.tr/eskiler/2013/02/20130228-12.htm. Accessed 11 June, 2018.

Official Gazette. (2014). Millî Eğitim Bakanlığı eğitim kurumları yöneticilerinin atama ve yer değiştirmelerine ilişkin yönetmelik. Sayı: 29026 ve Tarih: 10.06.2014. http://mevzuat.meb.gov.tr/html/egikuryon_1/egikuryon_1.html. Accessed 11 June, 2018.

Official Gazette. (2017). Millî Eğitim Bakanlığı eğitim kurumlarına yönetici atama yönetmeliği. Sayı: 30046 ve Tarih: 22.04.2017. http://www.resmigazete.gov.tr/eskiler/2017/04/20170422-6.htm. Accessed 11 June, 2018.

Official Gazette. (2018). Millî Eğitim Bakanlığı eğitim kurumlarına yönetici görevlendirme yönetmeliği. Sayı: 30455 ve Tarih: 21.06.2018. http://www.resmigazete.gov.tr/eskiler/2018/06/20180621-8.htm. Accessed 08 July, 2018.

Recepoğlu, E., & Kılınç, A. Ç. (2014). Raising and selecting school administrators in Turkey, present problems and solutions. *Turkish Studies, 9*(2), 1817–1845. https://doi.org/10.7827/TurkishStudies.6136.

Şahin, I., Kesik, F., & Beycioğlu, K. (2017). Chaotic process in the assignment of school administrators and its effects. *Elementary Education Online, 16*(3), 1007–1102.

Şimsek (1997). 21. Yüzyılın eşiğinde paradigmalar savaşı ve kaostaki Türkiye, İstanbul: Sistem Yayınları.

Şimşek, H. (2002). Türkiye'de eğitim yöneticisi yetiştirilemez. In C. Elma & Ş. Çınkır (Ed.), 21. *Yüzyıl eğitim yöneticilerinin yetiştirilmesi sempozyumu bildirileri kitabı* (ss. 307–312). Ankara: Ankara Üniversitesi Eğitim Bilimleri Fakültesi Yayınları.

Şişman, M., & Turan, S. (2002). Yöneticilerinin yetiştirilmesine ilişkin başlıca yönelimler ve Türkiye için çıkarılabilecek bazı sonuçlar. In C. Elma & Ş. Çınkır (Eds.), 21. *Yüzyıl eğitim yöneticilerinin yetiştirilmesi sempozyumu bildirileri kitabı* (ss. 239–254). Ankara: Ankara Üniversitesi Eğitim Bilimleri Fakültesi Yayınları.

Şişman, M. (2007). *Örgütler ve kültürler* (2nd ed.). Ankara: Pegem Akademi.

Smylie, M. A., & Bennett, A. (2005). What do we know about developing school leaders? A look at existing research and next steps for new study. In W. A. Firestone & C. Riehl (Eds.), *A new agenda for research in educational leadership* (pp. 138–155). New York: Teachers College Press.

Süngü, H. (2012). Recruiting and preparing school principals in Turkey, Germany, France and England. *Sakarya University Journal of Education, 2*(1), 33–48.

Taşdan, M. (2012). Turkish primary school teachers' perceptions of organizational trust. *The New Educational Review, 30*(4), 176–190.

Terzi, A. R., & Çelik, H. (2016). Relationship between perceived organizational support and leadership styles of school principals. *Journal of Research in Education and Teaching, 5*(2), 87–98.

Tezcan, M. (1985). *Educational sociology* (4th ed.). Ankara: Ankara University Press.

Üstüner, M., & Cömert, M. (2008). An analysis of the graduate courses and theses in educational administration, supervision, planning and economics. *Educational Administration: Theory and Practice, 55*(55), 497–515.

Yılmaz, K., & Taşdan, M. (2009). Organizational citizenship and organizational justice in Turkish primary schools. *Journal of Educational Administration, 47*(1), 108–126.

Yılmaz, D., & Turan, S. (2015). Distributed leadership view in schools: a structural equation modelling study. *Educational Administration: Theory and Practice, 21*(1), 93–126.

8 The 'Westernised' Map of the Field of Educational … 151

Kadir Beycioglu is Associate Professor of Educational Administration at *Dokuz Eylul University Buca Faculty of Education in the Department of Educational Sciences, Izmir, Turkey.* His study topics are mainly on educational change, school development, and educational leadership. He is also interested in the ethical use of ICT in education. He is Member of the *International Study of Principal Preparation (ISPP) project and International School Leadership Development Network—Social Justice Leadership Strand by BELMAS and UCEA.* He has published several articles in leading international journals. He has also acted as Guest Editor for some international journals and books and has published a number of chapters. He is (Founding) Editor of the *Research in Educational Administration & Leadership (REAL, a journal by Turkish Educational Administration Society)* and has been serving as Member of the editorial board or as Reviewer for some leading international journals. He has been Member of the *European Educational Research Association, British Educational Leadership, Management & Administration Society*, and the Commonwealth Council for Educational Administration and Management.

Ali Çağatay Kılınç is Associate Professor of Educational Administration at Karabuk University, Faculty of Letters, Department of Educational Sciences, Karabuk, Turkey. His research topics are mainly on educational leadership, school development, and organisational behaviour. He has published a number of articles in international journals including *Education and Science, Educational Studies: Theory and Practice*, and the *Alberta Journal of Educational Research*. He has also published a number of chapters and participated in a range of national and international conferences on educational management and leadership. He has been serving as Reviewer for leading national and international journals and is also Member of editorial or referee boards.

Mahmut Polatcan is Research Assistant of Educational Administration at Karabuk University, Faculty of Letters, Department of Educational Sciences, Karabuk, Turkey. His research topics are mainly on educational administration, organisational commitment, organisational socialisation, organisational social capital, and organisational cynicism. He has also published a number of chapters and participated in a range of national and international conferences on educational administration.

Chapter 9
A Reflection on Teaching Educational Administration in Iran: A Critical Approach

Arash Rastehmoghadam

Abstract Nearly half a century has passed since the teaching of educational studies and educational administration (EA) in Iran; however, a significant scholarly and practical progress has not been made. Therefore, reflecting on the status of the current situation is important. This chapter focuses on the teaching status of EA in Iran using the analytical-critical method to examine and analyse the constraints governing this area. The chapter is structured in three sections. The first provides a brief overview of the history of the traditional and modern education systems and the formation of educational studies and EA in Iran. The second part is devoted to the analysis of EA backwardness factors under the heading of macro- and micro-limitations. Macro-limitations refer to the historical-political background of the Iranian education system, which has had a direct and indirect impact on the field of EA. Micro-limitations refer to a set of factors related to the internal conditions of the EA field and are classified in three groups: scholarly weakness of the researchers, research poverty, and deficiencies in EA curriculum. Finally, in the third section, suggestions are made to improve the status of the EA field.

Introduction

The origin of Educational Administration (EA) is from the USA and Canada (Bates 2010; Campbell 1981; Campbell et al. 1966). The first EA students were graduated from Columbia University in 1905 which are sometimes called the grandfathers of EA (Campbell and Newell 1973). Later on, this field was extended to other continents such as Asia (Hallinger and Chen 2014). EA is also an historical discipline (Samier 2006) and multidisciplinary area and has interaction with various subjects such as economics (Miller 1965), political science (Ball 2012; Campbell et al. 1965; Samier 2008), sociology (Bidwell 1965; Hailer 1968; Weick 1976), social and behavioural sciences (Boyan 1981; Campbell et al. 1987), psychology (Bush 1999), organisation

---

A. Rastehmoghadam (✉)
Allameh Tabataba'i University, Tehran, Iran
e-mail: rastehmoghadamarash@gmail.com

© Springer Nature Singapore Pte Ltd. 2019
E. A. Samier and E. S. ElKaleh (eds.), *Teaching Educational Leadership in Muslim Countries*, Educational Leadership Theory,
https://doi.org/10.1007/978-981-13-6818-9_9

theory (Johnson and Fauske 2005), policy-making (Campbell and Mazzoni 1974), education (Wang and Bowers 2016), and recently neurosciences and cognitive sciences (Lakomski 2008).

This field has a long history as the literature demonstrates the predating of EA to other fields such as public administration. However, there is dissidence in the issue dates of the first EA publications; some scholars attribute the first one to 1882 (Wall 2001) and others to 1829 (Glass 2004). In spite of a long history, its theoretical foundation has always been controversial (Oplatka 2009). Therefore, after World War II, efforts have been made to legitimise EA such as the 'theory movement' (Culbertson 1983), 'humanistic and interpretive movement' (Greenfield and Ribbins 2005; Samier and Schmidt 2010), 'effectiveness movement' (Angus 1986), 'critical movement' (Bates 1984; Foster 1986; Smyth 1989), 'postmodernism movement' (English 2003), and recently the 'naturalistic coherentism' approach (Evers and Lakomski 2015). The advent of these movements has led to ontology (Newton and Riveros 2015), epistemology (Evers 2017; Eyal and Rom 2015) and methodology (Scott 2010b) of EA, and today the appearance of thoughts of philosophers such as Michel Foucault (Anderson and Grinberg 1998; Niesche 2011; Niesche and Gowlett 2014), Jacques Derrida (Niesche 2013a), Jean-François Lyotard (Niesche 2013b), Pierre Bourdieu (English 2012; Gunter 2002; Lingard and Christie 2003; Scott 2010a; Wilkinson and Scott 2013), Hannah Arendt (Gunter 2013; Veck and Jessop 2016) and Jürgen Habermas (Dolmage 1992; Kochan 2002; Milley 2008; Whiteman 2015).

These efforts, along with attention to the training of EA professors and curriculum (Samier 2014), have been conducted to achieve a global theoretical and practical improvement of EA so that today the accumulation of knowledge in many countries such as Asian countries (e.g., Hong Kong, Israel) is considerable (Hallinger and Chen 2014; Hallinger et al. 2013). In spite of these attempts and progress, and more than five decades from the entrance of EA into Iran, educational studies and EA have not yet been well-developed with respect to its theoretical and practical foundations (Abbaspour 2013; Alaghband 2001; Kardan 2002; Rastehmoghadam et al. 2016; Shamshiri 2005).

The main objective of this chapter is to investigate the pathology of theoretical and practical developments and teaching limitations of EA in Iran by using an analytical-critical method. The chapter is structured in three sections. The first is a brief overview of the history of the traditional and modern education systems and the formation of educational studies and EA in Iran. The second part is devoted to the analysis of EA backwardness factors under the heading of macro- and micro-limitations, macro-referring to the historical-political background of the Iranian education system, which has had a direct and indirect impact on the field of EA, and micro to factors internal to the EA field, classified into three groups: scholarly weakness of the researchers; research poverty; and deficiencies in the EA curriculum. Finally, in the third section, suggestions are made to improve the status of the EA field.

A Concise History of Education in Iran

This section reviews the education history, trends of stabilising educational studies and the formation of EA in Iran. As a general classification, the education system can be divided into three distinctive periods. The first period is that of ancient Iran, in which education was influenced by teachings of the Zoroastrian religion. The second was initiated by the entry of Islam into Iran in the Sassanid era during the twelfth and thirteenth centuries when 'Maktab', 'Nezamiyeh' (military school) and Mosques were among the most important child educational centres and considered to be the golden era of Islam (Sadiq 1960). The interval between the second and third periods (from the end of the twelfth century) is called the Middle Ages of Iran, in which the lights of science and knowledge were quenched for various reasons (Alamolhoda 2002).

The third period was initiated in the late nineteenth century, when the Qajar kings encountered the West, and is associated with political modernisation and the formation of a modern educational system (Shahriari 2017). The reason for the establishment and adaptation of this system was successive failures during battles with Russian armies in the Qajar era. The Iranians found a solution to the backwardness and disadvantages from obtaining knowledge from and modelling of the Western educational model (Shahvar 2009). Accordingly, under the administration of Abbas Mirza, the first group of Iranian students was sent to study abroad in 1811 (Menashri 1992; Sadiq 1960). In total, 84 people in five groups were sent to Europe in this era (Moradi Nejad and Rahimi Shariati 1974). The 'Dar al-Fonun' (polytechnic) was then established in 1852, through the endeavours of Mirza Taghi Khan Amir Kabir, the Chancellor of Nasser al-Din Shah, and had a tremendous influence on the modernisation and development of the Iranian educational system (Alaghband 1973; Menashri 1992; Tamer 2010). In 1889, the first Western-style school was opened by Mirza Hassan Roshdiyeh (Levers 2006), the 'Roshdiyeh School,' although some others such as 'Alborz College' (1873) and the 'Sepahsalar School' (1879) were active using a traditional approach. Whilst religious lessons were still taught at 'Dar al-Fonun' (Takmilhomayoun 2018) and the Roshdiyeh School, the imitative nature of these centres was strongly opposed by the clerics (Menashri 1992). Of course, the aim of the founders in adopting a foreign modern system was to empower Iran and emancipate the people from ignorance and injustice (Iravani 2014), but some analysed this in line with the project of cultural imperialism and secularism (Alamolhoda 2002). In any case, despite opposition, the modern educational system was established in Iran and created an oppressive morale in the people which eventually led to the constitutional revolution in 1906 (Takmilhomayoun 2018). One year after the revolution, the parliament and constitution were established in Iran for the first time. Despite all of its advantages, legislation in Iran led to a governmental (central) educational system (Menashri 1992). The fundamental Law of Education was passed in 1911, according to which all educational matters were put under the direct supervision of [the] Ministry of Education (Alaghband 1973).

At the end of the Qajar dynasty, the 'Pahlavi' regime began in 1920 and continued until February 1979. In this era (1928), according to law, it was decided that 100 people a year be sent abroad for higher education (Arasteh 1962; Moradi Nejad and Rahimi Shariati 1974; Sadiq 1960). In the Pahlavi era, Iran's educational system was stabilised centrally and authoritatively (Vejdani 2014), and the students who studied abroad were employed in senior positions (Arasteh 1962; Kardan 2002). Reza Shah used the education system as a tool for realisation of the nationalism, Westernisation, modernisation, and secularisation that provoked the protest of the clergy and the religious class of society (Alamolhoda 2002; Iravani 2014; Khaki and Bhat 2015; Levers 2006; Tamer 2010; Yazdani 1998). In this period, the establishment of the University of Tehran was realised in 1934, as the idea of one of the first practitioners of science in Iran (Menashri 1992; Sadiq 1931, 1960). Reza Shah's rule did not last long, and following the conquest of Iran by the Allies during World War II, he was forced to assign rule (power) to his son, Mohammad Reza. Although the status of the education system continued through its imitation of the West and dictatorship approach during his rule, a little improvement was made in the political atmosphere as religious people were allowed to choose the type of school and education for their children. Since then the possibility of establishing the religious and nongovernmental (private) schools in Iran was provided (Rai Golouyeh and Rahmanian 2017), including the Alavi School, Alborz School and Farhad School that have been considered to be successful cases of schooling in Iran (Qasemi Pooya 2008).

In 1979, the Islamic Republic was established upon the failure of the imperial system. The Islamic Revolution of Iran was an ideological revolution and took care of cultural issues, especially education (Mehran 1989, 1990; Paivandi 2012). Accordingly, since the beginning of these times, the leaders of the system Islamicised and religionised education in Iran by creating various regulatory organisations including the 'Cultural Revolution Council' (Levers 2006; Tamer 2010). During this period, emphasis was placed on religiosity, Islamisation, and a focus on religious rituals in education through a mandatory approach.

Establishment of Educational Studies and Educational Administration in Iran

Educational studies in their current forms are the product of modernity (Ahanchiyan 2005; Shamshiri 2005), of which EA is a major branch (Mialaret 1985). First, it is necessary to characterise the history of educational studies literature in Iran. There are two approaches to the formation and teaching of educational studies as academic fields: the first considers the entry of educational studies in Iran to be at the establishment of the 'Dar al-Moallemin' (Teacher's Training College) in 1919; the second attributes it to the beginning of 1932, which was taken by teaching of Issa Sadiq Alam in the higher education institute called 'Danesh Saraye Ali' (Kardan 2001; Sadiq 1960). However, the necessity of passing studies in the field of education for those teaching at higher education institutions and teacher training centres led to the development of the first texts by a number of primary actors in this field and by using Western references. Some of these are as follows (Mohsenpour 2011):

- *A New Method of Education*, by Issa Sadiq Alam, 1936.
- *A Brief History of Education*, by Issa Sadiq Alam, 1938.
- *Science of Self or Psychology in Terms of Education*, by Ali Akbar Siasi, 1939.
- *Principles of Education*, by Mohammad Baqer Houshiyar, 1957.
- *Philosophy of Education*, Fathollah Amir Houshmand, 1957.
- *The Foundation of Modern Education*, by Mohammad Talimi, 1958.

The entry of educational studies into the Iranian higher educational system and establishment of specialised colleges are indebted to the efforts of pioneers in 1964. The teaching of educational studies before that time was conducted along with philosophy and sociology. After the establishment of the first faculty of education and psychology in 1964 at Tehran University, educational studies developed as an academic field in B.Sc. and M.Sc. The period between 1964 and 1979 (the victory of Islamic Revolution) is called the age of 'development and specialisation of educational studies'. To increase education studies colleges and establish new fields, the education system was revised in 1971, imitating the 'Langevin-Wallon' in France leading to the formation of three stages—primary school, guidance school, and high school—but was an incomplete adaptation from the France system (Sadiq 1942).

The first curriculum of education studies in Iran included six syllabi entitled 'psychology in terms of education', 'sociology in terms of education', 'philosophy of education', 'foundations of secondary education', 'history of education,' and 'principles of education'. In order to train in these syllabi, the first references of educational studies in Iran were codified by Issa Sadiq Alam, Ali Akbar Siasi and then Mohammad Baqer Houshiyar who were influenced by American, French and German experts in this field, respectively. Issa Sadiq Alam had graduated from Columbia University where his thoughts were inspired by John Dewey, while Mohammad Baqer Houshiyar was an alumnus of the University of Munich, and therefore, his book was a reflection of the German philosopher, Kershensteiner (Kardan 2002). After the Islamic revolution, in pursuit of the goals and slogans of the Islamic revolution, educational syllabi were controlled and revised by the Supreme Council for Cultural Revolution (SCCR) and the Ministry of Science, Research and Technology during the 1989–1993 period (Nowroozi 2012). After more than two decades, the curriculum of this field has been recently revised:

> At present, educational sciences is presented at undergraduate level through four fields named as 'Educational Planning and Administration', 'Educational Technology', 'School and Preschool Education' and 'Education of Children with the Special Needs'. The undergraduate period of educational sciences takes about four years including 140 educational courses: A) Basic courses: 20 units, B) Main courses: 70 units, C) Professional courses: 18 units, D) Optional courses: 10 units and E) General courses: 22 units. (SCCR 2015)

The turning point of EA can be placed in the time of Tehran's higher education institute independence, the Danesh Saraye Ali, which led to teaching it as a course by Mohammad Ali Toosi and Mohammad Mashayekhi (Naeli 1996). The introduction of EA courses at universities began in the 1940s, and then, the MA degree (1969) was offered in the newly established faculty of educational studies at the University of Tehran (Alaghband 2001). However, in some universities such as Kharazmi University, EA is part of the Faculty of Management and Accounting. The first EA books entitled 'Culture Organisation and its Leadership' (1964) and 'Management and Educational Leadership' (1968) were written and translated by Mohammad Ali Toos (Rastehmoghadam 2017). Since then, some other activities have also been conducted including commissioning of graduate-level programmes, publishing books, articles and establishing specialised journals.

Limitations on Teaching and Theoretical Development of EA in Iran

In this section, limitations of the teaching and theoretical development in Iran are discussed based on an analytical-critical method. EA limitations refer to a set of factors and issues that have caused problems in the development of the field, the relevant ones discussed in two general categories, named the macro-limitations (outfield) and the micro-limitations (infield). Macro-level limitations are a set of factors and socio-political variables that inhibit the development of EA, whilst the micro-level limitations include the scholarly weaknesses of the researchers, research poverty, and deficiencies in the EA curriculum.

The Macro-limits (Outfield)

As pointed out in the historical trend of education discussed above, the confrontation of Iranians with the new educational system resulted from successive defeats in military wars. Hence, attention to modern education and scholarship was used to gain power and overcome enemies (Shahriari 2017). Thus, from the outset, an emphasis on military and medical sciences was preferred to humanities (Takmilhomayoun 2018), and attention to humanities was also pursued to foster the spirit of homeland defence and patriotic friendship (Siasi 1958a). On the other hand, the traditional and religious system that formerly authorised education could not change itself in the time available and despite the numerous resistances of clerics and religious scholars; the new educational system was finally developed throughout the country. Therefore, the new educational system in Iran was imposed, imitated and used as a tool to pursue political power. In such a system, schools were not completing the path of the 'Maktab' and 'Seminary', but regarded as an imported commodity that was intended to pave the way for the country's progress and modernisation. In this process, no constructive interaction was found between tradition (Maktab) and modernity (School), and even some of the positive points of the Maktab such as the practice of having male and female students in the same class (Nasiri 2008) were forgotten. Despite four decades passing since the establishment of the Islamic Republic of Iran, the education system is still wandering between tradition and modernity symbols (Paivandi 2012). Considering the way in which modern education has been introduced into the country, it is natural that its corresponding management was also formal, imitative, and instrumental.

EA has more administrative responsibility to implement the orders and circulars from government than paying attention to educational affairs (Alaghband 1985). In general, education, and consequently EA, since the Qajar dynasty to the present time, has always been a means for legitimising the values of the rulers in society. In the Qajar period, an imitative management obtained from Western educational institutions was used as a model in the country (Iravani 2014). During the Pahlavi era, using the 'White Revolution' and in Islamic Republic using the 'Cultural Revolution,' rulers tried educating people according to their desires through the educational system (Tamer 2010; Menashri 1992). On the other hand, the trend of revolutions in EA opposed the international intellectual and scholarly standards. For example, just when the West introduced the issue of management and ownership by *The Principles of Scientific Management* (1911) by Frederick Winslow Taylor, the 'Constitution of Education' was released in Iran in the same year, as the administration and ownership of schools were taken over by the government and the freedom and authority of schools were eliminated (Naeli 1996).

On the other hand, at a time when international education emphasised freedom and respect for students as well as the authenticity of the human being and his rights, in Iran, the Pahlavi era was ruled as a dominating and authoritarian system that misused education in the consolidation of his thought including the promotion of the concept of royal affairs (Hamraz 1997), as the educational principals became affiliates and associates of senior officials (Alaghband 1985). Therefore, there was an asynchronicity and contradiction between the evolution and demands of education on worldwide and internal levels. It is worth noting that even after the Islamic Revolution, not only did authoritarianism and concentration of power (as the heritage of the previous period) not disappear, but the existing authoritarian capacity was used to develop the degree and formalism of religious activity with an emphasis on the implementation of Islamic rituals (Iravani 2014), whereby the educational system became a tool for legitimising the twelve Imami Shia of Islamic ideology (Levers 2006; Mohsenpour 1988). As a result, there was no significant difference in political views and their type of management and educational policies (Saee et al. 2012) and, consequently, all of them pursued the same policy.

In addition to these issues, the adoption of an ideological approach to the humanities after the Islamic Revolution included an 'Islamisation of science' project that had the greatest impact on the curriculum of these fields (Godazgar 2001; Paivandi 2012; Shorish 1988). Educational studies and EA were no exception (Mohsenpour 2005; Nowroozi 2012). Undoubtedly, the educational visions in every society are based on its political philosophy and worldview which can have a metaphysical aspect. However, how to achieve these goals in educational studies are affected by innovation and modernity. Nevertheless, the Islamisation Project considered education procedures as well as its goals and values. Looking at EA from a religious point of view means to extract EA principles and practices on the basis of Islamic references. As in previous periods, an imitation prevailed in Iran's educational system, but governed by Islamic and religious teachings instead of Western principles. The spirit governing the education system and EA was propelled forward contrary to conventional academic routes at a time when world-class EA scholars had begun to pay attention to cultural differences (Hallinger and Chen 2014; Hallinger and Walker 2011). The actual conditions of schools and EA in Iran were arranged on the basis of Islamic and religious sources, unaware that religious propositions tend to explain and describe the spiritual world rather than focusing on cultural and social realities (Shamshiri 2005) and did not necessarily tolerate cultural and social differences in society. This policy has led to a neglect of the practical and historical heritage of this field both in the traditional pattern (Maktab) and in the new model (the experiences of successful schools such as Farhad School and Alborz School). As a result, some books such as 'Seeking for the Methods of Education' by Turan Mirhadi (1983), 'School Director' by Jalal Al-Ahamad (1958), and 'Excavation of Educational Issues in Iran' (1957) written by Samad Behrangi, which described the conditions and issues of the educational organisations of the country, were rarely addressed by policy-makers and EA scholars. Of course, this policy did not have successful results. So, despite the creation of multiple centres, allocation of funds, and holding of several conferences on the subject of Islamising humanities studies, there is still a long distance between the current state of education with the expectations of the officials (Ramazani and Hamani 2014) and secularism as the dominant approach of Iranian scholars towards education (Alamolhoda 2002).

Collectively, all of these factors show that EA in Iran has not been historical, because the history of each discipline or field of study is shaped by problematisation. This refers to the research discovery process that asks questions in a historical and social context of society. Up to now, few issues related to EA have been explored in the country's historical and indigenous background, because education and its administration are seen as a tool not intrinsically important but serve other purposes. Therefore, analysing the current state of EA in the country requires examining the governing political and social limitations.

Minor Limitations (Infield)

In addition to the macro-limitations noted above, EA also suffers from internal limitations as follows: 'the scholarly weakness of EA researchers', 'research poverty,' and 'deficiencies in the EA curriculum'.

The Scholarly Weakness of EA Researchers

One of the most important limitations on this level is attributed to the students and researchers of the EA field. Many professors are not familiar with the names of major international scholars, associations, awards and accredited journals, but they have taken responsibility for the training of a wide range of master's and Ph.D. students. The depth of the professors' insight into the evolutionary trends of EA in the global arena is low. Historically, the first group of EA professors in Iran graduated from Western universities in 1970s. Formation of the EA field in Iran coincided with the failure of the 'Theory Movement' in 1969 (replaced by later movements). EA in Iran was turned into an academic discipline when the researchers' efforts for a more rigorous scholarly standard were developing in the West, but Iranian researchers faced the 'unfinished EA' project. Although in a few works, attention has been paid to the background and evolution of the conceptual evolution of EA (Alaghband 2001, 2010), a general weakness and lack of attention to trends and theoretical movements are evident in most of the educational textbooks. In fact, knowledge of the domestic investigations of EA was achieved not through studying classical and authoritative works but articles published after development of EA journals after the 1970s. Following the worldwide declining trend of the review and conceptual studies of EA and the domination by positivist paradigm (Bush and Crawford 2012), Iranian EA scholars also began to import research issues and conduct decorative studies that lacked depth and value in resolving problems. Iranian EA researchers could not correctly understand the message of the 'Theory Movement'. Therefore, instead of paying attention to the conceptualisation of the real conditions of educational organisations, they adopted the positivistic approach and theoretical borrowed from other management, administration, and leadership fields. Whereas the experiences of the 'Theory Movement' was contrary to the current trends in Iran, research in this field not only contributed to the scholarly identity of EA in Iran, but also influenced the content of textbooks strongly through the fields of psychology, public management and organisational behaviour. It seems, ignoring the history of EA, along with the retirement and loss of pioneering scholars, concerns have developed that EA will face a lack of history on the global scale in the future (Rastehmoghadam et al. 2016).

Along with the lack of historical insight, the status of the EA researchers' scholarly communities, the associations, and networks that play an important role in the development of specialised knowledge, is also undesirable. The history of the formation of world-class academic and professional circles of EA dates back to the 1930s. Nevertheless, the 'Iranian EA Association' has existed for only nine years. Although improvements of EA have been achieved in light of personal dedication and a continuity of individual activity (Hallinger 2011), it should not be forgotten that scholarly development means the production process, distribution, and critique of knowledge through channels used for creating a collegial atmosphere of dialogue among the researchers of this field. The weakness of dialogue space and critique, individual activities, and lack of academic interactions internationally are some of the features of EA in Iran. The activities of the Iranian EA Association are limited to organising educational workshops and setting up representative offices in the provinces, with fewer spaces provided for discussion of opposite ideas, theorising, publishing, and critiquing. It seems that diffusion of individualist values hidden in Asian culture has also been effective in this regard, so that in addition to Iran, the culture of research cooperation is also very weak and disappointing in the best educational institutions of East Asia (Hallinger 2011).

In addition to the above cases, the status of volunteers and students in EA is not satisfactory. Students entering the field do not have the adequate capacity to develop it. Many of them had to study EA as a result of their failure to be accepted in the other disciplines. Some are staff members of governmental organisations studying to obtain an undergraduate degree in order to get promotions in their organisations. On the other hand, inability to function with English language skills reduced them to a level of literacy more dependent on Persian books and references. The totality of the above factors caused EA in Iran to suffer from the lack of talented human resources for conceptual development.

Research Poverty

The content of EA research published in the form of papers and books is a result of several factors. The first is the weakness of interdisciplinary research in the field. Facing these complex phenomena requires comprehensive and multidimensional research. Ironically, due to its multidimensional nature, EA often needs such studies. Schooling is not merely the educating-learning environment, but it has political, social, economic, and legal functions. Several studies have been carried out on a global scale using an interdisciplinary approach, but in Iran, such studies have rarely been conducted through this approach. EA research in Iran, similar to the neighbouring country, Turkey, does not interact effectively with the other academic disciplines (Beycioğlu 2006).

Most studies have been conducted using public management concepts and the positivist approach in the context of educational organisations. On the other hand, a large part of EA research has been limited within the framework of educational studies concepts. Therefore, the status of EA research in Iran is fluctuating between the academic imitation of management fields and scholarly isolation in science fiction, whereas EA is beyond the simple combination of management and education fields (Campbell 1981). Therefore, it is necessary to avoid adopting a particular approach that prevents reviewing the patterns of other countries' thought. Only through establishing a link between EA studies and other academic disciplines will we be able to capture new concepts and theoretical developments. For example, application of postmodernism critiques or the use of a critical-realism approach includes a new attitude toward the school and its administration (Pounder and Johnson 2007).

The second point is that EA research in Iran is highly disconnected from problems in the educational system. Of course, the political and social contexts governing educational organisations are highly influential in this regard, but it should not be ignored that the researchers in this field have been less able to resolve educational problems through interaction with the true subjects of the educational environment at the micro-level (school) and macro-level (policy-making). Therefore, production of knowledge in the field has not been significantly usable by practitioners or policy-makers. As a result, the gap between research and practice has increased, and there is little relationship between the content of academic journals and the current problems of the educational system. Academics are less aware of the situation of educational organisations, and the executive managers are unaware of the progress of academic studies in the EA field.

Deficiencies of the EA Curriculum

One of the limitations in a theoretical development of the EA field in Iran is related to its curriculum which is not adequately compatible with the business, social and practical needs and focuses more on theoretical and disciplinary aspects rather than the operational and practical ones (Arefi 2005; Keramati and Ahmadi 2011; Rahmani-Kochghani and Behrangi 2009; Shadfar et al. 2011). This has led to a decrease in the impact on graduates (Yarmohammadian and Salmanizadeh 2006). Also, the contribution of a number of disciplines in the arrangement of the curriculum is unbalanced. Despite the important effect of psychology, philosophy, and sociology, they play an extremely small role in curriculum of EA (Aali and Hosseingholizadeh 2010), even though pedagogy is not possible without psychology (Siasi 1958b). On the other hand, various studies demonstrate the need for reviewing the traditional curriculum in undergraduate and graduate studies (Aali and Hosseingholizadeh 2010; Arefi 2005; Hosseingholizadeh et al. 2018; Noorabadi et al. 2014; Rahmani-Kochghani and Behrangi 2009; Yarmohammadian and Salmanizadeh 2006). Recently, after more than two decades, educational studies curricula have been revised in a focused way by decision-making authorities (SCCR 2015). The new curriculum has been arranged based on the Islamic approach, as among the total of 140 study units, 16 units are directly devoted to Islamic thought in education. On the other hand, only a two-unit case lesson, called 'internship', deals with the practical aspects of EA. Finally, it seems that regarding the centralised approach in the design of curriculum and, consequently, reduction of professors' participation, meeting various regional and local needs will also remain in the midst of ambiguity.

Content of the EA curriculum in Iran is a combination of public management, organisational behaviour, and behavioural issues. A number of studies have shown that although over 40 books have been written about EA in Iran, up to now, none of them have paid attention to the Lakomski (2008) and Evers (2017) epistemological viewpoints introduced to the global arena two decades ago. Also, EA movements, including the 'Theory Movement', the 'Effectiveness Movement', and the 'Standardisation Movement', have remained unnoticed in the textbooks of this field. In addition, despite a half century elapsing since the introduction of the EA into Iran, many of the important foreign works of this field have not yet been translated into Persian.

Part Three: Conclusion and Suggestions

In this chapter, the establishment of a new education system and formation of educational sciences and consequently EA in Iran were first described. Then, limitations of its theoretical development were analysed in two categories: the macro and micro. Impacts of the historical-political and ideological conditions were addressed in the macro-level, whilst some of the cases including the researchers' scholarly weaknesses, research poverty, and weaknesses of the curriculum were dealt on the micro-level as the most important limitations of the theoretical development of EA. Undoubtedly, presenting any kind of suggestion for its development on practical and theoretical levels needs to change policy-makers' attitudes towards the role and place of EA in the context of the Iranian educational system. Thus, by considering these points, suggestions are made here to improve EA conditions in Iran.

In order to improve the scholarly basis of EA in Iran, one recommendation is to reduce the volume of instructional and managerial activities of university professors to provide opportunities for thought, research, and monitoring of theoretical changes. Formation and consolidation of academic and professional communities, as well as improvement of English language capabilities, are among other solutions that can aide the development of international cooperation, exchange of ideas, and supervisor–student interactions. With regard to the lack of common educational background being one of the reasons for the prevention of knowledge production, it is also recommended that graduated students of the EA field be recruited as university faculty members. In addition, to prevent weak and less motivated applicants entering this field requires that entry requirements be increased by the decision-making authorities.

To increase the quality of EA studies in Iran, it is recommended that an increase in interdisciplinary studies needs collaboration of EA researchers with those of other disciplines. Of course, EA is a practice with a local–national character rather than international. So, with regard to ethnic, religious, regional, and racial differences in Iran, it is essential to study schooling models and avoid imposing a uniformisation in this respect. Fortunately, a study has been recently done with an historical approach in order to document the management pattern of one of the famous religious Iranian schools (Kashani Vahid 2016). The EA field in Iran is really in need of such studies. On the other hand, national studies require the formulation of a research agenda and a coherent research map. This research route can be established through a coordination and division of tasks among academic centres, and in this way, conduct of repeated and non-related studies could be prevented. Eventually, EA studies in Iran must lead to the establishment of what is called Relevant Educational Administration (REA) in Iran. REA refers to the type of EA which deals with actual cases of the educational system through research programmes where schools are established next to EA faculties in order to facilitate the accessibility of professors and students to the actual research environment. Of course, implementation of internship courses would also help the connection of science and practice.

In order to improve and promote EA curriculum in Iran, it is also recommended that faculty members be more empowered through curriculum development through their own discretion. Additionally, a coherent and integrated approach should be developed for arrangement of educational studies by focusing on the new national and international topics such as educational justice, cultural diversity, and educational policy. Also, it is essential to pay more attention to philosophical and sociological issues in study programmes. In this regard, it is recommended that graduate courses be designed with the title of 'Philosophy and History of Educational Administration' and 'History of School Administration in Iran' in order to realise the role of philosophy and obtain knowledge of the philosophical origins of EA theories.

Finally, in order to improve EA in Iran, it is recommended that an 'EA Professional Research Institute' be established by participation of national scholars. The tasks of the aforesaid institute may include monitoring theoretical and empirical evolution of EA in the global community, policy-making for translation of books from original sources, including encyclopaedias and handbooks according to the domestic needs and conditions of the country, arranging a review meeting for new EA books (domestic and foreign), preparing an EA strategic plan in the country, and finally conducting an historiography of successful schooling experiences in Iran.

References

Aali, M., & Hosseingholizadeh, R. (2010). Evaluation and criticizing the curriculum of education science, the branch of administration and education planning. *Higher Education Letter, 2*(8), 35–51.

Abbaspour, A. (2013). From the theory throne to the depth of practice in educational administration: In search of drawing a management image in the education system of Iran. *Quarterly of Training in Military, 1*(2), 12–11.

Ahanchiyan, M. R. (2005). *Take a look at educational sciences in the mirror of postmodernism; the revision of great desires*. Paper presented at the first conference of the analysis and regulation of the educational studies system, Mashhad.

Al-Ahamad, J. (1958). *School director* (Vol. First). Tehran: Ferdowsi.

Alaghband, A. (1973). *The public school teacher in Iran: Social origin, status, and career orientation* (Doctoral thesis, Southern Illinois University).

Alaghband, A. (1985). Necessity and importance of attention to educational administration. *Quarterly of Education, 4*, 15–14.

Alaghband, A. (2001). Educational administration. In A. M. Kardan (Ed.), *Educational studies: Its nature and domain*. Tehran: The Organization for Researching and Composing University Textbooks in the Humanities (SAMT).

Alaghband, A. (2010). *Theoretical foundations and principles of educational administration* (5th edn., Vol. 22). Tehran: Ravan.

Alamolhoda, J. (2002). Influential thinking streams in contemporary Iranian education. *Book Review, 22*, 132–109.

Anderson, G., & Grinberg, J. (1998). Educational administration as a disciplinary practice: Appropriating Foucault's view of power, discourse, and method. *Educational Administration Quarterly, 34*(3), 329–353.

Angus, L. (1986). *Schooling, the school effectiveness movement, and educational reform*. Victoria: Deakin University Press.

Arasteh, A. R. (1962). *Education and social awakening in Iran, 1850–1968*. Leiden: Brill.

Arefi, M. (2005). Evaluation of educational administration curriculum in Iranian higher education from the perspectives of students, professionals and employers. *Curriculum Studies, 1*(1), 74–43.

Ball, S. J. (2012). *The micro-politics of the school: Towards a theory of school organization*: Abingdon: Routledge.

Bates, R. (1984). Toward a critical practice of educational administration. In T. Sergiovanni & J. Corbally (Eds.), *Leadership and organizational culture* (pp. 260–274). Urbana: University of Illinois Press.

Bates, R. (2010). History of educational leadership/management. In P. Peterson, E. Baker, & B. McGaw (Eds.), *International encyclopedia of education* (pp. 724–730). Oxford: Elsevier.

Behrangi, S. (1957). *Excavation of educational issues educational issues in Iran* (Vol. 10). Tehran: Shabgir.

Beycioğlu, K. (2006). Research in educational administration & leadership. *Educational Administration: Theory and Practice, 47*, 317–342.

Bidwell, C. E. (1965). The school as a formal organization. In J. March (Ed.), *Handbook of organizations* (pp. 972–1019). Chicago, IL: Rand McNally & Co.

Boyan, N. J. (1981). Follow the leader: Commentary on research in educational administration. *Educational Researcher, 10*(2), 6–21.

Bush, T. (1999). Introduction: Setting the scene. In T. Bush, L. Bell, R. Bolam, R. Glatter, & P. Ribbins (Eds.), *Educational management: Redefining theory, policy and practice* (pp. 1–12). London: Paul Chapman.

Bush, T., & Crawford, M. (2012). Mapping the field over 40 years: A historical review. *Educational Management, Administration & Leadership, 40*(5), 537–543.

Campbell, R. (1981). The professorship in educational administration—A personal view. *Educational Administration Quarterly, 17*(1), 1–24.

Campbell, R., Thomas, F., Jackson, N., & John, B. (1987). A history of thought and practice in educational administration. New York: Teacher College, Columbia University.

Campbell, R., Corbally, J. E., & Ramseyer, J. A. (1966). *Introduction to educational administration*. Boston: Allyn and Bacon.

Campbell, R., Cunningham, L. L., & McPhee, R. F. (1965). *Organization and control of American schools*. Columbus, OH: Charles E. Merrill.

Campbell, R., & Mazzoni, T. L. (1974). State governance models for the public schools. Ohio State University, Columbus: Educational Governance Project.

Campbell, R., & Newell, L. J. (1973). A study of professors of educational administration: A summary. *Educational Administration Quarterly, 9*(3), 3–27.

Culbertson, J. (1983). Theory in educational administration: Echoes from critical thinkers. *Educational Researcher, 12*(10), 15–22.

Dolmage, W. R. (1992). The Quest for understanding in educational administration: Ahabermasian perspective on the 'Griffiths-Greenfield debate'. *Journal of Educational Thought/Revue de la Pensée Educative, 26*(2), 89–113.

English, F. (2003). *The postmodern challenge to the theory and practice of educational administration*. Springfield, IL: Charles C Thomas.

English, F. (2012). Bourdieu's misrecognition: Why educational leadership standards will not reform schools or leadership. *Journal of Educational Administration and History, 44*(2), 155–170.

Evers, C. W. (2017). Epistemology and educational administration. In M. A. Peters (Ed.), *Encyclopedia of educational philosophy and theory* (pp. 755–759). Singapore: Springer.

Evers, C. W., & Lakomski, G. (2015). Naturalism and educational administration: New directions. *Educational Philosophy and Theory, 47*(4), 402–419.

Eyal, O., & Rom, N. (2015). Epistemological trends in educational leadership studies in Israel: 2000–2012. *Journal of Educational Administration, 53*(5), 574–596.

Foster, W. (1986). *Paradigms and promises: New approaches to educational administration.* New York: Prometheus Books.

Glass, T. E. (2004). *The history of educational administration viewed through its textbooks.* Oxford: Scarecrow Education.

Godazgar, H. (2001). Islamic ideology and its formative influence on education in contemporary Iran. *Economía, Sociedad y Territorio, 3*(10), 321–336.

Greenfield, T., & Ribbins, P. (2005). *Greenfield on educational administration: Towards a humane science.* London: Routledge.

Gunter, H. (2002). Purposes and positions in the field of education management putting bourdieu to work. *Educational Management & Administration, 30*(1), 7–26.

Gunter, H. (2013). *Educational leadership and Hannah Arendt.* Abingdon: Routledge.

Hailer, E. J. (1968). The interdisciplinary ideology in educational administration: Some preliminary notes on the sociology of knowledge. *Educational Administration Quarterly, 4*(2), 61–77.

Hallinger, P. (2011). Developing a knowledge base for educational leadership and management in East Asia. *School Leadership & Management, 31*(4), 305–320.

Hallinger, P., & Chen, J. (2014). Review of research on educational leadership and management in Asia: A comparative analysis of research topics and methods, 1995–2012. *Educational Management Administration & Leadership, 43*(1), 5–27.

Hallinger, P., Lee, T. H. T., & Szeto, E. (2013). Review of research on educational leadership and management in Hong Kong, 1995–2012: Topographical analysis of an emergent knowledge base. *Leadership and Policy in Schools, 12*(3), 256–281.

Hallinger, P., & Walker, A. D. (2011). School leadership in Asia Pacific: Identifying challenges and formulating a research agenda. *School Leadership & Management, 31*(4), 299–303.

Hamraz, V. (1997). Cultural institutions in Reza Shah's government. *Contemporary History of Iran, 1*, 63–50.

Hosseingholizadeh, R., Ahanchian, M. R., Kouhsari, M., & Noferesti, A. (2018). The experience of revising the educational management curriculum at Ferdowsi University of Mashhad. *Higher Education Letter, 10*(40), 97–124.

Iravani, S. (2014). Introduction to explaining the nature of the education system in Iran from the beginning of the modernization period to today. *Research Foundations in Education, 4*(1), 110–183.

Johnson, B. L., & Fauske, J. R. (2005). Introduction: Organization theory, educational leadership and educational research. *Journal of Educational Administration, 43*(1), 5–8.

Kardan, A. M. (2001). The history of education. In A. M. Kardan (Ed.), *Educational sciences; Their nature and domain* (pp. 70–100). Tehran: Organization for Researching and Composing University Textbooks in the Humanities.

Kardan, A. M. (2002). *The trend of education knowledge in contemporary Iran.* Paper presented at the Proceedings of the First National Iranian Seminar, Tehran.

Kashani Vahid, M. (2016). *Conversation with Masoud Kashani-e-Vahid.* Tehran: Institute for the Study of Generation Excellency.

Keramati, M. R., & Ahmadi, A. (2011). The quality curriculum evaluation in postgraduate studies of educational management and planning in the public universities of Tehran City. *Procedia-Social and Behavioral Sciences, 15*, 3723–3730.

Khaki, G., & Bhat, M. A. (2015). Pahlavi's the pioneers of education in Iran: A study of Reza Shah. *International Journal of Education, 3*(3), 45–50.

Kochan, F. K. (2002). Hope and possibility: Advancing an argument for a Habermasian perspective in educational administration. *Studies in Philosophy and Education, 21*(2), 137–155.

Lakomski, G. (2008). Functionally adequate but causally idle: W(h)ither distributed leadership? *Journal of Educational Administration, 46*(2), 159–171.

Levers, L. (2006). Ideology and change in Iranian education. In R. Griffin (Ed.), *Education in the Muslim world: Different perspectives* (pp. 149–190). Cambridge: Cambridge University Press.

Lingard, B., & Christie, P. (2003). Leading theory: Bourdieu and the field of educational leadership. An introduction and overview to this special issue. *International Journal of Leadership in Education, 6*(4), 317–333.

Mehran, G. (1990). Ideology and education in the Islamic Republic of Iran. *Compare: A Journal of Comparative and International Education, 20*(1), 53–65.

Mehran, G. (1989). Education in post-revolutionary Persia 1979–95. *Encyclopedia Iranica* (230–233). Costa Mesa: Mazda.

Menashri, D. (1992). *Education and the making of modern Iran*. Ithaca: Cornell University Press.

Mialaret, G. (1985). *Meaning and scope of science*. Paris: Tehran University. Press.

Miller, V. (1965). *The public administration of American school systems*. New York: Macmillan.

Milley, P. (2008). On Jürgen Habermas' critical theory and the political dimensions of educational administration. In E. A. Samier (Ed.), *Political approaches to educational administration and leadership* (pp. 54–72). New York: Routledge.

Mirhadi, T. (1983). *Seeking for the methods of education* (Vol. second). Tehran: Mahdiyeh.

Mohsenpour, B. (2005). In search of a template for the preparation of educational sciences textbooks based on Islamic sources. In K. Akrami (Ed.), *Analysis and regulation of the educational sciences system*. Tehran: Institute for Humanities and Cultural Studies.

Mohsenpour, B. (1988). Philosophy of education in postrevolutionary Iran. *Comparative Education Review, 32*(1), 76–86.

Mohsenpour, B. (2011). Pathology of academic texts in the field of educational sciences. *Ayar, 24*, 80–67.

Moradi Nejad, H., & Rahimi Shariati, P. (1974). Research on sending students abroad during the Qajar and Pahlavi periods. *Sociological Studies, 4*, 115–190.

Naeli, M. A. (1996). The role of specialized educational management in the effectiveness of the education system. *Journal of Psychology and Educational Sciences, 3*(1–2), 33–16.

Nasiri, M. (2008). Study of the evolution of school (Maktab Khaneh) system in the Qajar and Pahlavi periods. *Area, 25*(150), 278–195.

Newton, P., & Riveros, A. (2015). Toward an ontology of practices in educational administration: Theoretical implications for research and practice. *Educational Philosophy and Theory, 47*(4), 330–341.

Niesche, R. (2011). *Foucault and educational leadership: Disciplining the principal* (Vol. first). London: Routledge.

Niesche, R. (2013a). *Deconstructing educational leadership: Derrida and Lyotard*. Abingdon: Routledge.

Niesche, R. (2013b). Politicizing articulation: applying Lyotard's work to the use of standards in educational leadership. *International Journal of Leadership in Education, 16*(2), 220–233.

Niesche, R., & Gowlett, C. (2014). Advocating a post-structuralist politics for educational leadership. *Educational Philosophy and Theory, 47*(4), 372–386.

Noorabadi, S., Ahmadi, P., Dabiri Esfahani, O., & Farashkhah, M. (2014). Necessity and the possibility of changing the curriculum approved by Iran's higher education system into a consolidated curriculum. *Journal of Instruction and Evaluation, 7*(25), 122–102.

Nowroozi, M. (2012). Possibility of Islamicization and localization of educational sciences curriculum. *Culture Strategy, 19*, 168–140.

Oplatka, I. (2009). The field of educational administration: A historical overview of scholarly attempts to recognize epistemological identities, meanings and boundaries from the 1960s onwards. *Journal of Educational Administration, 47*(1), 8–35.

Paivandi, S. (2012). *Education in the Islamic Republic of Iran and perspectives on democratic reforms*. Dubai: Legatum Institute.

Pounder, D., & Johnson, B. (2007). Reflections on EAQ's past, present, and future. *Educational Administration Quarterly, 43*(2), 259–272.

Qasemi Pooya, I. (2008). Explaining and analyzing the characteristics of successful schools in contemporary education. *Quarterly of Education, 96*, 201–239.

Rahmani-Kochghani, M., & Behrangi, M. R. (2009). Study on the content and design the course of principles of educational administration in master's degree of educational administration from the perspective of professors and students. *Higher Education Letter, 2*(7), 58–41.

Rai Golouyeh, S., & Rahmanian, D. (2017). Politics and education in the second Pahlavi period; Case study of the causes, modes and process of changing issues and approvals of the supreme council of culture, 1332–1320. *Al-Zahra University Quarterly of Islam and Iran History, 27*(35), 80–58.

Ramazani, M. A., & Hamani, K. (2014). The history of islamic human sciences: After islamic revolution in Iran. *Cognitive Studies at Islamic University, 18*(58), 5–20.

Rastehmoghadam, A. (2017). *Visualization of global scientific map of educational administration, Based on web of science and its explanation from expert's (well-grounded's) view* (Doctoral dissertation, Allameh Tabataba'i University, Tehran).

Rastehmoghadam, A., Abbaspour, A., & Jalali, A. (2016). Reflection on global scientific legacy of educational management. *Journal of Management and Planning in Educational Systems, 9*(16), 51–84.

Sadiq, I. (1931). *Modern persia and her educational system.* New York: Columbia University Press.

Sadiq, I. (1942). Investigation of Iranian culture. *Mehr Journal, 73,* 137–139.

Sadiq, I. (1960). *History of education of Iran (Persia) from the earliest times to the present day.* Tehran: Tehran University Press.

Saee, A., Gharkhani, M., & Momeni, F. (2012). State and education policy in Iran from 1981 to 2001. *Journal of Social Sciences, 19*(56), 166–117.

Samier, E. A. (2006). Educational administration as a historical discipline. *Journal of Educational Administration and History, 38*(2), 125–139.

Samier, E. A. (2008). *Political approaches to education.* New York: Routledge.

Samier, E. A. (2014). Western doctoral programmes as public service, cultural diplomacy or intellectual imperialism? Expatriate educational leadership teaching in the United Arab Emirates. In A. Taysum & S. Rayner (Eds.), *Investing in our education: Leading, learning, researching and the doctorate* (pp. 93–123). Emerald: Bingley.

Samier, E. A., & Schmidt, M. (2010). *Trust and betrayal in educational administration and leadership.* London: Routledge.

SCCR. (2015). *The curriculum of the bachelor of educational sciences, approved by the meeting of the 170th council for the promotion and transformation of humanities.* Tehran: Supreme Council of the Cultural Revolution.

Scott, E. (2010a). Bourdieu's strategies and the challenge for educational leadership. *International Journal of Leadership in Education, 13*(3), 265–281.

Scott, E. (2010b). Studying school leadership practice: A methodological discussion. *Issues in Educational Research, 20*(3), 220–233.

Shadfar, H., Liyaghat Dar, M., Javad and Sharif, M. (2011). Study of the degree of adaptation of the curriculum of management and planning with the needs of students. *Quarterly of Research and Planning in Higher Education, 62,*146–123.

Shahriari, K. (2017). Modernization process in Iran: Historical overview. *Journal of Social Science Studies, 4*(1), 269–282.

Shahvar, S. (2009). *The forgotten schools: The Baha'is and modern education in Iran, 1899–1934.* London: Tauris Academic Studies.

Shamshiri, B. (2005). *Culture, the most fundamental territory of the field of educational sciences.* Paper presented at the first conference of the analysis and regulation of the educational sciences system, Mashhad.

Shorish, M. M. (1988). The Islamic revolution and education in Iran. *Comparative Education Review, 32*(1), 58–75.

Siasi, A. A. (1958a). Education. *Educational Principles, 4–5,* 5–9.

Siasi, A. A. (1958b). Psychology and pedagogy—Their relationship with each other. *Educational Principles, 2,* 14–16.

Smyth, J. (1989). *Critical perspectives on educational leadership.* London: Psychology Press.

Takmilhomayoun, N. (2018). *Darolfonun*. Tehran: Cultural Research Bureau.

Tamer, Y. (2010). *Basic changes in Iranian education system before and after Islamic Revolution* (Unpublished master's thesis, Middle East Technical University, Ankara, Turkey).

Veck, W., & Jessop, S. (2016). Hannah Arendt 40 years on: thinking about educational administration. *Journal of Educational Administration and History, 48*(2), 129–135.

Vejdani, F. (2014). *Making history in Iran: Education, nationalism, and print culture*. Redwood City: Stanford University Press.

Wall, N. E. (2001). *A critical analysis of the theories, models, and policies of educational administration*. Masters thesis, University of New Brunswick, Canada.

Wang, Y., & Bowers, A. J. (2016). Mapping the field of educational administration research: A journal citation network analysis. *Journal of Educational Administration, 54*(3), 242–269.

Weick, K. E. (1976). Educational organizations as loosely coupled systems. *Administrative Science Quarterly, 21*(1), 1–19.

Whiteman, R. S. (2015). Explicating metatheory for mixed methods research in educational leadership: An application of Habermas's theory of communicative action. *Leadership, 29*(7), 888–903.

Wilkinson, J., & Scott, E. (2013). 'Outsiders within'? Deconstructing the educational administration scholar. *International Journal of Leadership in Education, 16*(2), 191–204.

Yarmohammadian, M. H., & Salmanizadeh, M. (2006). Evaluation of students' and graduates' opinions about curriculum of management and educational planning of Islamic Azad University of Khorasgan. *Knowledge and Research in Educational Sciences, 9,* 86–77.

Yazdani, M. (1998). History of education in Iran: Revising a report on the Iranian approach to the development of culture and the establishment of educational institutions. *Treasury of Documents, 31–32,* 25–10.

Arash Rastehmoghadam is the visiting professor of Allameh Tabataba'i University (Tehran, Iran) and has experience in teaching public administration, sociology of education and educational supervision. He received the bachelor's degree of Educational Administration from Birjand University and subsequently Master's and Ph.D. degrees from Allameh Tabataba'i University, Iran. He has several research papers and publications regarding learning organisations, organisational culture, educational administration, financing of higher education, and educational policy-making. Arash has a solid experience in reviewing research studies and serves as a reviewer for a number of national peer-reviewed journals. He has several years of experience in human resource development, organizational structure and administrative transformation in governmental organizations in Iran.

Chapter 10
K-12 Education Reforms in Saudi Arabia: Implications for Change Management and Leadership Education

Bader A. Alsaleh

Abstract The Saudi education system has been experiencing continuous reforms during the past two decades. However, despite the financial support education reforms are granted by the government, impact of those reforms on education outcomes, if any, remains minimal. The author argues that reviewing Saudi education reforms based on Rogers' (2003) characteristics of innovation (internal factors) and Ely's (1990, 1999) conditions of change (external factors) as a framework demonstrates that shortcomings of these reforms could be attributed to a lack or at best to weak change management and leadership that failed to provide for those factors during the implementation stage. Taking these factors into consideration by Educational Administration Departments at the Colleges of Education in Saudi universities should improve teaching topics and issues of educational administration and leadership at these departments as well as improving school's principals in their role as change managers. This chapter starts with an overview of the Saudi education system and the Tatweer education reform project followed by an overview of Rogers (2003) and Ely's (1990, 1999) proposed frameworks. Next, it critically reviews Saudi education reforms based on this framework. The chapter ends with proposed curriculum outlines in change management and leadership for the preparation of future graduates of the colleges of education at Saudi universities.

Introduction: An Overview of Saudi Arabia Teaching of Educational Administration and Leadership

The education system in the Kingdom of Saudi Arabia, both government and private, is composed of general education which is organised into three stages of elementary school for six years, intermediate school and secondary school for three years each and university and technical and vocational education. Only recently preschool has received special support with the Saudi Vision 2030 (Preschool Development Programme 2018). The Ministry of Education (MOE) (2018a) runs more than 38,000

B. A. Alsaleh (✉)
King Saud University, Riyadh, Saudi Arabia
e-mail: ba_alsaleh@yahoo.com

© Springer Nature Singapore Pte Ltd. 2019
E. A. Samier and E. S. ElKaleh (eds.), *Teaching Educational Leadership in Muslim Countries*, Educational Leadership Theory,
https://doi.org/10.1007/978-981-13-6818-9_10

schools, with six million students and half a million teachers. Post-secondary education includes universities that offer bachelor's degrees in almost all academic majors in humanities and sciences and masters and PhD degrees in many majors. Presently, there exist 28 government universities, 10 private universities, and 42 private colleges (MOE 2018b). Further, the Technical and Vocational Training Corporation (2017) runs 71 technical colleges and many vocational training institutes.

The Saudi education system is centralised with a top-down management approach. K-12 education is managed at three levels; at the school level, principals manage the daily routine operations of the schools; at the district level, the education directorates manage schools in their districts; and at the national level, the MOE is responsible for setting educational policies and curricula, allocating financial resources, hiring staff, selecting and or authoring textbooks and maintaining the education system (Badawood 2003, cited in Meemar 2014, p. 14).

Until recently, the Saudi Universities were under the authority of the Ministry of Higher Education. However, a royal decree in 2015 merged the Ministry of Education and the Ministry of Higher Education into one entity which is now the Ministry of Education (Sack et al. 2016). The Technical and Vocational Training Corporation, which runs two-year and four-year technical colleges and vocational institutes for boys and girls and used to be an independent entity, has recently become under the authority of the MOE as well. The rationale behind this merger is to encourage alignment between universities and technical colleges' graduates and job market demands, develop qualified teachers, and improve system-wide efficiency (The Boston Consulting Group 2018). Even though Saudi education has witnessed huge expansion, and despite costly education reforms during the last two decades, reform outputs in terms of graduates ready for a highly competent job market have been criticised for their low quality (Mackenzie 2015; Pennington 2017; Saudi Transformation Plan 2020 2016; Saudi Vision 2030 2016).

Education reform implies change that is a complex and lengthy process because of many human and non-human factors involved. Thus, the success or failure of education reforms cannot be attributed simply to one cause. Taking this into consideration, the author argues that examining Saudi education reforms using a change management and leadership framework based on Rogers' (2003) characteristics or internal factors of innovation and Ely's (1990, 1999) conditions or external factors that facilitate innovation implementation will reveal that weak or an absence of well-planned implementation and change management and leadership of Saudi education reforms is a major factor of their shortcomings or failures. This suggests that educational administration and leadership graduate degrees need to cover more on change and innovation that is relevant to the Saudi context. To present this argument, the chapter begins with an overview of Rogers' characteristics of innovations (2003) and Ely's conditions of change (1990, 1999) followed by an overview of the Tatweer education reform project. Next, a critical review of Saudi education reforms based on the proposed framework is presented. The last part of the chapter proposes curriculum outlines in educational change management and leadership at the colleges of education in Saudi universities. In this chapter, change, innovation, and reform terms are used interchangeably.

Tatweer Education Reform Project

Education is the resource that nations heavily invest in to fuel and expedite their economic, social, health, etc., developments. The 2016/2017 annual budget for general Saudi education alone exceeded $35.2 billion (MOE 2018a). With the inception of a huge k-12 education reform, namely the King Abdullah Project for the Development of Education (publicly known as Tatweer means to develop or to reform) in 2007 with a budget of $2.4 billion, educational reform initiatives have gained more governmental support. Tatweer is managed by the Tatweer Holding Company which runs four companies aimed at transforming the Saudi school system into a twenty-first century model of education (Meemar 2014). Education reform has recently gained more momentum with the inception of the 2020 National Transformation Plan and became one of the main pillars of this very ambitious social and economic plan towards a knowledge- and service-based economy (Alnahdi 2014).

Tatweer's goals include the following: empowering districts and schools to manage and lead change; improving curriculum, instruction, and assessment; professionalizing teaching practice; leveraging technology to improve school and student performance, and improving governance, leadership, and policies to sustain change (Meemar 2014). Presently, Saudi education is focusing on three priorities: 'improving the basic level of education, ramping up vocational education and training; and improving the flow of young people, including university graduates, from education to employment' (Mackenzie 2015, n.p.). The GCC countries have implemented many education reforms but research of their impact is limited, which creates challenges for policy-makers and leaders in implementing further reforms (Alfadala 2015). Though research-based evidence of the impact of Saudi education reforms is sparse (Alyami 2014), Tatweer has been criticised for not having tangible impact on schools' improvement (Al-Essa 2009, cited in Tayan 2017, p. 68) which indicates the need to focus more on change management by faculty involved in teaching educational administrational and leadership.

Rogers' (2003) theory of the diffusion of innovations addresses the process from a social change perspective. The main components of this theory are the elements of innovation diffusion (the innovation, communication channels, time, and a social system), the stages of the innovation-decision process (knowledge, persuasion, decision, implementation, and confirmation), and the characteristics of the innovation itself. He defines five characteristics (internal factors) inherited in the innovation that can speed up its diffusion and adoption:

1. Relative advantages: The degree to which an innovation is perceived by a target audience as better than the old practice. Advantages may include ease of use, time or money-saving, etc. The greater the perceived relative advantages of an innovation, the more rapid its rate of adoption is expected.
2. Compatibility: The more the innovation is compatible with values, beliefs, and current practices as perceived by target audience, the more rapidly it will be diffused and adopted.

3. Ease of use: The innovation that is perceived as easy to understand and used within available skills and knowledge is expected to gain rapid acceptance and adoption.
4. Trialability: The innovation that gives the target audience an opportunity to try it out before making the decision to adopt it increases its likelihood of adoption.
5. Observability: The more the innovation results are easily observed by the target audience the more likely it will be adopted.

Ely (1990, 1999) argued that there is more to the successful implementation and adoption of innovation than the inherited qualities of the innovation itself. Therefore, he focused on conditions that exit in the innovation's environment (external factors) which facilitate its implementation; these conditions are:

1. Dissatisfaction with the status quo: Something must necessitate a need for change.
2. Knowledge and skills: Intended adopters must have the knowledge and skills required to implement the innovation.
3. Availability of resources: Resources necessary to implement the innovation must be available.
4. Availability of time: Provision of time to intended audience to learn and adapt the innovation to their needs.
5. Reward or incentives: Provision of intrinsic or extrinsic incentives or reward to motivate audience adoption of innovation.
6. Participation: Intended audience must have their inputs into the innovation process.
7. Commitment: Leaders must show continuing support to the innovation.
8. Leadership: Leaders must provide encouragement, support and inspiration for adopters.

Saudi Education Reforms: Education Administration, Change Management, and Leadership

Literature related to the causes of the failure of education reforms over times and across cultures reveals patterns or common factors that explain this phenomenon (e.g. Ely 1990, 1999; Fullan 2007; Rogers 2003). Akkary (2014) attributed failure of education reforms in the Arab countries to the following common factors:

- reforms are rigidly run by top-down management,
- lack of basic knowledge about effective education reform,
- lack of implementation management plan, and
- lack of professional capacity on the part of those targeted by reform.

Unfortunately, these factors are present in the case of Saudi education reforms that need to be focused on in education administration and leadership graduate programmes. A review of literature of those reforms (e.g. Alzaidi 2008b, cited in Alyami 2014; Alsalahi 2014; Oyaid 2009; Tayan 2017) reveals similar factors hindering the implementation of Saudi education reforms. Dealing with these factors from a change management perspective is a prerequisite for successful implementation of education reform (Pont et al. 2008). Innovations may fail during the implementation stage if prerequisite conditions do not exist (Ely 1990, 1999; Fullan 2007, Rogers 2003). Therefore, I argue that despite the generous financial support education reforms are provided by the MOE, shortcomings or failure of those reforms can be attributed to a lack or weak change management and leadership during the implementation stage. This has been manifested through the absence of internal and external factors that facilitate implementation of education reforms as well as lack of change leadership's accountability, timetables of tasks implementations, effective change tracking procedures and timely interventions. In short, I believe that a major problem in Saudi education reforms lies in change management and leadership during the implementation stage which necessitates re-evaluation of educational administration and leadership programmes in terms of content and teaching to effectively and efficiently manage those reforms.

While Rogers (2003) emphasised the role of the characteristics or internal factors of innovation in its rate of diffusion and adoption, Ely (1990, 1999) addressed external factors that exist in the innovation environment and influence its implementation. Ertmer (1999, cited in Albugami and Ahmed 2015, p. 40) categorised factors hindering ICT implementation into internal factors (views and attitudes of school staff) and external factors (ICT resources and technical support). According to Alwani (2005, cited in Albugami and Ahmed 2015, p. 41) in the case of Saudi education reforms, external factors are related to the MOE. Likewise, Fullan (2007) argues that implementation is the 'big hurdle' of educational change for several interactive factors. These are internal factors (characteristics of change), local characteristics of change (district, community, principals, and teachers) and external factors (government and other agencies).

It appears then, based on related literature, that both characteristics of innovation (internal factors) and conditions in the innovation environment (external factors) are influential in determining the degree to which the innovation well be adopted and successfully implemented. This means that graduate programmes for educational administration and leadership are inadequate in preparing their graduates in change management. Change is a process composed of stages that happen over time; effective change management is a prerequisite for a smooth transition through those stages. Of those stages, the implementation stage is particularly critical (Fullan 2007). Based on this argument, educational change leadership must consider the provision of both internal and external factors of education reform.

Rogers (2003) specified five characteristics of innovations. When applied to Saudi education reforms based on related literature, one finds that Saudi authority responsible for leading and managing education reforms either ignore or at best does not give enough attention to those characteristics when planning and implementing educational reforms; this situation may be attributed to ill knowledge of the basics of change management and leadership and inadequate graduate programmes in educational administration and leadership. Below is a brief discussion of Saudi education reforms based on Roger's characteristics of innovation.

As mentioned earlier, the Saudi education system is centralised; decisions about reform agendas are taken at the education minister cabinet level; thus, input from a target audience into this agenda is almost absent (Akkary 2014; Algarni and Male 2014; Tayan 2017). Teachers are usually informed of reforms by circulars; thus, they are not well informed about their features and goals; consequently, teachers are not aware of the relative advantages of those reforms. Fullan (2007) considers clarity of change features an important factor of its success and points out that clarity of problems about teachers' new duties appears in virtually every study of change. Even with recent efforts by the MOE to involve teachers and school principals in matters related to education reforms initiatives by electronic means via e-portal, those initiatives are not well articulated as to what roles are expected of teachers and principals ahead of their implementation. This shortcoming needs to be addressed by educational administration and leadership curriculum as well as through the provision of professional development programmes.

A large part of Tatweer's project is related to digital technology with the goal to transform Saudi schools. This means that Tatweer implementation requires teachers well-trained in technology integration. However, review of related literature (Alyami 2014, 2016; Al Mulhim, 2014; Alnahdi 2014; Meemar 2014; Tayan 2017) reveals that teachers lack sufficient knowledge, skills, and technical support; consequently; they perceive reform as hard to implement (complexity); and because of sparse information about reform's effectiveness (Alfadala 2015; Alyami 2014), teachers have no knowledge of reform results (observability). In this context, teachers are expected to react negatively towards reform's initiative and not willing to try it out (trialability). It is worth mentioning that repetitive negative experiences with education reforms will eventually encourage teachers to be indifferent about them because they know from their past experiences will not last long.

Compatibility of innovation with existing school culture, the values and beliefs held by its staff is an important factor of innovation acceptance while its absence may cause resistance (Rogers 2003). Any type of change introduced to schools is often met with resistance if it is contrary to current practices (Hinde 2014, p.2). According to Alyami (2014, p. 1522), staff resistance in Tatweer's schools was up to 70%; teachers preferred to leave for other schools rather than to change their practices. Therefore, school leaders must be sensitive to school culture when initiating change (Fidler 1996, cited in Alyami 2014 p. 1523). In addition, school culture needs to be addressed in teaching educational administration and leadership. Numerous studies support the finding that a change supportive culture is necessary for its success (Hinde 2014). In a study of the relationship between school culture and teacher change, Schweiker-Marra (1995, cited in Hinde 2014, p. 8) found that teachers' qualities facilitated change, and in some cases, a new culture must be instituted to accommodate change. In Tatweer's case, some globally recognised educational systems such as Finland's and Singapore's were used as benchmarks to Saudi education reforms but without giving much thought to cultural differences and the need for an adaptation vision to accommodate those differences (Tayan 2017). According to Kotter (1995), a change process occurs through phases and that transition from a current tradition to a new state of practice may not be achieved if culture is in direct contrast with intended change (Kotter 1995); this and other related issues should be included in the graduate programme of education administration and leadership.

External Factors of Innovation

Contrary to Rogers' (2003) emphasis on the characteristics of the innovation itself, Ely (1990, 1999) focused on external factors that exist in the environment and affect the implementation of innovation. In other words, he notes that even when the innovation is well designed, it may not succeed if certain conditions do not exist in the environment in which it will be implemented. This contention supports the concept of readiness mentioned by Abedor and Sachs (1978); according to them, readiness is necessary at the individual and organisational levels for the successful implementation of change. The more the change deviates from the status quo, the higher the level of readiness is needed at both levels. Readiness and other concepts related to innovation adoption should be part of education administration and leadership curriculum at the graduate programme at the colleges of education in Saudi Arabia. Fullan (2010, cited in University College of the Cayman Island, 2013) indicated that change success requires creating the right conditions and developing organisational and individual capacity. In the following section, review of Saudi education reforms based on Ely's (1990, 1999) conditions that facilitate implementation of innovation is presented. Topics reviewed in this section are: dissatisfaction with the status quo, knowledge and skills, availability of resource, availability of time, incentives or rewards, participation, commitment, and leadership.

Dissatisfaction with the status quo is probably the condition that most concerned educators and education leaders in the country agree with. In the Yidan Prize Summit in Hong Kong (Pennington 2017), the Saudi Minister of Education, Ahmed Al-Issa criticised the Saudi current education system as 'being the product of the past, not an enabler of the future' (n.p.). Tatweer's project itself is a strong indication of the urgency to improve Saudi education. The 2020 Saudi Transformation Plan (2016) and the Saudi Vision 2030 (2016) both have emphasised the urgent need to reform the Saudi general education to prepare young Saudis for the job market and increased global economic competitions. This reform should include the improvement of educational administration and leadership programmes. A rationale to transform Saudi education has been emphasised in both initiatives (MOE 2018b). These are clear articulations of the dissatisfaction with the status quo of Saudi education.

Probably, knowledge and skills in addition to availability of resources are the problems repeatedly mentioned by Saudi teachers. Alsalahi (2014) found that teachers need to be empowered with needed skills and knowledge to practice their roles as leaders and that preservice programme neglects training them with the knowledge and skills they need to practice this role. Not only teachers that need to be empowered in education administration and leadership skills but schools principals too;

Meemar (2014) for instance, found principals in Saudi schools perceive themselves as having a low to medium level of ability to implement administrative and technical authorities. For example, Alenezi (2017), who studied technology leadership in Saudi schools, reports that Saudi teachers are not well trained to integrate ICT into teaching. Al-Degether (2009, cited in Tayan 2017, p.65) calls for the need to improve Saudi teachers' skills and instruction via professional development to enhance the quality of Saudi education. Such professional development should include opportunities for training in educational administration and leadership teaching.

Ertmer (1999, cited in: Oyaid 2009 p. 43) indicated that teachers may not be able to integrate ICT into instruction due to the low availability of resources if schools do not provide enough support, training, time, and equipment. Al Mulhim (2014, p.491) discussed three factors that prevent teachers in Saudi schools from using ICT frequently and appropriately into their teaching; they included lack of access to technology, effective training, and time. Several Saudi studies about education reforms and ICT technology status in Saudi schools (e.g. Alenezi 2016; Alyami 2014, 2016; Al-Zahrani 2015; Meemar 2014; Oyaid 2009) found that problems of resource provision in schools including lack of software to support subject matters content and lack of technical assistance present major obstacles towards successful implementation of reforms. Alyami (2014) indicated that Tatweer's smart schools lacked human resources to use Intel programmes. Albugami and Ahmed (2015) found many factors hindering ICT implementation in Saudi schools among which are lack of management and technical support, lack of ICT policy, lack of ICT resources, and lack of teachers training. These findings highlight the important role of teaching education administration and leadership for those involved in change management to enhance the likelihood of adopting education reform.

Ely's (1999) fourth condition of successful implementation of innovation is the provision of time for teachers to practice and try out new teaching approaches. Time is one of the four elements of Rogers' (2003) theory of innovation diffusion. Realising that change usually takes considerable length of time can improve the chances of change success (Kotter 1995). Maroun et al. (2007) assert that reforms implemented with less time pressure have higher chances of success, and if teachers do not have enough time to learn about, implement, and reflect on intended change, effects remain questionable. In their study of time and school reform, Adelman and Walking-Eagle (1997, cited in Hinde 2014, p.6) explain that there are three stages in a reform process that are time-related: first teachers need time to learn about and practice new behaviours; second, in the implementation stage, teachers need time to integrate new change in their daily routine; and third, teachers need time to evaluate reform results. Over and over, related literature (Ertmer 1999; Franklin et al. 2001, cited in Oyaid 2009, p. 43; Muir-Herzig 2004,) identifies lack of time as a major barrier facing implementation and integration of ICT in schools. School leaderships have a major role in eliminating such barrier to see education reform realised in their schools.

Educators are usually very eager to see results of education reform soon after its implementation, but relevant literature (e.g. Ely 1990; Kleiman 2000; Kotter 1995; Rogers 2003) shows that those results are not easily tangible and take a considerable length of time. Kleiman (2000, p. 5) notes that full integration and use of technology in k-12 schools 'takes years not weeks or months'. Al Asmari (2011, cited in Albugami and Ahmed 2015, p.41) stated that Saudi teachers do not have enough time to prepare ICT materials for their lessons. Alnahdi (2014, p.4) advises Saudi education officials to be patient in dealing with reforms process because it is 'complex, difficult, and very slow process and that the chance of seeing tangible results quickly after applying reforms and changes is minimal'. These characteristics of reforms need to be addressed by education administration and leadership curriculum.

Literature on change resistance emphasises the importance of incentives or rewards in the adoption process of change (Ely 1990, 1999; Hardy 1997; Hiatt 2006; Rogers 2003). Ladner and Brouillette (2000) describe three categories of education reforms: rules-based reform (e.g. extending school days and class time, changing teacher certification); resource-based reform (focusing on funds increase, Internet access, remodelling school facilities, etc.); and incentive-based reforms through public school choice (e.g. charter schools, choice among private schools by vouchers). They note that incentive-based reforms encourage traditional public schools to improve through market-based incentives which recent research indicates that it has had greater success than the rules or resource-based reforms. Evans (2001, cited in Alyami 2014, p. 1522) argued that teacher's pay system must be related to performance to generate motivational impact. According to Alyami (2014), participants in her study indicated that there was not any system of incentive to use Intel programmes in Tatweer's schools. Obviously, incentive should be given special consideration by education administration and leadership curriculum and teaching because of its direct influence on teachers' performance.

Research indicates that school autonomy is vital for the successful implementation of education reform and provision of leadership for improved learning (Pont et al. 2008). Ely (1999, p. 6) emphasised 'shared decision-making' in the implementation process of innovation. Hargreaves and Shirley (2009, cited in Tayan 2017, p. 66) argue that teacher's autonomy is fundamental to the success of education reform. Though the MOE (2018a) recently has been trying to involve teachers in decisions related to education reform via e-portals (e.g. MOE future gate), decisions to implement those initiatives are still largely dominated by the MOE. Tayan (2017) indicates that Tatweer is led and managed by a centralised approach that has not given needed authority to teachers to work as leaders and change agent; for example, Tatweer's smart schools were decided and introduced by the MOE authority without input from teachers, principals, or students. Also, Alzaidi (2008b, cited in Alyami 2014, p. 1517) argues that lack or weak authority given to head teachers in Saudi schools was the most important factor of teachers' dissatisfaction. It is important to consider perceptions of teachers and head teachers about any planned changes for school reform if they wish to implement it effectively which it did not happen with Tatweer's project (Alyami 2014).

In his study about the challenges of teachers' leadership in Saudi schools, Alsalahi (2014) found that all participating teachers were disempowered to play their role as leaders in planning their schools' strategic development. In another study, Al-Essa (2009, cited in Tayan 2017, p. 66) found that education reform implementation failed to effectively address and support teacher autonomy.

Commitment to support education reform during the implementation stage is vital to its sustainable and resource provision. According to Fullan (2001, p. 3), 'schools that sustained reforms had ongoing support from district and state allies'. While Tatweer's project relied heavily on technology integration in its second phase which included 50 smart schools, it failed to provide technical provisions for those schools (Alyami 2014). In Tatweer's schools, principals have little support in performing the new administrative and technical authorities granted to them (Meemar 2014). Fullan (2001, p. 3) emphasised the importance of commitment of change leadership to provide needed support during the implementation stage; according to him, continuation of the change will be jeopardised unless commitment for support and continuous follow up is present. This implies that graduate programmes in education administration and leadership at the Saudi colleges of education needs to cover the commitment of change leadership concept.

Leadership plays an important role in realising an effective educational system. Many reforms have failed because of lack of quality leadership (Hinde 2014 cited in Pont et al. 2008). Educational policy in the Organization for Economic Co-operation and Development (OECD) countries considered school leadership as a priority for motivating and empowering teachers to improve school outcomes (Pont et al. 2008). According to Fullan (2007), the role of school principals as change leaders is vital to the success of educational change. Scheerens and Bosker (1997), Teddlie and Reynolds (2000) and Townsend (2007, cited in Pont et al. 2008, p. 33) report that the past three decades of research findings about school effectiveness and improvement have repeatedly demonstrated the central role of school leadership. According to Pont, Nusche and Moorman (2008, pp. 33, 32), the general conclusion reached based on reviewing more than 40 studies indicates that 'school leaders have a measurable, mostly indirect influence on learning outcomes'; and that 'effective school leadership is essential to improve the efficiency and equity of schooling'.

Alfadala (2004, p. 6-7) states that education reforms in the Gulf Cooperative Countries (GCC) shifted the roles and relationships in school communities and created challenges such as weak leadership skills among principals, lack of clarity on methods of reforms and lack of student motivation and increased drop-out rates. These are important challenges that need to be focussed on by the education administration and leadership graduate programmes.

Because of the dominance of top-down decision-making, school staff have a long-held belief that the education reform process is the sole responsibility of the MOE; Bashshur (2005, cited in Akkary 2014, p.7) argues that 'teachers view change as something that happens to them rather than something that they initiate'. To Fullan (2010, cited in University College of the Cayman Island 2013, p.16), top-down management does not bring about successful educational change. Almannie (2014) found that Saudi schools' principals have limited leadership roles to perform tasks related to schools' improvement because they are not prepared for such tasks; they are more of managers rather than instructional leaders. Algarni and Male (2014, pp. 45, 46) criticised educational leadership in Saudi education for 'considering educational leadership as the responsibility of a single person and for its relying on maintaining the status quo instead of development and on management instead of leadership';

they suggest the 'devolution of much decision making from central authority to the schools and let the principals and teachers be catalysts change agents'. Almudarra (2017, p. 36.) supports this finding pointing out that the dominant leadership style in Saudi schools is mostly transactional where the focus is mainly on maintaining the day-to-day operations using the power of rewards and where future strategic planning and readiness for change implementation including training, incentives, and resources are not of concern and indicating a need for a different training in education administration and leadership that gives special consideration to these issues of change implementation.

The MOE has felt the need to delegate some tasks to school principals to minimise the centralisation of Saudi schools (Alyami 2014; Meemar 2014). Therefore, in 2001, 31 administrative authorities were conferred to school districts (Meemar 2014), and in 2011, 21 new authorities were conferred to school principals. Moreover, the MOE has realised the need to equip its educators with leadership competencies. Thus, as indicated in its 2016/2017 annual report, the MOE (2018a) initiated two professional development programmes: one is to train managers of education directorates at Harvard University; the other is to train school principals and teachers in universities abroad in such areas as managing school functions and become instructional leaders, creating a school culture that encourages teaching staff collaboration and diffusion of innovation among schools and the effective use of technology for teaching and learning purposes, and promotes schools–community relationships. The rationale for this programme is to strengthen the values, skills, knowledge, and attitudes of teachers, counsellors, and principals through practical experience in high-performing k-12 schools and to prepare school principals to serve as change agents when they return to their schools (MOE 2017, p. 3).

Technology is one of the main drivers of school transformation around the globe. Tatweer's project relies heavily on technology to transform Saudi schools into twenty-first-century learning. In this regard, graduate programmes in education administration and leadership should include technology leadership topics and issues in these programmes. The MOE (2018a) is currently implementing digital education initiative (Future Gate) and iEn (national education portal), and it has established a digital transformation unit to promote digital transformation in education. In this era of technology-oriented knowledge economy where digital culture is becoming more pervasive, a strategic vision for technology adoption and integration in education becomes a priority. This strategy needs school leadership and staff well informed about infusing technology into education. Al-Zahrani (2015) stressed the importance of the role of technology leadership in Saudi schools if ICT integration is to be realised; however, problems identified above also present with technology leadership. Alenezi (2016) points out that there is a lack of teacher preparation and training in digital technologies. Lack of this preparation may be attributed to ineffective school leadership and support. Also, Alyami (2014) notes that Tatweer smart schools lacked technical provisions. Further, Saudi school principals are often unable to solve problems in their schools due to limited decision-making power, lack of resources, and lack of training (Meemar 2014). Kleiman (2000) interprets the reasons k-12 schools face difficulty in their efforts to integrate technology into teaching as being inadequate training provided to teachers, lack of technology resources, and insufficient technical support.

Change Management and Leadership Curriculum

The implications of the above review of Saudi education reforms based on Rogers' (2003) characteristics of innovations (internal factors) and Ely's (1990, 1999) conditions of change (external factors) as a framework show that Saudi education reforms suffer a real problem of lack or at best ill change management plan and leadership during the implementation stage. This plan had failed to consider the internal and external factors necessary to facilitate successful implementation of reforms as suggested by this framework. Schools and classrooms are the environments where implementation process of education reform takes place; hence, the roles of school principals and teachers in this process are vital. Below is an outline of suggested education curriculum in administration and leadership at the colleges of education in Saudi universities to prepare them for this role.

As reported above, the MOE (2017) has initiated a professional development programme to provide school principals with leadership competencies with the goal of preparing them to play their roles as change agents and be able to transform their schools into twenty-first-century learning. However, in-service training must not be a replacement of well-planned pre-service education. Therefore, pre-service education should be improved to include change management and leadership curriculum to equip future graduates of teachers, supervisors, and principals with fundamental skills in this field.

Curriculum to equip education staff with skills and competencies in management and leadership can be offered at two levels: the first is to provide all education majors with foundational concepts related to educational change management and leadership; the rationale behind this suggestion is to enable teachers, supervisors and schools' principals to be instructional leaders. The second level is directed to those majored in graduate educational administration. This level should go into more depth in the following topics: theories and models of change management and leadership, tools and techniques of change management; project management; tasks of change agent; educational change leadership; definition, concepts and types of leadership; building change leadership team; handling crises and conflict, transformative, pedagogical, and digital leadership; emotional intelligence; education reforms' case studies; and best practices. Soft skills of change management and leadership are equally important. Examples of these skills may include understanding why people resist change and how to overcome it, how to help people transit through change stages and provide them with needed support, how to involve school staff in change vision and strategy, shared responsibilities, collective leadership, skills for effectively communicating change and motivating target audience.

Administrators on the job at education directorates in cities, provinces, and districts also need to be equipped through in-service education with necessary skills in change management and leadership. Workshops, coaching, and short summer courses can help meet this need. However, ongoing professional development for all education staff should be provided whenever needed.

The types of readings that are suitable for graduate programmes in educational administration and leadership at the colleges of education in Saudi universities should include and adapt to the Saudi local context topics and issues of educational change addressed in such references as Ely 1990, 1999; Fullan 2001, 2007; Havelock and Zlotolow 1995); innovation diffusion theory of Rogers (2003); Owen (2015) on how to lead; and issues related to the Saudi contexts in educational administration and leadership addressed by Saudi theses and papers such as Alnahdi (2014), Alyami (2016), Algarni and Male (2014), and (Alsalahi) 2014 to name but a few.

Conclusion

This chapter discussed Saudi educational reforms based on a change management leadership framework of Rogers' (2003) characteristics of innovations (internal factors) and Ely's (1990, 1999) conditions facilitating implementation of innovation (external factors) in order to address needs in the educational administration and leadership curriculum. The author's critical review of those reforms based on this framework showed that weak or absence of change management and leadership explains to a large extent the failure or at best the minimal impact of those reforms on the improvement of k-12 education. The chapter ended with proposed curriculum focusses in change management and leadership for prospect graduates of the colleges of education. In conclusion, the Saudi education authority must build education reforms initiatives with well-designed change management plan and leadership during the implementation stage while paying special attention to the internal and external factors that facilitate the implementation and adoption of intended reforms in addition to the provision of pre-service education in change management and leadership. Finally, the author recommends the MOE to adapt Rogers' (2003) characteristics of innovation and Ely's (1990, 1999) conditions that facilitate implementation of innovation as a framework for the implementation of education reform initiatives and to serve as guidelines for the educational administration and leadership curriculum needed in these programmes.

References

Abedor, A., & Sachs, S. G. (1978). The relationship between faculty development, organizational development, and instructional development: Readiness for instructional innovation in higher education. In R. K. Bass & B. D. Lumsden (Eds.), *Instructional development: The state of the art* (pp. 1–20). Columbus, OH: Collegiate Publishing.

Akkary, R. K. (2014). Facing the challenges of educational reform in the Arab world. *Journal of Educational Change, 15*(2), 179–202.

Albugami, S., & Ahmed, V. (2015). Success factors for ICT implementation in Saudi secondary schools: From the perspective of ICT directors, head teachers, teachers and students. *International Journal of Education and Development using Information and Communication Technology, 11*(1), 36–54.

Alenezi, A. (2016). Technology leadership in Saudi schools. *Education Information Technologies, 22*(3), 1121–1132.

Algarni, F., & Male, T. (2014). Leadership in Saudi Arabian public schools: Time for devolution. *International Studies in Educational Administration, 42*(3), 45–59.

Almannie, M. A. (2014). Leadership role of school superintendents in Saudi Arabia. *International Journal of Social Science Studies, 3*(3), 169–175.

Almudarra, J. B. (2017). Leadership and supervision in Saudi Arabian educational context. *International Journal of Developing and Emerging Economies, 5*(11), 34–47.

Al Mulhim, E. (2014). The barriers to the use of ICT in teaching in Saudi Arabia: A review of literature. *Universal Journal of Educational Research, 2*(6), 487–493.

Alnahdi, G. H. (2014). Educational change in Saudi Arabia. *Journal of International Education Research, 10*(1), 1–6.

Alsalahi, S. M. (2014). Challenges of teacher leadership in a Saudi school: Why are teachers not leaders? *Academic Journal, 9*(24), 1416–1419.

Alyami, R. H. (2014). Educational reform in the Kingdom of Saudi Arabia: Tatweer schools as a unit of development. *Literacy Information and Computer Education Journal, 5*(2), 1515–1524.

Alyami, R. H. (2016). *A case study of the Tatweer school system in Saudi Arabia: The perceptions of leaders and teachers* (Doctoral dissertation, University of Reading, Institute of Education).

Al-Zahrani, A. (2015). The place of technology integration in Saudi pre-service teacher eEducation: Matching policy and practice. *The Turkish Online Journal of Educational Technology, 14*(1), 151–162.

Ely, D. P. (1990). Conditions that facilitate the implementation of educational technology innovations. *Journal of Research on Computing in Education, 23*(2), 298–305.

Ely, D. P. (1999). *New perspectives on the implementation of educational technology innovations*. https://files.eric.ed.gov/fulltext/ED427775.pdf. Accessed May 15, 2018.

Fullan, M. (2001). Whole school reform: Problems and Promises. Ontario Institute for Studies in Education, University of Toronto. http//michaelfullan.ca/wp-content/uploads/2016/06/13396044810.pdf. Accessed April 14, 2018.

Fullan, M. (2007). *The new meaning of educational change*. New York: Teachers College Press.

Hardy, G. (1997). *Successfully managing change*. New York: Barron's Educational Series.

Havelock, R. G., & Zlotolow, S. (1995). *The change agent's guide*. Englewood Cliffs, NJ: Education Technology Publications.

Hiatt, J. M. (2006). *ADKAR: A model for change in business, government and our community*. Loveland, CO: Prosci Learning Center.

Hinde, E. R. (2014). *School culture and change: An examination of the effects of school culture on the process of change*. https://www.researchgate.net/publication/251297989_School_Culture_and_Change_An_Examination_of_the_Effects_of_School_Culture_on_the_Process_of_Change. Accessed May 25, 2018.

Kleiman, G. M. (2000). Myths and realities about technology in K-12 schools. *The Online Journal of Leadership and the New Technologies Community, 14*. https://ncdli.fi.ncsu.edu/resources/docs/myths_realities_kleiman.pdf. Accessed June 28, 2018.

Kotter, J. P. (1995). Leading change: Why transformation efforts fail? *Harvard Business Review*, March/April 1–8. http://eoeleadership.hee.nhs.uk/sites/default/files/leading_change-why-trtansformation-efforts-fail.pdf. Accessed July 6, 2018.

Ladner, M., & Brouillette, M. J. (2000). *The impact of limited school choice on public school districts*. A Mackinack Center Report. https://www.miworkerfreedomorg/archives/2000/s2000-04.pdf. Accessed June 11, 2018.

Maroun, N., Samman, H., Mouzas. C. N., & Abouchakra, R. (2007). *How to succeed at education reform: The case for Saudi Arabia and the broader GCC region*. 1–36. Booz & Company Ideation Centre analysis. http://citeseerx.ist.psu.edu/viewdoc/download?doi=10.1.1.585.515&rep=rep1& type=pdf. Accessed June 13, 2018.

Meemar, S. S. (2014). *Tatweer school principals' perceptions of new authorities granted in the initial steps of decentralization*. Western Michigan University. http://scholarworks.wmich.edu/dissertations/384. Accessed May 22, 2018.

Microsoft Corporation. (2014). *Education transformation framework overview*. www.microsoft. com/education/. Accessed June 20, 2018.

@@@Oyaid, A. A. (2009). *Secondary school teachers' ICT use: Perceptions and views of the future of ICT in education* (Ph.D. Thesis, University of Exeter). htpp://ore.exeter.ac.uk/repository/bitstream/handle/10036/69537/OyaidA.doc.pdf. Accessed May 6, 2018.

Owen, J. (2015). *How to lead*. London: Pearson Education.

Pennington, R. (2017). *Saudi plans major overhaul to poorly performing education system*. Yidan Prize Summit Hong Kong. https://www.thenational.ae/uae/saudi-plans-major-overhaul-to-poorly-performing-education-system-1.683557. Accessed June 23, 2018.

Ministry of Education. (2018). *Preschool development program* (2018). https://kids.tatweer.edu.sa/ in Arabic. Accessed April 25, 2018.

Pont, B., Nusche, D., & Moorman, H. (2008). *Improving school leadership*. Organization for Economic Co-operation and Development (OECD), vol. 1 (Policy and Practice). http://www.oecd. org/education/school/44374889.pdf. Accessed May 16, 2018.

Rogers, E. M. (2003). *Diffusion of innovations*. New York: Free Press.

Sack, R., Jalloun, O., Zaman, H., & Alenazi, B. (2016). *Merging education ministries: Lessons learned from international practices*. UNESCO http://unesdoc.unesco.org/images/0024/002473/247344m.pdf. Accessed June 22, 2018.

Tayan, B. M. (2017). The Saudi Tatweer education reforms: Implications of neoliberal thought to Saudi education policy. *International Education Studies, 10*(5), 61–71.

Technical and Vocational Training Corporation. (2017). http://www.tvtc.gov.sa/English/TrainingUnits/Pages/default.aspx. Accessed on March 26, 2018.

The Boston Consulting Group. (2018). *New blueprint for education in Saudi Arabia*. https://www. bcg.com/industries/education/new-blueprint-for-education-in-saudi-arabia.aspx. Accessed April 25, 2018.

The Ministry of Education. (2018a). *Education annual report for the year 2016–2017*. https://drive. google.com/file/d/1Dms201KlLTuthlkK7lpFEYCNH1G99lKE/view. Accessed July 26, 2018.

The Ministry of Education. (2018b). *Education and vision 2030*. https://www.moe.gov.sa/en/Pages/vision2030.aspx. Accessed April 12, 2018.

The Ministry of Education. (2017). *Building leadership for change through school immersion (Cohort 2)*. https://www.britishcouncil.org/sites/default/files/rtp-building_educational_leadership_for_change_cohort_2_final.pdf. Accessed April 13, 2018.

The National Transformation Program. (2016). http://vision2030.gov.sa/sites/default/files/NTP_En. pdf. Accessed April 23, 2018.

The Saudi Vision 2030. http://vision2030.gov.sa/sites/default/files/report/Saudi_Vision2030_EN_2017.pdf. Accessed April 23, 2018.

University College of the Cayman Islands. (2013). The changing nature of educational leadership. *Journal of the University College of the Cayman Islands, 6*. http://www.ucci.edu.ky/_docs/jucci/JUCCI-Issue-6_Dec-2012.pdf. Accessed May 16, 2018.

Bader A. Alsaleh is a retired professor from King Saud University, Riyadh, Saudi Arabia. He has a Ph.D. from Michigan State University in Educational System Development (term used for Instructional Design and Technology at MSU), a Masters in Instructional Media from the University of Northern Colorado, and a BA in Arts and Education from King Saud University, Riyadh. His research interests are in the application of instructional design theories and models for learning and training, integrating instructional technology into teaching and learning, the diffusion and adoption of instructional innovations and educational change management. He is a Distinguished Arab scholar, granted by the Arab Association of Educational Technology (AAET), Cairo University, 2008. He translated and co-translated into Arabic five books of which two are 21st Century Skills: Learning for Life in our Times and Instructional Technology: Definition and Domains of the Field and has co-authored two books. He has delivered keynotes at more than fifteen conferences, forums and meetings at international, regional and local levels, has published over 25 articles in his field, and regularly reviews for a number of journals. In addition, he has regularly presented at local and regional meetings, forums and conferences as well as designed and delivered training workshops and programmes for teachers and professors for the Saudi Ministry of Education, a number of Saudi universities, and private and public schools. He also reviews research studies, research projects, academic programmes and faculty promotion in Saudi and Arab universities.

Printed in the United States
By Bookmasters